Happy Baby Mamas Make Good Wives

Happy Baby Mamas Make Good Wives

Notes on Restoring the Black Family in Post-Modernity

Von Gneisenau

Bourgeois Post-Pavilion Publishing

Publishing Information
Published by Bourgeois Post-Pavilion Press
Atlanta, GA
©Bourgeois Post-Pavilion Publishing 2023

ISBN: 979-8-218-31497-2
ISBN: 979-8-218-31500-9

In the normal course of events I would not mind doing a dedication page, however being associated with my opinions cannot at this point do any of the persons, organizations, and entities I have associated with in my life any good. And yes, included in that is God. Like the rappers and the denizens of R&B, I'd love to say all sorts of wild stuff in recordings, get an award (or do a public dedication), and then thank God effusively with a bottle of Champaign in my hand, and three in my blood stream, blunted like my whole life felt like I was a mime; just moving way faster and more smoothly. And yet in my books I go hard, and it would be highly presumptuous of me to holler bout God and cuss, fuss, and disparage certain types of things more than I think God would find necessary or prudent. In this volume I do not cite God, Judaism, Christianity, and Islam because I am Holy or even worthy of calling the names of these venerable religions. Where I cite religious themes and texts, I cite them because in my exposure to these themes in my life experiences, I have found them to be true. While I am on the subject, let me say in advance that I do not encourage or condone discrimination or violence against anyone. I am 100% non-violent (yes even in child rearing). I am for legalized abortion (because I do not want to see women back in the back alleys and with root doctors, and it is a hearts and minds issue, not a issue for conservatives to legislate). To the extent I crack jokes against, or critique the socialist-atheist-LGBTQIA Black Liberal Democrat Movement, I am not, I repeat not, arguing against individuals, or their individual rights, I am arguing against a political movement and its institutionalization in a society that presumes to want to continue propagating itself and the human species. Thus I ask the Negro public to think of it like when German philosopher Friedrich Nietzsche wrote the book 'Nietzsche contra Wagner' (Nietzsche vs. Wagner). For those of my readers not familiar with the situation, Nietzsche and composer Richard Wagner were very good friends early in their lives as young men. They were similarly gifted, talented and intelligent in their chosen studies and professions, and similarly broke financially (much of the reason for Wagner's later anti-Semitism). Not quite overnight, but dramatically nonetheless, Wagner gets a famous patron or two, then the King of Bavaria Ludwig, and Wagner was riding on top of the world, feted and hailed a genius and the inheritor of the great German Artistic tradition. Wagner was hailed as a saint of German Opera. Meanwhile Nietzsche was still broke, disrespected as an intellectual and public thinker, and marginalized. Nor did Wagner put his old friend 'on" when Wagner came to power. Nietzsche's only consolation at the time was prefacing one of his books with the statement that his readers are not of this time, which is to say he will come to be appreciated for his worth in the future. And indeed this was true. If Nietzsche and Wagner would have both remained broke and under appreciated, Nietzsche never would have written a book that seemed oft times cruel in its polemic against his old anti-Semitic friend. But the critique was not personal, or rather it was precisely personal. To Nietzsche, the intellectual and artistic giant he knew, would never have allowed himself to be feted by princes, kings, elites, or bourgeois and mass sentimentalism. We would do well to remember the 'revolutionary' Wagner who had to struggle not to get his career caught up in the 1848 'Revolution' once the 'elites', the King and the military came back into power. Nietzsche's main point, was that the Wagner he knew, before being wined and dined by the ignorant and buffoon like Munich court of aristocrats surrounding the childish Bavarian King Ludwig, and before being feted by the ridiculously pompous and arrogant Prussian Junker Aristocrats, '**that**' Wagner was better than this (his use by Ludwig, the Prussian aristocracy, the aristocratic, and bourgeois classes). Nietzsche's argument was that the old Wagner, was better than even the man/musician he became after the applause of the bourgeois middle classes and elites and fulfilling their silly bourgeois/elite/princely lowbrow expectations. So yes Kecia Lance Bottoms, Stacy Abrams, Raphael Warnock, and the host of Black elected officials in the Democrat party turning tricks for their new masters, I am 'contra' you, but it is only because like Nietzsche felt about Wagner, 'I know you can do better', and you are better than simply what your rich White Liberal and Conservative patrons, Hollywood public acclaim, and princely titles and positions pay you to do.

CONTENTS

One

The Majesty of the Blues

Introduction & Clarion Call (7ChambersofNiggerdom)

Here in Atlanta, the mother of all urban cities in Niggerdom, I watched a local news segment absolutely horrified. In the wake of school shootings, teen violence and underperforming schools, representatives of the 'all Black' school board and scholastic community had an anti-violence pep rally. They took away from instructional time to host a pep rally, complete with cheer style led chants and promises and oaths not to bring guns to school or be violent in in dealing with misunderstandings. There were rappers there that I'd never heard of, but I have long ceased trying to figure out who are the latest rappers and denizens of the R&B world. They all seem to be talking about the same things anyway, notably absent from their predilections are discussions about strong families, respecting parents, elders, slowing down on drug and alcohol use and falling in love and getting married.

Ladies and gentlemen pep rallies and trite raps are what a people does who have absolutely no idea of any practical steps to take towards solving the problem. Pep rallies are held in support of a team, win or lose matters not, and no one in their right mind thinks that if the pep rally is good and exciting enough, the school basketball or football team is going to win! But somehow 'all Black' school boards and niggers with degrees in varying aspects of childhood education and counseling seem to think that the quality of the pep rally has something to do with whether our children stop attacking teachers and administrators, and stop attacking each other like animals for the benefit of the 6 o'clock news in the hallways. Is it too much to ask our youth whom we feed and clothe to start behaving in ways that reflect that our youth respect education and respect education's power to increase their individual quality of life and the quality of life in our communities...but we get pep rallies and trite social justice chants. And yes that is the same reason no urban majority or significantly Black school system has had particular success in hiring and retaining good superintendents, increasing test scores and/or decreasing incidences of violence.

They are playing musical chairs with superintendents and what is altogether worse they are hiring million-dollar consultants to find them candidates that won't last 3 years. African America please listen to me, if Jesus came back (no disrespect intended) and the first thing he did was suggest that he should be superintendent of schools, with the intent of fixing them, and his ideas didn't include stronger nuclear and extended families, discipline, good ole Judeo-Christian values, I'd be really surprised, but yet we think we can hire niggers and White liberals so smart they wouldn't do what Jesus would do to fix the schools. Yeah, they're going to relax discipline, in favor of hunting for children's learning styles. These are the same children who don't know what they want for lunch today or tomorrow, so the idea that they would know their 'learning style' and be able to communicate it to adults, and that adults should follow it is ridiculous. And these are the monstrosities of injustice that liberal socialist atheist largely Black urban female run school systems are birthing in America.

After the teen shootings on the 14th street bridge near the upscale Atlantic Station shopping development, local unnamed rappers, city politicians like Mayor Dickens and preachers held press conferences imploring our children that 'this has got to stop'. And yet it never does and appears to be getting worse. These shootings and examples of teen violence prompted city officials to suggest that curfews were the 'solution'. And yet, the pink elephant in the room is that curfews and restrictions are being suggested for Black children's issues. Not a soul has ever broached the subject in the context of mainstream metropolitan Atlanta that Jewish children or Arab American children, of African children or yes, even Hispanic children need a curfew to curb any youthful tendencies towards indiscretions.

Social justice warriors love hollering about how our children are singled out and criminalized but when social justice liberals like Keshia Bottoms and Dickens and the city council get in power, the first thing they do is single out our children for extra-special police supervision that other races of children don't seem to need. Is that not embarrassing? Why not? That is precisely how bankrupt they are in terms of ideas for preventing violence in Black communities generally and Black youth. These Black female liberals spent the 'woke-wake' of the George Floyd Black Lives Matter era trying to 'defund the police' and now as crime has spiked and exploded, the only solutions they have are the same ones Republicans and conservatives have been trying to put on us since Reconstruction; curfews, Black Codes, Jim Crow laws about where it is proper for us to be at certain times of night, law enforcement, legalism and tougher punishment. That is how bankrupt post-modern Black liberal politicians and thinkers are today.

Local Atlanta news programs show fight after fight, it seems on a weekly basis of Black students jumping on each other, and jumping on teachers and administrators; all on the 6 o'clock news outlets making our children look like animals and us look completely impotent in solving the problem. Thus, it seems we prefer that someone else, be it the government, White mainstream socialist atheist LGBTQIA Liberals, reparations, or even school choice White partisan conservative Republicans to solve our problems for us and we don't mind stinking up the 6 o'clock news because maybe it may spur Whites and the White mainstream to feel sorry for us and fix its nigger problem (The Black Urban Poor Question). Only, you'd be surprised how far, the far right can spin that narrative. So far that after 19th Century Germany being so, so modern and prosperous, that Jews in Germany were happy to assimilate, shed themselves of racial and cultural stereotypes of Judaism and be modern, to being a Germany that in the 1920's the Nazis would come to power. They came to power by blaming every single social problem Germany ever had on the presence of Jews as an impoverished minority and the culture they 'bred', from crime to the mongrelization of the culture and German women's morality, and the 'blame' for infusing pure German art and culture with Jewish (nigger loving) values. Even the presence of 'acceptable' niggers, who may even have renounced Judaism and truly embraced German culture and values did not keep the Nazi's from blaming every single socio-economic problem Weimar Republic Germany had on the Jews. The Nazi's rose to power blaming everything on the Jews. Black people are the problem in 2023 today. The political argument being made by the Republican right greatly resembles these notions that liberal Negroes have integrated powerful positions and thus endangered the whole pure Americana thing. A fall of culture is thus predicted. Go woke go broke. The face of wokeness is the Black female and the gay-trans Black man. That certain political persuasions would see in this not only a problem but an easily identifiable target for political purposes is standard these days. The homosexuals came out of the closet in Weimar Republic Germany too, hooked on jazz, cheap liquor and the culture symbolized in the musical Cabaret. It is the same thing here in America with the jazz age, F Scott Fitzgerald, speakeasies, gangsters, pimps, prostitutes, etc. And White Conservative and right of center groups have taken advantage of now having an identifiable target to go after and to symbolize everything you think is evil and 'White folk gone wrong' in the world. As a matter of fact, that is really what a Donald Trump presidency represents, the triumph of the political argument 'White folks gone wrong' starring Black women and social atheist LGBTQI Sith Lords in high places.

Bud Light, I will teach you a lesson. The problem was not any God-fearing Capitalist American having a problem with gay people or trans people drinking beer, or Budweiser or anyone else acknowledging that they have customers of all races, creeds, religions, sexualities. All are united in drunken frivolous wasting away their lives. The problem and perhaps unforgiveable sin was in putting a face with it, the face of Dylan Mulvaney. So now they inherited all of his baggage (intended and unintended). The White mainstream socialist atheist Democratic Party is in the same boat as Budweiser. They have made the mistake of for 'representations sake', going out and putting face(s) on woke radical racial socialist atheism, and that face is 'Black Women' (Kamala, Stacy Abrams, Ketanji, Robin from the Today show, Britney Griner, Ru Paul, Oprah, Billy Porter, etc.). The tragedies in that are multi-fold. Black people as a whole, and certainly not just Bible belt Black southerners and others of the real heirs of the quite Christian Civil Rights Movement, did not choose Democrat Party socialist-atheism or it's necessary by products in the LGBTQIA movement. Not na'an nigga in the 50's, 60's and 70's knew that by his marching, civil disobedience and protesting, he was protesting for the atheist BLM/LGBTQIA agendas and that would be the ultimate direction of where he was 'driving' his and his people's political agenda and what they would come to be defined by. So, the first problem was that we did not choose that veering off from the quite Christian Civil Rights movement. The second problem is that if we could have seen the consequences, the blowback, we may have trodden a little more carefully. For instance, do you think the niggas and Black lawyers pushing affirmative action in the 60's and getting it, would have predicted the day the blowback would come in 2023 and conservative courts would nearly completely gut, decapitate and undermine affirmative action programs? Could they have predicted that White people conditioned by decades of political innuendo and 'dog whistling' (Goldwater, Reagan and Welfare Queens, Gingrich, Donald Trump) to resent affirmative action and perceived correlated 'entitlements' like welfare etc., to then go out on a White man's mission to file lawsuit after lawsuit, and send high powered lawyer after high powered lawyer, and send Conservative nigga after conservative nigga from Thomas Sowell to Larry Elder to argue against affirmative action and set asides? Did our Civil Rights era affirmative action era warriors think the White blowback would be that strong? Like Shannon Sharp said, "did they really want that smoke?"

Part II

And now Crime in our communities is off the charts (even by minority standards going back to the Jim Crow era). Before integration Black people were just as poor (if not poorer) and had just as few opportunities, but the internal (read Black on Black) crime rate was less and this should clearly prove that money and academic and professional opportunities in themselves, do not create safe spaces in schools or communities. How is it that we of Negritude are more afraid of each other and our children, in 2023 than we were at any point during Jim Crow days and probably even slavery! How is it, that in 2023 Black men and women fear going to gas stations, grocery stores and mall parking lots. This fear is so intense that as a grown 250-pound big ugly nigga (self-description), I exercise extreme caution in observing the environment in these places. Once sold to us as a matter of convenience, it is hard to go the ATM without having the fear of God in your heart and bank account, as not only will someone perhaps knock you over the head and take your money, but they may also follow you home and take way more than what you had in the ATM. Not only that, even though we of Negritude seem to prefer the old fashion methods of robbery to the new White-collar criminality, one still need be afraid of hacked bank accounts, skimmed credit card numbers and pins and getting scammed and hacked by every two-bit thief scattered across the globe!

Having to take all those precautions and the necessity of having to fear what your fellow American citizens are capable of in terms of thievery and violence, it is no wonder why Americans of all stripes feel themselves to be anxiety ridden and under extreme pressures. Honestly, how many more usernames and passwords must I remember? The list keeps growing. Is the answer simply trusting in storing them in the AI Cloud, which for all its presumptions of cyber encoded security, still seems to me perfectly compliant with Jesus' admonition not to store your precious things where the violent and crafty can 'seize it by force'. Is the answer simply storing things in a nebulous AI cloud where computer algorithms can take our data storage and usage patterns and design (just for me) sales content, sales items that cater to my addictions and supply me with info that instead of freeing my thinking, simply YouTube, Instagram, "Facebooks' and 'threads' me feeds of my own predilections and vain imaginations, creating an echo chamber which to the extent that it is controlled by algorithms and the forces of AI, in essence controls us by controlling what we see and shaping how we think about it by conveniently using influencers and cyber notions of peer pressure. Do you think cyber peer pressure doesn't exist? Think about Sales patterns and patterns of teen girls with self-esteem esteem issues preceding from their interactions with social media; buying clothes, shoes and other products, patterns of dumb ass tik-tok challenges getting millions of dummies to participate. Hundreds of thousands of millions of Swifties and devotees of Queen Bey et al, pissed off or supportive because of what their idols seem to encourage them to do, like the Muslims follow the Sunnah and Hadith of the Prophet Muhammad, they follow the sayings and the practices of Taylor Swift and Beyonce? Really?

Gangs are terrorizing our streets and schools and there seems to be not enough police or enforcement. Police or law enforcement that make mistakes are pilloried, tarred, and feathered by the denizens of 'wokedom', as woke leaders make enough money off 'wokeness' to live in gated communities with private security. Nor would these denizens of 'wokeness' ever send their children to our inner-city schools. These liberals send their children to private schools along with the conservative elites they 'joan' in front of you, but love when they get by themselves at PTA and the like when their children marry amongst each other. Black liberals and Black elected officials will not embrace nuclear and extended family and family responsibility to the elderly. They will embrace and promote bigger and bigger forms of government to 'potentially' solve the problem. More intrusive and intensive government is their answer to everything. And so the elderly are left to rot as family members think it beneath them and not their responsibility to intervene, because such loyal and dutiful behavior does not result in them having time and the ability to freely pursue their ability to 'live their truth'. And because the government or some government sponsored home will take care of them anyway.

Part III

There are record and myriad feelings of alienation and anxiety reflected in the spate of calls for 'mental health' personnel and wellness in reaction to random senseless daily outbursts of public violence, for which the only explanation we can make is that the person has/had mental health issues. This is reasoned better than calling it a demonic or foul spirit as would have been done in Jesus times and prior to Jesus times. Even when we humans were in cultural and evolutionary psychological terms, animists, and deists of all stripes, there was an assumption (rational or not), about what a foul spirit was, and what it did inside a person. I suppose one might make the argument that if a wild random killer is on the loose, killing for no apparent reason, then he/she has mental health problems; yet if wild random killers are on the loose (repeatedly and seemingly daily), killing for no apparent reason, then perhaps it is not the individual that has mental health problems, but the society and culture itself the individual lives in. Similarly, if a wild random killer is on the loose, killing for no apparent reason, then the man or woman doing the killing has a demonic or foul spirit; and I hope you see where I'm going with this, if repeatedly and daily, a wild random killer is on the loose, killing for no apparent reason, then that society and culture has a demonic and foul spirit. Let them that have ears to hear, hear that one, ladies and gentlemen.

Record alienation and anxiety, record violence, record hostility between the races even though the question must be asked how the hell it could have been better 50 years ago considering all that we thought 'forced' integration, public education about unity, enlightenment, affirmative action, lip service about racial love and harmony, and the Civil Rights Movement were supposed to bring both Blacks, Whites and America as a country. But it has seemingly done the opposite. America is polarized and parties either push racial/sexual agendas or the political opposite of racial/sexual agendas and that is what makes Trump so effective. Like him or not, he is the face of the blowback against 'wokeness' and the fact that 'wokeness' must be defended is the very proof that in the post-Civil Rights era forms it took, something went wrong. Instead of bringing the 'promised land' or something that looked like what Martin Luther King Jr., described in his famous speech, it brought Asians suing Harvard because their test scores and student attributes are way above what Black and White people score that get into Harvard and other elite schools for varying reasons. Asians call it discrimination against them.

Instead of bringing the promised land it brought a living hell, where White people resent us as Blacks openly, and as a matter of political conviction (conservative), even going so far as to openly politically and academically aver that the Civil Rights era strategies weakened America by lowering standards in everything from Medical Schools to the Military to the Coast Guard. At the very same time, Black people and Black self-centered leadership had an economic incentive in the new apparent social mobility afforded by White liberalism and it became more important to sell your political self to White liberals as 'representing Black people', rather than to (actually) represent Black interests. Thus, in the post-civil rights era we have elected many Black elected officials that have included men and women over the years, but the trend now is towards Black women with radical socialist-atheist LGBTQIA agendas. The reason for that shift in the post-Civil Rights era towards 'wokeness' is that it is more lucrative for a Black politician to sell him or herself to the White liberal Democrat machine (or the White Conservative Republican machine), than it is to (actually) lead Black people and have to do the hard work that comes with leadership. That is to say, designing and creating strategies for African American development that are not 'dependent' on White mainstream culture affirmations or government programs.

That is why the policies coming out of the Black political and cultural left are so ridiculous. Stacy Abrams says abortion rights helps Black women and Black economic opportunity. A whole host of Black political and cultural liberal elites think it is more important to teach and preach the perfect normalcy of the LGBTQIA lifestyle in high school health class, hosting trans reading hours for little children and putting laundromats in schools so that teen moms can feel more comfortable at school than it is to make sure they can read and write on grade level! These wild-eyed woke liberals apparently think that agenda more important in terms of public education policies than old fashioned issues like discipline, home training, and respect for fellow students, teachers, and administrators. Time these liberal Negroes get in power they are affirming the LGBTQIA community like our (Black Lives Mattering) depended upon it; as though the only way Black Lives can matter is if Ru Paul and Billy Porter can prance around on TV and in movies as successful examples of Black masculinity every day. I'm not making the argument they aren't successful Black men, I am not the arbiter of maleness or success, but it seems they tend to get way more press and affirmation than us average nigga men with, shall we save, average appetites and habits. These Black liberal radicals and radical feminists even tell us that the key to raising more healthy Black males is if they affirm and teach gender fluidity. This they claim will reduce male toxicity. These liberals sell and push gender studies above SAT tutorials, gender studies above discipline, gender studies above music and the arts, and gender studies above ensuring Black children get a competitive K-12 education so they can compete more effectively post-graduation in college and university or wherever life sends them. Black liberal politicians know damn well we are raising generations of Black children in inferior schools and scholastic settings (the proof is that they don't send their children to urban schools, preferring to live and send their children to White mainstream schools). Ladies and gentlemen, that is criminal. It is criminal to have leaders that know we are not raising our children to be competitive in the world; setting them up for defeat and failure, all the while enforcing White liberal political agendas that can neither produce the stated desired improvement, nor result in the improvement of mental health in general.

Part IV

Black professional athletes get bigger salaries than ever before, but the impact of 50 years of success in athletics and entertainment if viewed through the lens of Black poverty, Black schools, the Black family, and economic development, has meant nothing but having tokens of acceptability and respectability all conveniently at the disposal of much larger corporate forces. As I write, the 2023 NBA playoffs are going on at arenas owned or sponsored by major White mainstream corporations all over the country. Look closely when the camera pans to the cheering and jeering crowds, and the sea of rich White faces is many. There are 30 or so rich Black faces I suppose. I'd like to argue, not a single Black ghetto born star has put a dent in the poverty rate of the ghetto that 'borned' him. This is the case with so called gangsta or hood rappers as well that magically end up with homes in Buckhead and other elite White mainstream neighborhoods.

Ladies and gentlemen of Negritude and Niggerdom, these are holes in the political and cultural puzzle that need to be solved (do children even put puzzles together anymore, I hope my metaphor isn't lost). So confused and perplexed am even I, that I look at all the pieces that came in the box and my lack of progress in putting it together into something that looks like what came on the box, that I wonder if a mistake has not been made and maybe the manufacturer didn't send all of the pieces or some kind of way, some incongruous puzzle pieces from another picture got mixed up in it somehow. What are the constituent important pieces of the puzzle in the context of African America, in order to sincerely and earnestly improve the quality of life for Black people in America; thus contributing towards increasing the stability and quality of life for Americans in general. This is especially important as American power seems to be fading from its heights in the wake of Russian and Chinese intransigence, perfidy and just plain old 'real politique'. American and

Western European personalities, politicians and corporations were flattered and felt powerful at the idealistic hope that the Chinese 'freer markets' and post-Soviet 'free markets' would make them rich and reinforce a new Western economically led (if not politically and militarily), world order to boot. However, China and Russia were not so enamored of the economic and political systems of the Americans and Europeans, and only pretend(ed) to embrace those values long enough to use western technology and other practices to restore their ancient imperial nations to their 'proper place' in the world's global leadership.

But I digress, crime, dysfunctional juveniles, dysfunctional schools, economic underdevelopment in our communities, these are all holes in the picture of Black quality of life that we would like to picture with the pieces in the boxed puzzle that to many other citizens looks like the 'American Dream'. Ladies and gentlemen, I will belabor the point a little further for the sake of being thorough. Mayor Andre Dickens and his 'Midnight Basketball' will not work; anti-gang and youth violence task forces will not work; youth pep rallies and trite motivational chants will not work. The saints and geniuses working at DFACS cannot improve the situation, the saints and geniuses working at the Police Department can not do it, even if such a thing were possible. Big Brothers and Big Sisters, United Ways and near perfectly enlightened judges, more jails, less jails will not do, turning Atlanta City Jail into a 'Help Center' just like Weezie and Helen used to work in and raising them from the dead in nationwide séance in order to lead it would not help Black women and children, the homeless, the regular insane, the criminally insane, etc. Those are but small pieces in the real puzzle of what it takes to really increase the quality of life for Black people in America. There is but one answer, one huge puzzle piece staring us in the face and because of our liberal Black elected official leadership cadres and the fact they are beholden to the White liberal Democrat power structure, we have been ignoring it like the plague.

This puzzle piece has been staring us in the face while we pretend to believe that 'midnight basketball' can trump crime and dysfunction, and while we continue to believe that citywide mandated curfews backed up by law enforcement can trump juvenile crime and dysfunction. And in the face of the obviousness of the 'missing puzzle piece' to other races of people around us, it makes Black elected officials and the Black community look insane or absolutely blinded by anger and resentment against White people. We have for so long ignored the elephant in the room that now Asians, Africans, Republicans, conservatives, and White culture in general considers it a truism that our families are fucked up and most of our children don't have fathers of note in their lives. Furthermore, it seems that Black men and Black women no longer respect or love each other enough to get married anymore and have resigned ourselves to the fact that 70% of our children are born out of wedlock. To add insult to injury, we think White racism and the lack of reparations has more to do with crime, juvenile dysfunction and violence, dysfunctional schools, economic underdevelopment et al than the state of our families.

Part V

African America, descendants of Africa in the West, Nigrodom and Negritude; in this book I will submit evidence that one of the big pink elephant missing pieces in the room, is staring us in the face. This one missing piece is the most important piece of the puzzle in improving the quality of life for Black people in a wholistic way. And that is by strengthening the Black family. By wholistic, it is meant inclusive of economic, academic, cultural, political, and intergenerational wealth considerations. The strengthening of the traditional Black family, familial units, and relationships will affect our problems faster, and in a way that will prove more stable than any temporary or short term (throw money at it) solutions like more police, curfews, washing machines in high schools, free lunch, Black and brown liberal judges, reparations etc. I will submit varying forms of evidence; you be the judge and jury. If the case I present doesn't make sense, live your life, live your truth. If the case I present in this book makes any sense at all, then pay your due diligence to your God, your family, the ties of kith and kin, education, commerce, and industry, quite nearly in that order and enjoin those same values amongst your friends family, community, and municipality and America will experience a new post-modern Religious Revival, Renaissance and Enlightenment for which the heart and future of the nation are at stake. If we continue in the direction we are headed, we will be weakened and divided; hellfire bound in this world and the next. As our families go, so will go our nation go and that is why Black people get what we get out of America (welfare and affirmative action dependence) and America will experience the same disunity and dysfunction that comes from disunified and dysfunctional nuclear and extended families, but it will have far greater regional and international political effects that don't bode well for White mainstream American and European culture like exponentially declining birthrates.

Part VI

Is it not true that the family (our nuclear and extended families resulting from long term pairing throughout the entire range of human and our ape cousins and common ape ancestor's histories) were the original DFACS. The very things DFACS does for children; that is to say, enforcing a bare minimum approach to care and providing for the core needs of children whose parents are unable to care for them for whatever reason. Because the 50 year reign of today's liberal socialist atheist LGBTQIA Black elected officials and cultural elites, family and social splintering has meant many children are not experiencing the positive developmental care that the old-fashioned family, as a socio-eco-cultural institution gave. What cannot be reproduced in DFACS, philanthropic, and government programs is that the family, more often than not, goes above and beyond a child's bare minimum, core needs, whereas the state doesn't. State supervision is never as good as the family, even in the case of exceptional case workers, presumably like Mariah Carey's character in the movie Precious. Clearly (by default), the family did its historical job well throughout human, ape, and primeval mammal history, and DFACS is simply an expensive, unwieldy and oftentimes brutal ersatz version of the essential characteristics of the traditional family. And now a society that calls itself technologically and politically advanced has decided the traditional family is unnecessary, and all types of ad hoc families can do the job the good old fashioned mammalian defined family did. Supposedly these man-made families can do the job the biblically old-fashioned defined family did, just as well too. DFACS, the Welfare system and all sorts of ad hoc families supposedly can raise strong, sound, peaceful, educated healthy children just as good? 50 years of that and the evidence has proven none of those institutional forces are good substitutes for the family, and cause attachment problems in children who do not have the benefit of the love, care and support of traditional families. Evidence of the failure of the state and these post-modern ad hoc family structures can be seen in African America on the 6 o'clock news. Look at prison records, has abortion on demand, welfare dependency, mom's new boyfriends and girlfriends, the foster system, DFACS, WIC, etc., dented the statistical analysis that shows 70% of the people incarcerated have problematic relationships with their fathers. Now we depend on the government and devalue family values and life. We are all supposed to be ok with the government taking responsibility for our children? Judge the results by anecdote and your own experiences. Older aunts, uncles, cousins, gram and granddaddy them, took up the slack and still are. It is largely grandparents bearing the burden today of their grandchildren, the innocent children of wayward sons and daughters. An important benefit to children is that it gives children care givers related to them, providing a sense of rootedness to time, place, community, religion, culture, and spirituality. Why does the government want us to believe that it can do just as good a job as the family? The post-modern liberal LGBTQIA socialist atheist Democrat Black woman run political elites have been way more successful at defunding and bankrupting the family, as opposed to their equally misguided efforts to defund the police. As a matter of fact, our liberal Democrat government presently construed here in America will support anything but the traditionally empowered family, and put it on a poster to prove how much they respect freedom. Freedom at whose expense; our children, social stability, the law? Why? Where is our government's dog in the fight over what a family is…after 2000 years and untold millennia of mammalian evolution?

Ladies and gentlemen, it is in someone's interest to foster dependence and reliance upon technology, government and common law as opposed to (God, Family and Tradition). Post Modernity unfortunately is purposely weakening the bonds of God, family, tradition and roots and it is literally driving people crazy. Mental health issues and crises have risen exponentially. More and more people are unhinged from the traditional things and values that gave people's lives identity and meaning. Post-Modernity says the ancient traditions we once valued, are just passing whims and cultural fancies, like whether a boy is a boy or a girl. People are confused, diabolically and damn near demonically confused and it is causing horrible adjustment problems. How is it indeed, a boy somehow gets the message from his environment at 8 that his penis is his problem, and he wants to cut it off, thus changing his identity, which hitherto was rooted in physical DNA based family, community, religion, culture etc. Post Modern materialism is also purposely weakening the bonds of God, family, tradition, and roots in people's consciousness, in order to replace them with perpetual obedience to the latest influencer and the reward of consumerism and binge watching movies all day, high off drugs (legal and otherwise). Many young men are not socialized to or sociable enough to even want to have real sex and get married, and waste their lives away being entertained by a series of porn-hub algorithms that magically seem to only to cater to your adolescent fetishes. In this new consumerist AI post-modern reality, we are not even in control of our own habits anymore let alone spending habits. AI is. That is how they want you; conditioned to think it a good thing to order your porn from porn hub and food from Grub hub. You can have stuff delivered to you instead of going to the market and having to socialize amongst the other hoi polloi, and you escape 'the prison' of eating communally prepared meals at home around biological family and loved ones. Drones will make deliveries, be used for general surveillance and law enforcement and eventually the crime will get so bad we will empower and weaponize the drones and AI to combat crime. Presently construed if a policeman causes a couple chain reaction accidents chasing a suspect, suspected, and documented on surveillance camera to be a dangerous felon, the policeman involved must face certain questions as to the appropriateness of his actions relative to the safety of the general public. But if a robot drone causes some collateral damage after a clear AI match in the database for a convicted felon, are you going to question the robot tactical pursuit software, programming and technology, the drone footage used to match the human perpetrator; furthermore is it even possible to punish a robot without in some sense questioning the 'guilt' of the entire system that created it and justifies its existence. The self-driving car thing is just the testing of the waters. What an auto-driven car does accidentally, or, by the will of God in that it was unpredictable and due to an unforeseen in the programming event or series of events, exculpates the robot and the systemic technologies and software it is dependent on, but it does not exculpate the human being. It is thus giving technology benefits of the doubt and rights that we don't give other human beings that is especially dangerous.

Our life savings are somewhere up in the banking cloud somewhere; just a number I see when I log into my account on my smartphone and use my debit or credit card or write a check (if anyone really does that anymore in favor of sending money through various other digital means). You'll see hell with your own eyes before you put your money in your brother's safe in his home but have little or no qualms about putting your money somewhere up in the cloud, only able to access it when the power is on. That is one of my central problems with bitcoin though I am told there is philosophical or technological wrap around that covers my inhibitions. If you buy land or a business, or a home or a golf course, let us say real estate in general and do the sales properly and it is properly deeded and the like with such authorities as are appropriate; if all else fails you can go to that land and sleep on it if you want to, though the appropriateness of that might be called into question except under extreme circumstances. The same can be said for gold or precious metals and the trade in such things. It is something you can hold in your hand. It is also why I prefer recordings to streaming. Growing up in the classic age, going into record stores reading and looking at the covers of albums and searching the stacks was a kind of discipline and practice reading in itself. I'd spend at least 15 minutes or so, engaged in reading the back liner notes to my favorite band's latest or previous albums that I couldn't afford at one time.

Now artists discographies are a click away to a kid with wi-fi, minus the adoration, discipline and reading skills that come from reading liner notes standing up in a record store with people all around you and the music blasting and avoiding getting in people's way. Oh yes, and remember being a teen in the drug or grocery store selling 'teen mags' or 'Black teen mags' or 'rock band mags' and standing there the whole time your mother was at the store reading through magazines with interviews of your favorite musicians, stars and people. Kids are on their phones now a days. That's why they can't concentrate. As a teen kid in 87' we were standing in the middle of aisle 2 with the magazines and offices supplies and a cascade of people going by. We were gung-ho concentrating on 'the reading', and getting the gist of it as fast as possible and drawing conclusions, because you knew damn well your mama wasn't and/or couldn't buy the magazine, and your only exposure to the information would be standing there in the middle of aisle 2 with your mother in the line telling you to be at the front door by the time she gets through check out. As a matter of fact, most of us knew the last sane thing we could ask our Black mothers, while they are struggling to pay for the food the family eats and make it go as far as possible, was to ask for the latest 'Teen Beat' with Duran Duran on the front cover, with a fold out of them in '7 and the Ragged Tiger' pose. I inhaled the article and read as fast as I could while my mother was in line, hoping and praying she sees my interest and tells me 'bring it up here boy'. But that didn't happen, and truth be told, I wanted to put the Duran Duran fold out poster up on my bedroom wall. That is because all of the coolest and hippest dudes I knew had artistic, musical and shit on the walls like chicks in bikinis.

It is the same with the difference between physical libraries and streaming content digital libraries in a sense. What is physical cannot be altered post-production per se, but what is digital, is subject to all sorts of alterations and iterations at every stage of its life, of which none but the computer knows. And the computer knows full well the average person won't notice the alteration of a word or two. To be dependent upon digitally streamed and streaming versions is to present ourselves 100% vulnerable to this new AI Chatbox generation where Republicans are crazy and/or dumb enough to do an AI generated commercial and God knows where else this kind of madness will lead and how as it gets realer and realer, the possibilities for sheer chaos grows and grows.

Indeed, a new world order has been created and it is based on dependence on technology, the authority of common civil law (as opposed to the triumvirate of family, religion, and culture), and social media friends and associates (aka chatbots designed to ingratiate themselves using algorithms to certain personality types) instead of God as the ultimate public authority and family. Where is the authority when our children do Tik-Tok trends instead of chores? Where is the authority when our children are on commercials celebrating (worshipping) the fact that they have high speed internet connections in every room in their house, and can handle multiple streaming devices at once. Our children seem to be so excited by wi-fi and their smartphones, that they celebrate that with the same fervor as though they were catching the Holy Ghost in a store front church. Compared to wi-fi and technology, our children think everything else looks and feels boring like books, the natural world, and simple conversations with others. And we look at it and think it advantageous for some child actors, and cute and appropriate that our children are sold to in their youth, in such crass commercial terms; enslaving them to the idea that wi-fi and connectivity is a value in itself, i.e., there is no reality except it and it is the base value of their lives because it prevents them from being bored by normal life. Wi-fi supports their varying gaming consoles, the phone, their laptops, their tablets, on Instagram getting fucked by the latest trend, which I hear today on the news is a Tik Tok Trend. Tik Tok is a company that for all intents, purposes and claims otherwise, is owned by America's political, military, and economic international rival (China). In this Tik Tok trend, where presumably otherwise sane American youth are challenged on TikTok to jump off a moving boat at speed into the water, like some James Bond shit or something. Ladies and gentlemen 20 American youth have died in the past month. Why would China need to attack America, Tik-Tok is doing it for them and they make money infantilizing American children and adults too. It's a win-win for the Chinese. Remember the Tik-Tok trend where supposedly sane adults dump cold water on their heads to raise money for some charity. This is sold to us as a better option than simply sending the charity some money directly. That is not exciting enough for we technologically infantilized Americans.

But let us not belabor the time with simply demonstrated proofs from your own experiences and interactions with public and social media culture in America. Let us content ourselves with this argument; the family, was the original employment agency, i.e. the role that the local DOL Department of Labor suggests it can and should play in people's lives today. The boy is no scholar or athlete, the boy got somebody pregnant. Let him go down to the plant or the factory or the fields or the docks with Uncle Mike or Aunt Joan. It quite often happened that children and adolescents did or wanted to do what (industries, fields of commercial activity) their aunts, uncles and cousins did or tended to do. In this wise they got actual skills simply from being around family members and observing them perform professionally. In a family, this happens in a context where the child does not even notice his family members work in the store and it cannot be said that someone 'made' them do it. They observed older brothers, siblings and cousins do, and they took great pride in doing 'it' too, acting like their older siblings and big cousins. Ever seen the kid with the plastic lawn mower following dad and the real mower? The patriarchy, the family, didn't make these kids mimic the activities and behaviors of their older siblings, parents, and cousins, as the case is made when liberals and the transgender communities suggest that the traditional family 'indoctrinates' youth into vocational, sexual, and familial roles. Within the dynamics of those familial relationships, and the skill sets by various family members and willingness to go far beyond letting your little cousin watch what you do, and actually teaching them to do what you do, senses of competency and confidence are encouraged and gained that are good for a child's psychological health. So far from being limiting, even in the worst-case scenario, it gives a child the freedom to know what they don't want to do after the fact of having been exposed to it for so long in their family. But we are told the DOL (Department of Labor) can do just as good a job doing all those functions the family used to do.

Let us also endeavor to say the family (nuclear and extended) was the original United Negro College Fund, the Original Student Loan Association, the Original Vocational Rehab Education and Training and perhaps most importantly, the original Small Business and Entrepreneurial Loan Association. For that matter, The Family was the original Credit Union too! Even today as we are in the dominant phase of the faceless, nameless, highly legalized, and commodified world of modern industry, there are still tech companies that trace their roots to being started in the suburban garages of parents and relatives, the early financing by grandmothers and grandfathers, cousins, aunts, and uncles. As I think on this trend in Tech companies, it is ironic how important family was to the early founders. This dependency on family is not limited to the corporate or tech world either.

Leontyne Price and Jessye Norman, renown opera singers families contributed to their study of professional classical music vocal training. You know damn well these families from Augusta, GA (Jessye Norman) and Laurel, Mississippi (Leontyne Price), in these small rural Black communities didn't know shit about classical music in the main. But they believed in their granddaughter, cousin, niece, sister, and contributed sacrificially to the cost of lessons, and the expense of advanced professional training. Quite often travel expenses were required as European teachers taught Black voices before traditional White mainstream American teachers and institutions would accept and develop Black operatic voices because of racism. This happened to Mattiwilda Dobbs, of the important Dobbs family in Black Atlanta who became a very accomplished European Classical Music singer. But like Marion Anderson, she was at her height before integration could give them the exposure and commercial opportunities they well deserved. Price and Norman rose after the Civil Rights Movement and thus we know of their accomplishments more than we are familiar with the accomplishments of Dobbs and Andersons. The training in Europe had the additional effect of bestowing upon Black singers like Price and Norman a privilege no White American Impresario could deny. Once the 'masters' themselves (the Germans, Italians, etc.) of European Classical Music endorsed a Black singer, to deny the qualification of 'the masters', even in the face of racism, still meant Whites denying themselves, because that is the pedigree the White mainstream impresario claims is what distinguishes him and separates him from 'common' pop American culture as well. And with all of that, Divas Price and Norman began life in the deep country with no other support than their families...and guess who...their churches and community support. The very churches that supported and nurtured Black talent long before the government, philanthropists, and White mainstream socialist elites ever thought about it. They have abandoned these little Black churches and their antiquated values and all the hard work they did prior to the Civil Rights Movement, Jim Crow, Reconstruction and the antebellum age in favor of the socialist-atheist LGBTQIA agenda.

Yes, many of our old-fashioned Black churches essentially have never recovered from the one two punch of the silly impotent extravagance of prosperity preachers and the abuse by atheists, sectarian religionists and 60's Black radicals that the Black church itself is complicit in Black people's dysfunction. With its 'pie in the sky' theology, dependence upon the pastor/preacher who is often enough manipulative and exploitive, and seeming capitulation to the obedience to the White man's religion, traditional Black Christianity was a prime target for radicals of all stripes that needed a target. The effect has been generations of Black people who openly manifest the self-hatred required to detest the religion of their fathers and grandfathers which they suggest is 'the White man's religion' in favor of the Arab man's religion, the Indian man's religion, and the Chinese man's religion and still the White man's religion in the form of atheism, LGBTQIA self-determinism, and atheistic notions of stoic self-reliance which is idolatry. Even making that argument, let us note that in most cases our ole fashion Christian grandma and grandad loved you and supported you even when you apparently rejected their religion in favor of some other foreign religion. They didn't agree with or understand your particularized version of 'living your truth' but they loved you anyhow. I find it rare that the favor of unconditional love flowed both ways.

And yet we can go on and on ad infinitum trying to replace things that need not be replaced. The family was the original Uber, Lyft; the original Christian Mingle and other forms of dating and matchmaking sites. And let me pause here on The Family as the original Dating App. Male or Female, you could and quite often did 'socialize' with your family member's friends and associates from the wider community. It used to be a truism that older aunts were always introducing single nieces and nephews to 'nice young people' of the opposite sex they thought were nice, came from good homes and would make a good match. They were always (as it were) trying to set you up. As exciting as self-selection is, and falling in love at complete random, with 70% divorce rates, and falling birth rates, a strong case could be made that self-selection and whatever we are currently doing is not working! The truth of the matter is that some of us do need help and maybe your auntie has a hard working co-worker from a good home she thinks you would make a good match with. How can we even suggest that a computer algorithm and paying $75 for an assessment test could get you any better?

The question of whether you'd be happier depending upon such familial arrangements and considerations as that in a world of online dating, hooking up, etc., I don't know. But as I said, none of that is making our families stronger, nor does hooking up and perpetual dating statistically make us happier. Oftentimes people in such situations self-report themselves as unhappy with the quality of their relationships. Are we any happier and satisfied sexually or emotionally because an app exists that shows you the location of other human beings within a 3-5 mile radius (or the selected range) of your home that are desirous of hooking up and want to fuck? Even if the bestiality and carnality of such behavior doesn't get you, it will not take long for you to view it as unfulfilling. Were it fulfilling, you wouldn't continue to do it, like the addict must continue to ingest greater and greater amounts of the drug to even pretend that it is satisfying.

Plus, the fact that trusted cousins, uncles, or aunts have introduced you to somebody puts an unspoken onus on the relative and the potential mate. If they really like, respect, and love your (aunt, uncle, friend/ etc.) they will not want to disappoint them by treating the beloved poorly. Hey, I know it's not exactly a guarantee, but it has got to help on some level, and you never know if it might make the difference one day between divorce and staying together. Another corollary effect regards domestic violence. The fact that his girlfriend/wife's cousins, brothers, he not only knows personally, but may have been involved in their introduction, would tend to reduce verbal abuse and domestic violence. That is even if it is just in making the person think twice. My favorite example of the 'onus' required in this is the guy that happens to fall in love with his best friend's sister (of similar age). If that is really your road dog, your ride or die nigga, you wouldn't disappoint or disrespect him by cheating on his sister and making her miserable and sad where she is complaining to their loved ones about how unhappy and miserable you have made her. And God forbid if you hit her or stole her check or some shit like that. A real nigga who you would be proud to call your friend because he has honor, would beat your ass himself for cheating on or hitting his sister. All of these forces make a muthafucka think twice before nutting up and requiring police or 911 intervention.

Part VII

As we prepare to close let us turn towards a somber reality. Post-Modernity and Democrat socialist atheist, LGBTQIA, abortion as a lifestyle, Dr. Kevorkian culture of the humane, has told the Black community (and any other cultures and groups of people without strong enough religions and cultures to withstand it), that we can neglect our filial and family duties and that it's ok. It is ok because the government and White mainstream benevolence and benevolent institutions will 'take care' of our aged, loved ones, or children of family members whose family members are unable to care for them. Or perhaps we have the money we can simply pay someone to take care of them. Perhaps it is as easy as depending upon government care or simply going to a website like 'whattodoaboutmama.com' and big mama and big daddy will be taken care of, and we can go out there using the free time to go searching for 'our truth'. And yet I find it hard to believe that if we can't find enough teachers, policemen and hospital nurses, we can find adequate numbers of personal attendants who our loved ones are dependent upon to wash them, feed them and in all the other small ways look after and care for them. Who'd want to do that job when you could be flipping houses or be a social media influencer or be Kim Kardashian, who I am told recently made her child wait at the MET Gala while she walked the red carpet alone...truly fulfilling the biblical note and mandate to 'trod the winepress alone' and that as the old hymn tune averred, ' I come to the garden alone'.

The family was the original old folk's home. Honestly in terms of human evolution and evolutionary psychology, the responsibility of caring for the aged (even in our ape ancestors) necessitated certain social behaviors and adaptations that helped to facilitate human development and civilization. Without that impetus we go back to beasts even if we give ourselves the illusion that the government or 'someonetocarefor-mom.com' can calm our consciences. Furthermore, it is good for a child to have chores involving taking care of previous generations; not to the point of suffering, but to the point of learning the lesson that one day, somebody your present age (12 or 13 for instance) will be taking out a stinking plastic trash bag full of your adult diapers. What the fuck are we hiding our children from, and it may be more destructive to them to encourage in their minds the idea that you will never, nor should you ever be asked to do unpleasant but righteous duties and good deeds. And yes, a lesson is to be learned, is that sometimes 'your truth' doesn't preclude you from family obligations (Harry and Meghan)! In my truth I am a great writer and theologian, political wit, bon vivant and aristocrat born for high office and responsibility. That's my truth. But I still have to wipe my great aunt's ass for her (no disrespect intended). Quite the contrary, find yourself an old ass to wipe and do your duty to the older generations. It is a far better and perhaps more effective tradition than the one we Christians have of washing people's feet during Easter.

And yes, the Family was the original food stamps, WIC, Aid to Dependent Children and Soup Kitchen. There is 'a whole tradition in and of itself' of Black people romanticizing their mothers, aunties or grandmothers regarding food. Tyler Perry and many, many others have pilfered the theme throughout the years. Yes, indeed, something magical happens in Grandma's kitchen. Recently I've grown fond of the phrase regarding a spiritually and gastronomically savory meal, that 'grandma/auntie must have put her foot in it'! What a striking phrase, indeed most horrifying, unhygienic and macabre. Did grandma dip her foot in the pot, only taking it out when it became unbearable because of the heat? Or did grandma cut her foot off and put it in the pot, along with the broth, vegetables, and stew? Was grandma turning us into cannibals...which not coincidentally the Romans, Jews and foreigners accused the early Christians of being in the whole notion of 'this is my body broken for you broken for many', 'this is my blood, shed for you, shed for many', love feast? In some way is even the food ritual symbolism of grandma and auntie's table done...in remembrance of them?

Forgiving myself in advance for wild speculations and extrapolations, most of our grandmothers sacrificed, whether it was racism, sexism, etc. Perhaps they sacrificed their career to support a husband, and their child's development of their potential in the world. Many a woman that played piano, was good at math, science and business cut off a limb, that is to say, cut herself off from doing that skill or talent at the highest level, in order to allegorically and literally (as it were) nourish her family, and her husband and children's careers and livelihoods. So the next time you hear 'grandma must have put her foot in that potato salad', know indeed that she more than likely did in sacrificing a whole lot of her own life's expression ('her truth' to use a phrase) to so do. And knowing 'her foot' is in the potato salad are you going to respect her all the more, or are you going to disrespect her and say because she isn't dunking like Britney Griner, White House spokesperson like Karine Jean-Pierre, running for Governor like Stacy Abrams or superrich, elite and independent like Oprah, her life is meaningless and that grandma is living a less than a fulfilled life?

And yet there is much time remaining in this volume of work (book) to introduce corollaries to the destruction of the Black families. Can a concluding argument to this particular essay be asked, if not and whether in the post-Civil Rights Era we acquiesced to the weakening of theBlack family ideologically and in terms of first lines of social stability and defense, in favor of exalting the government and socialist atheist entitlement driven materialism in the form of reparations, philanthropy and good will, as the responsible party for Black quality of life? But in exchange for depending upon the government, social programs and White good will, we have accepted the destruction of our families. The government has in essence proved our families are no longer necessary. What WIC can't do, public education can't do, food stamps can't do, government sanctioned therapy and counseling will do, judges, jails and institutions will do, all of which the traditional family and religion once did. Technology will do what motive and will once did, becoming the new arbiter of what is 'real' as AI shapes and distorts reality in small steps and increments until the whole of it is completely fake.

Just to belabor a point for the sake of belabors, the family was the original Angies List. What have we gained and what have we lost? Is there a consequence of grandma's foot not being in our food that transcends its nutritional value? Is your cousin or older brother teaching you how to ride a bike better than learning on YouTube? Perhaps not always but it does provide for continual active connection and thus a sense of rootedness that decreases anxiety in children and adults. We gained the government and technology but what have we lost, and the idea that we Negro post-moderners aren't even asking the question is the shocking part that leads me to think we are already on the road to self-destruction. There is a moment when one is lost in the woods perhaps, that being lost is not that bad an omen and it seems easy to aright oneself. It is a bad omen when you are lost and do not know you are lost, and thinking that you are going the right direction, only to realize much later that you have been lost for so long, the chances of going back are futile. Thus, a kind of brutal realism sets in that come hell or highwater, or the Thelma and Louise fact that this road ends off a cliff, we have no other course but to go over it, lest we suffer the humiliations of getting captured, humiliated, and killed.

There is this admitted effect all over post-modernity and its weakened families, that children and adults are suffering from the symptoms and effects of increasing anxiety. With Jordan Peterson we might even add to that an increase in the kind of 'mass hysteria' that makes numbers of people seriously question whether they should cut their dicks and titties off, is taking hold of America and Europe! And we wonder why our children are anxious and anxiety filled. We are explaining to them at eight years of age, that in addition to learning addition and subtraction, they need to know about LGBTQIA so they can understand they have the freedom to pick any sexual identity they want. Did it give you a sense of comfort as a child to walk in Baskin Robbins with their 31 flavors only to realize your parents only gave you $1.50 for one small cone (and if you mix two flavors it is more expensive). Or did you stand there paralyzed in front of the counter trying to decide and, in the end, just picked chocolate or vanilla. (Let them that have ears to hear, hear). Confronted, confused, conflated, and confounded by the sheer volume of the choices, including wi-fi and constant connections to Youtube, Instagram, social media, etc., adults sense that we must put children on Ritalin and other forms of stimulants and depressants just to think that they can control themselves. But really that is not our primary motive in this Balenciaga bongo world of grooming, the reason to put them on stimulants is so that unscrupulous parents can control them. What is worse, we are not asking the question if part of the anxiety many children sense is coming from the fact that if you did not have a relationship with your father or extended family and did not (as it were) sense yourself to have a role in that family, you would, like any child sense yourself vulnerable and subject to far more anxieties than children situated differently in stable families.

Sensing that vulnerability, some youth take refuge in gangs. The only reason to join a gang is because your original gang, your family, religion, education, commerce, and industry have failed you. So you resort to gangs and criminality, and the proponents of such lifestyles will say to themselves as a means of justification that these are types of things they had to do to survive and eat, like gang bang, sell drugs and use women as prostitutes. We can do more than presume that it is these gangs that are disrupting scholastic life for our children, disrupting peace and security by random gun violence, and by the disruptions in peace and security, that makes economic development virtually impossible; and yet to the liberal Black female run socialist atheist LGBTQIA political elite, the very #1 anti-gang unit itself, strong nuclear and extended families is a non-starter and ignored as a strategy?

Stacy Abrams will never standup in front of Black people and say Black men and women need to strengthen their nuclear families in order to stabilize our schools! That is not in keeping with her agenda of things to promote. The Black family is not on her list of things to promote?

No, she will fight for LGBTQIA rights leading a Pride Parade before she says Black children need strong fathers, uncles, brothers, and cousins in their lives. Can we imagine the current crop of Black feminist/womanists ever coming to the public conclusion that perhaps Black girls especially, who seem susceptible to thinking Meg tha Stallion, Cardi B, Black Chyna (pre the Lord), Nikki Minage, Kim Kardashian, Lizzo and a host of other half naked women or Da Brat & Judy, Janelle Monae (thank you India Arie) are valid role models, need fathers who protect them from sexualization until they get old enough to have developed enough skills and talents where their sexuality is not the only thing they can depend on?

What kind of civilization do we live in, if it is damn near illegal to talk about the traditional biological family, rooted firmly in mammalian and reptilian and even plant nature to varying degrees in positive terms? Is it really the fear of offending someone? Normative is only a social construct if you tout it in a social construct. If you root it in biology, mammalian biology, and recognize the fact that it is precisely due to sex variation in mammals that we avoided inbreeding, took advantage of genetic advantageous mutations through distance and intermingling between sexes and groups of humans throughout human history. One of the other reasons mammals have been successful is because of the stability of children being raised by their fathers (in addition to their mothers) and both parents extended families. I would argue in evolutionary psychological terms that social, religious, and cultural networks played an important part as well extending back to the earliest days of humanity. The very thing of our success as mammals and as humans (because we just heightened those initial sex differentiated divisions of labors and skill sets) as successful mammals, was dependent on those early cooperative roots between the sexes and were just intensified in early humans, I believe requiring this big brain to deal with necessary communication and sense memorization skills that had to be learned. Because of the stability of the human nuclear pair and its extended family resources, human children could be children and play and learn in ways our ape and mammalian ancestors were not capable of, and for a longer extended childhood, because the lack of division of labor in Ape society did not give them the time to do so. So at the very heart of what it means to be a mammal and human is sex differentiation…but no one can talk about it in such terms with offending….uh…mammalians and early humans? The success of warm-blooded mammalians as a species is due to parents who birth their children live, and females nurse them from mammary glands. If that is a socio-patriarchal construct then tell me what society, culture, or polity invented male/female differentiation for early mammals? Who invented it for them if it is a man-made construct? Who at such a time as the differentiation of land-based mammals sexual organs, felt so strongly that it was patriarchally and socially necessary for control that they thought up the idea to differentiate and construct land-based mammalian sexuality and upon the physical differentiation of the sexes?

If we happened to run into a species of alien, whose males grew dicks like we grow body hair, perhaps cutting some of them off might be desirable on some level. But in as much as a man has one penis and woman just two titties, cutting them off for cosmetic reasons is hard to justify. Notwithstanding that; at the rate Japanese and White people are going, they will have to use invitro fertilization to have a chance to increase their birthrate. That is ridiculous when you consider that the dramatic decrease in birthrates is happening at the same time alternative sexualities are being promoted and hailed. At best homosexuality is a civilizational luxury of latent decadent civilization(s) (as Historian Oswald Spengler theorized; Peterson & Paglia concurring) and certainly not the standard.

I sincerely ask, have they not heard Marvin Gaye's greatest hits, Barry White, Teddy Pendergrass, the ballads of the American songbook, many sultry ballads filled with sexual innuendo sung by the greatest male and female singers of the 20th century? I have a feeling getting married and living happily ever after was presented in so many fairy tales because the ancestors knew that the reality of the situation would be far different, and if you wanted to hang on to the idea that the ancient intersectionality of men and women was ordained by God and even mammalian biological evolution, you would have to believe in the fairy tale aspects of it; the forces assailing it would be so ruthless. How ruthless is the socialist atheist LGBTQIA movement? Ruthless enough to demand mountains of cut off dicks, and cut off titties in sacrifice from supplicants and seekers? Ruthless enough to demand a lifestyle of purchasing and consuming hormones that are completely unnecessary to the maintenance of life and purely cosmetic and subjecting one's body to that rigorous regimen of pills, shots, and cosmetic surgeries. How ruthless a regimen, letting and even encouraging children to do it. Ladies and gentlemen let us believe once again in fairy tales that connect us to the essential truths of mammalian, humanoid, and monotheistic male/female sexual reality. Even if the fairy tales of a soul mate princess and prince charming are exaggerated, oversimplified and hyperbolic, they still represents truths as exaggerated, oversimplified and hyperbolic as that our ancient male and female ape ancestors fell in love and chose mates and mated for reasons completely unrelated to the bare mechanics of natural sexual selection. That is to say, the fairy tale of it. And yet, to the extent cavemen were knocking women over the head and dragging them home, perhaps they were both realities, subject to the same forces of upbringing, experience, genetics, and personality that make mates good or bad today. Does the reality preclude the fairy tale, or does the fairy tale preclude the reality? If you believe you have a soul mate, then you have a soul mate. If you believe your God will lead you to him or her, He will. It is not that far-fetched to believe that believing in your soul mate is like believing in the tooth fairy except that for as long as you could be fooled by such a thing, it was exactly the case that your parents made you believe in it.

2. The Most Successful team in mammalian and human history (The Evolutionary Biological Argument)

One woman and one man. The most successful team in mammalian and human history. In nearly any species of mammal, including ourselves, the greater the cooperation between mating pairs, the more stable the environment for the young and the greater the chances for not only the living success of that young, but the reproductive success of that young, ensuring the DNA survives (presumably in perpetuity). There are no lifestyle arguments that stand in the face of that and thus liberals are unfortunately in for some grim reality. Technology, for Da Brat and Judy can give us the 'choices', but the choices only imitate the natural means and as such can be no other 'thing' than by default an imitation of life; with its own forthcoming tragic mulatto story, as I am told they chose a White ethnic sire for their sperm donor. I guess they didn't want any weeded out, ballin' nigga sperm even though that is the life they owe their careers to, and the life they celebrated in their music. Apparently Da Brat and Judy didn't want no 'funkdafied' sperm donor.

To argue this (Da Brat & Judy Pregnancy Situation) is an advance over what God and mammalian evolution designed and endorsed over countless millennia is not only a vain and arrogant argument, it is completely ridiculous in light of the fact that for all the evils the LGBTQIA says are put upon them by the 'straight' world and its 'straight' assumptions, they seem intent on either imitating us (families) or infiltrating us and trying to pass. There are certain inconsistencies with that logic, like the rapper 'Young Thug' driving expensive European luxury automobiles and living in an expensive home in Buckhead...precisely where the White upper middle class and elites that live there, don't want him anyway. It is not political in that he is not patting himself on the back, nor is negritude patting him on the back for living there like we pat niggers on the back who integrate the White mainstream world and do good like Tiger Woods. They don't want Young Thug's children in the Buckhead daycare, don't want his kids in their schools, and his kids will not be invited to the sleepovers. He built a career off literally opposing their Buckhead bourgeois elitist values like education, family, art in favor of encouraging lifestyles of partying, thugging, schmurda, hustling, etc.?

I'm reminded of my feelings watching a great herd of elephants migrate hundreds, even thousands of miles with a matriarch and group of sisters and related females leading their young through the literal and figurative paths of life. Ancient water holes, ancient trails that loop and double back seemingly at random, but in actuality with the different patterns of season growth and times of peak ripeness...passed down from mothers and aunts to daughters, nieces and cousins who upon the death of the grand dame, the grand matriarch, will come next to lead the next generation of calves and the young. The family and the resultant community of interrelated and dependent smaller families is the nursery! Nursing mothers nurse their own and their relatives children of similar age in a communal effort dependent upon circumstances and these bonds lay foundations for future loyalties and relationships that have future implications for stability and increasing the chances of survival for the old and younger elephants. Furthermore, of the aunts, older sisters and cousins that learned the lessons (trade routes and seasonal climactic patterns) of the elder mothers better, they became better leaders. What the Greeks would call Paideia. An elephant Paideia.

A similar occurrence happens in the lives of Prides of Lions. They are usually a group of related sisters and related females. Unlike the elephant, whose success depends not so much upon memorization of ancient migration routes, seasonal patterns, water holes and fruit maturation and ripening patterns, but upon hunting together strategically as a unit and 100% in cooperation with one another; a band that can only be reinforced in the fact of being raised together, often times sucking at the same mothers, aunts and older cousins teats, observing the same aunts, mothers and older cousins hunting strategies, activities and patterns they observed from their elders....Paideia as Greek intellectuals would call it. That they excel in the Paideia and the working interpretation of the lessons learned from the ancestors (immediate and ancient), those individuals become leaders and model teachings, teaching, behavior, and ethics regarding family loyalty for the next generations. A generation will be born that will say they owe their success to the teachings of so and so; retained in even an animal's DNA memory. Grace be to God.

Part II

Let us now move on from our mammalian cousins and into the realm of the first man. Every time men and women went anywhere else in the world, they originated in what we today call Africa. This is long after our 'inferior' ape ancestors got run (swung) out of the trees by the superiorly endowed apes who whooped our human ancestors for the best territory, and thus our human ancestors though apes, were forced by necessity, survival and the genius and love of God to evolve very differently from our ape and mammalian cousins and shared ancestors. Once again 'forces' contrived' to present challenges, probably political, cultural, religious, familial and in terms of shifts in weather patterns, prey animal migrations and geographic changes were forced to move out of Africa and throughout the world. We might even be challenged not to come to the conclusion that the human world as we know it, is just large broken off pieces of Africa under water, lava, etc. and the resulting physical, cultural, political changes in the human genotype resulting therefrom. I'm not making that argument as scientist, just that in human terms it would be hard to argue we are not all Africans, in varying stages of physical and geographic evolution throughout the world.

As our ancestors traveled, in each stage and wave of early migration, Africans (presupposing Black ethnic) migrated out of Africa and into the exposed land masses in what we now call other parts of the world. In each wave of migration, Black men and Black women partnered and teamed together, creating not only families, but circumstances where the better their familial cooperation, the more successful they would be in colonizing other parts of the world and raising generations and their culture and history surviving in addition to finding food and shelter and defending your 'family/tribe' from animal threats and the threats of other humans. Let me restate that. Humans owe the entire success of our species and our mammal forebears to the success of males and females partnering in nuclear and extended family units. Ladies and gentlemen, considering that, how can we turn our backs on such an institution as has been foundational to mammalian and human evolution as the paired family, in favor of post-modern latent decadent phase sexual whims, in what Spengler et al, noted and documented in his book 'the Decline of the West'. This 'decline', post-modern liberals and progressives see as progress…literally the complete annihilation of the family and the powers that once derived from it, like the idea that you know better whether your child is a boy or girl as a parent, or that a 6-year-old child knows better whether it is a boy or a girl than what God presented it as. Government specialists and legalists, psychologists and surgeons are going to tell you what your child is?

Indeed, there have always been those who turn their backs on the traditional family, but hitherto common sense and a basic understanding of mammalian biology prevailed. But now, who is standing for the traditional family. Mainline western Christian denominations have apparently given up on the traditional family, in the name of appealing to everyone, and projecting God as being concerned about being perceived as a God of love and peace. Really? The atheists complain every day, nay even as one of their proofs that God doesn't exist, they argue that all this evil and suffering exists in the world because God is not good and loving and that a good God could not possibly do such things on this kind of mass scale. Once again, I ask the question, would a God, defined in those terms, give a damn about projecting himself as being a God of love and freedom, in general or even for the heck of it? All this mass killing, mass starvation, mass exploitation, mass suffering, the atheists suggest is going on, would such a God on a whim start being loving and super tolerant…super tolerant of all kinds of love and children die and are abused mercilessly for years in some unfortunate circumstances. Really, a God like that automatically affirms everybody and wants to see any old kind of love, 'same love', 'all love', because God is love...but the atheists swear God must hate people and not care or give a damn because of the suffering he allows to to happen to the weak, the innocent, etc.? My atheist friends you cannot have it both ways. Is it that same mad angry and hateful God, that is now legitimizing your behavior and now loves you and your 'same love' because the Bishop of Canterbury, the Bishop of the Presbyters in America and Europe, the Bishop of the North Georgia Conference in the middle of the Southern Bible Belt say so? The LGBTQIA peoples didn't start being gay when they were against the conservative family teachings of churches, why would you give a fuck now whether or not they are against the church, tolerate or are even for it? This is one of the misunderstandings of the mainline denominational church in Post-Modern America. They think that loosening the rules brings in believers. No, prophesying and what you say comes to pass is how you bring in believers. And there is no surer way and basis of prophesying than to know that sooner or later, that which is contrary to God's word will fail and receive its day of judgement. Men and women say they are on the right side of history and righteousness (presumably because they know God is love and endorses all love, whether he has spoken against it in mammalian nature, or in the past scripture for any reason, or not) in far, far too much haste! On its present trajectory America is bound for the hellfire and indeed it is coming to pass. Is a hateful God now realizing his mistake and affirming your lifestyles, or perhaps it is not that hateful, jealous God, that is legitimizing your behavior but simply the institutional church, the mainstream church, the website, and televangelism church. Institutional churches where they check your credit and your criminal history, make you go to seminary, and know the right things to say and you can get a gig. No Holy Ghost necessary. AI will write you sermons. You can learn to deliver them in homiletics classes in seminaries. These homiletics classes are special too, because they do not require extensive knowledge of the bible. Lord how the United Methodists celebrate their ebony liberal Bishops.

This is even though according to most readings of the biblical text, right alongside with things God ordained for us, like the sun, the moon, the stars, day and night, seed time and harvest, and celestial orbits, one of which was the traditional family; inviolable. What God has joined, let no man cast asunder. Are we going to choose the traditional family even though you can get an orgasm off a handheld device and even though there is an app for any sexual perversion or proclivity you could ever think to have? Will we choose family over dolls, robots, porn, general lasciviousness, sodomy, prostitutes, burlesque, etc. In themselves, those things may not be all bad for all people but to pass them off as normative, the way it is happening in America and Western Europe is ridiculous and as Spengler suggested, is a hallmark and sign of the inevitable decline of a civilization. And Spengler wasn't by any means, I would think a Christian, and whose interpretation of Christianity would be totally dependent on his historically models, not things like the Holy Ghost.

African men and women in waves of migration out of Africa over tens of thousands and hundreds of thousands of years bred the people whose descendants would be every race of people extant today, no matter what physical, cultural political or economic forms they manifest. The genius, the pluck, the aplomb in achieving such an undertaking and the fact that it was successfully done by men and women organized into nuclear and extended families and associated families, a community; a tribe, unites the timeline along the entire arc of the human narrative and by default the mammalian. Male and female partnering and the success of cooperation in raising young, and the next generation of young, as grandparents, precipitated the likelihood of not just individual survival, but family survival and the survival of the next generations. All were based on the quality and unity of our families!

Are we of post-modernity somehow so advanced we can now ignore something so ubiquitous as the tradition male/female-based mammalian family? What precisely, is different now about human and mammalian biology that distinguishes post-modern knowledge of sexuality from the demands of our mammalian, ape, and early hominid past? Are we to now think that there are no psychological and social consequences to generations of modern humans unhinged from such a basic understanding and institution as the family and its role in mammalian, ape and human evolution? Did all this post-modern angst, mental illness, all this anxiety, magically happen out of nowhere? To a Salmon, success is successful mating and he or she will literally kill themselves on a suicide mission to mate, seeking to spawn in the rivers and streams of their birth and youth. Success is not much more than successful mating to many species, to the point that the Salmon is not distracted by the vagaries of the sea, nor by ships, buoys, and beautiful islands when it is time to spawn, reproduce and die. The bright lights that sail along the backs of human vessels and ships on the surface of the ocean do not distract him or her. If there was such a thing as the Salmon lotto and a fish could win a gazillion dollars and a lifetime supply of open clear skies and fresh waters, it would not distract him or her from the mandate to mate. If he or she had a special friend or two or three, out there in the open ocean that made them feel the strongest love, as the biblical David would say of his love for his friend Jonathan, 'it excels that of a woman', it would still not distract him or her from the long journey back to the streams that birthed him or her in order to spawn, and do their duty in service to their ancestors and the creator and the bears and other wildlife that prey on them along the way; in the very same streams that birthed them and that their parents mated in. No matter how many dams humans have built and how high the spillways are along the route you see the Salmon jumping and leaping to go further and further upstream to mate, forgoing even food, the drive to mate is so strong. But we humans have invented better forces of sexual understanding and the justification of sexual activities? Really? We have improved sex and sexuality by the current anything goes approach. The data suggests otherwise.

In conclusion, we of niggerdom and negritude, considering our position relative to the other races in evolutionary terms; we have every interest in learning about and maintaining the physical, emotional, cultural, political and evolutionary manifestations of the traditional family (nuclear and extended) as our ancestors knew it for the purposes of reproduction, as a unit of cultural transmission, and as the foundation for social cohesion of the type that allowed human societies to flourish intellectually, artistically, religiously, throughout human history to the point of it being carried out through all recorded history etc. everywhere human beings went, no matter what physical and perhaps other changes they underwent making then into the vast physical array of human types we know today. Everywhere they went it was the successful families that thrived.

If I am against interracial relationships at all, it is for this reason only; peoples should preserve the physicality of their form, and this can only be done for the most part by breeding for the form. There is no more wrong with blond hair and blue eyes than there is with dark skin and brown eyes. No more wrong with 7 ft tall African tribes or than there is the shortest Asian or African pygmy. In the spirit of being thankful for what we have inherited we should take an interest in preserving the form. It is not a superiority argument; it is perhaps scholastic and thus historical if I need an excuse. As much as I love Christianity and its monotheistic Bible based sister religions, as an academic and historian, I would have liked to have collected the old heathen gods to file away or put on display in a museum of ancient gods, and deities in a museum of ancient civilizations. When the prophet Muhammad and his followers broke up and destroyed the pagan gods from the Kaaba it would have been an archaeological and ancient scholarly motherlode. When Hindus and Muslims in India and Pakistan fought and desecrated each other's temples and symbols of (G)od(s), quite a bit was lost in the fervor of the times; a fervor I must admit to my own scholarly horror, quite often appears to the faithful to be absolutely necessary and even some kind of test. I am sure there are a lot of Native American art and 'trinkets' that ended up in White mainstream flea markets all throughout the Midwest, Southwest and West; their religious significance completely lost on most Native Americans and everybody else.

If our DNA, our evolution as mammals, apes and humans was dependent upon the ancient means and methodologies of pairing and extended families of propagating the species, and the majority of our religions endorse the basic binary proposition and for all but the selected few ordain marriage and consider it a duty to be fruitful and multiply and raise the next generation of 'believers'; to supplant innovated and technological means and call it the equivalent of what our mammalian, ape and human ancestors depended upon to reproduce and express and solidify familial life in the nuclear and extended sense is insane. It is insane and it is driving our children and adults crazy here in America. In exchange for fresh air and active mentoring we have substituted techno-gaming, social media, and celebrity culture and then we wonder why our children are anxiety prone and angst ridden, literally hate themselves in terms of their physical features, taking all types of psychological medicines before the age of 9, bulimic and anorexic, getting nose jobs at 12 and cutting their dicks and titties off.

Trust me, I doubt any of our forefathers and mothers and the patriarchs and matriarchs of our foremost faiths thought a day would come where it would be politically correct to go around pretending like you have absolutely no idea what the difference is between a man and a woman is! And if you act like you interpret the difference between a man and a woman the old-fashioned way, what they look like at the genitalia, that they were born with, you will get fired from your job and everyone will say you are a crazy insane hater, transphobe, and simpleton. I'm sure they would have predicted that homosexuality and transvestitism would exist in smaller or greater numbers, theoretically at least hovering around 10% of the entire population in not just humans but perhaps mammals in general. But by default, for any other statistical exercise but a sexual one, no one in their right mind would call something that only occurs in the human and mammal world 10% of the time normative.

Our ancestors, religious and ape, never would have thought we would do such a thing and then pat ourselves on the back as intellectuals, theologians, and libertines for such a monstrous dereliction of duty.

This got me to thinking that in just such an environment as this, instead of not promoting the 'traditional family' and traditional religious reasons to involve yourself in traditional domestic simplicity, our ancestors would recognize this post-modern socialist-atheist materialist techno-trend and encourage us to actually model and teach the traditional family to our children, even if we have to represent it to them in fairy tale terms like Cinderella or other prince and princess happy ever after in never-never land tales. These speculations led me to an important truth; that is precisely what our ancestors did. Why did kids go to debutante balls, tom thumb weddings, junior proms, senior proms? Why were so many songs throughout human history in all cultures about love and romantic relationships? It is precisely that previous generations through the arts and a kind of fairy tale type setup were promoting marriage, and the belief that you do have a prince or princess out there. Our parents and grandparents put a lot of energy into making sure this happened.

Typical nigger that I was, when I was in elementary school, the idea of 'square dancing' did not appeal to me. But the idea of having a 'partner' (a young lady), was for a shy boy like me, my only opportunity to hold a girl's hand and get close to a girl. 'Swing your partner dos ee doh', and now switch partners. Yes, at the age of 8 or 9 I'm thinking to myself quite exactly that one day I will have a wife and we will dos ee dos the nights away in marital bliss. Ladies and gentlemen these were not random games and activities for our parents and grandparents to make up, nor were they simply exercises in patriarchy and getting girls and women used to the idea that some man would be swinging them around and 'dos ee dosing' forever if they didn't take control of their lives, rebel and become radical LGBTQIA feminist and womanist queers. Baby girl, as much as your mothers' and grandmothers loved you, do you really think they would view having you participate in certain traditional sexual roles as an effort to hold you back, make you submit to patriarchy and like a slave mother teach her child to be obedient as a survival skill? Rites of passage serve the role of these types of traditions like square dancing, prom, debutant balls, Prom King, and Queens, etc., in pre-modern societies and our own. The point here is that our ancestors did and were in effect teaching us that as we work with a partner of the opposite sex in square dancing, prom, debutant, King, and Queen type situations it was quite exactly a foreshadowing of what they saw as a the ultimate 'partnering' which is dating, marriage and childrearing; the most important functions members of any civilization have in raw terms.

3 The Religious Imperative to Family Values and Values of Education, Commerce and Industry

Nearly every major religion of any historical import finds itself prescribing sexual mores or notions of family life pleasing to the (G)od(s). Scattered throughout the present volume, I will refer to the Judeo-Christian and Islamic traditions to buttress my arguments on 1) the need to restore the Black Family to increase the general quality of life for African Americans and 2) some of the methodologies and modes of restoring Black families. I am buttressing my arguments in this way because I find it hard to believe it is possible to convince the 'world' of the benefits of the traditional family, if we of the big three sister faiths and similarly aligned faiths, cannot bring ourselves together to stop the chaos of immorality and sexual dysfunction (which spring from crude materialist-utilitarian notions about the 'purpose' of sexuality), that are presently crippling society and the human spirit.

Let us begin with a concept on marriage, family and the value of labor from the Jewish Talmud.

"In connection with this (social life) subject, a man is obliged to teach his son a trade, and whoever does not teach his son a trade teaches him to become a thief. The person who has a trade in his hand is like a vineyard which is fenced in, so that cattle and beasts cannot get into it or passers-by eat of it or look into it; and whoever has no trade in his hand is like a vineyard with its fence broken down, so that cattle and beasts can enter it, and passers-by can eat of it and look into it" (Tosifta Kid. I. I)

We find further words to this principle of 'work' in the Talmud is to the effect: "Whoever disregards the instructions of his employer is called a thief'. (B.M. 78a, b)

The biblical book of Ecclesiastes 9:16 counsels the wise (believer) that "whatever your hand finds to do, do it with your might." And in the New Testament we find Paul's classic admonition in 2 Thessalonians:

'for even when we were with you, we commanded you that if any should not work, neither should he eat'.

Take that you wild eyed radical liberal theologians that spin the Bible to be some kind of reductionist self-help guide that says others are responsible for you simply because you are poor or simply because you exist (excepting widows and orphans who can't work). Here again, in the old days, the family, not the government, not benevolent organizations, nor the unions, socialists and communists were the first line of defense for (as it were) taking care of their own.

Paul furthermore counsels us in the same chapter that...

'...we hear that there are some which walk among you disorderly, working not all, but are busybodies. Now them that are such we command and exhort by our Lord Jesus Christ, that with quietness they work, and eat their own bread'.

The phrase 'disorderly, working not at all, sounds a lot like our youth these days'. The need to 'eat one's own bread', and the feeling of self-satisfaction it gives a person are underrated sentiments in post-modern America. In Acts we find Paul refusing to take John Mark with him on an Apostolic journey because he remembered the occasion that John Mark was supposed to go with them 'to work' in Pamphylia before, and 'went not with them to the work'. While it is not specified why this one incident was enough for Paul, perhaps it is enough to say that this one incident was enough to make Paul's appreciation of John Mark's 'work skills', and discipline problematic enough to talk about it in negative terms in a chapter of the New Testament that whether Paul it knew or not, would come to define Christianity for the 2000 years or so since.

Ladies and gentlemen of post-modernity, are these biblical mandates to be considered genius and wisdom or do we need post-modern liberal theologian's and atheist Marxist's interpretations that end up arguing just the opposite as what is clearly the intention of the text in suggesting 'work', a profession, a business, a training, a skill, etc., and the need for the family to provide you with the basic means of such, as appropriate behavior for men and women.

Let us refer to the tradition of Islam and the Hadith of the Prophet Muhammad for another perspective on the dignity of work.

'By Him in whose hand is my soul, if one of you were to carry a bundle of firewood on his back and sell it, that would be better for him than begging a man who may or may not give him anything'.

-Sahih Bukhari 1401

We saw that the Talmud makes the argument that if a father does not teach his child a trade (or some profession) he has in effect taught his child to be a thief. We Christians often minimize the fact, but the bible states and most commentators believe that prior to Jesus active ministry, he was indeed 'a carpenter's son' and plied that trade at least to the standards of his father, the guild or union of local carpenters he, his father and brothers probably belonged to. To be honest, even more priceless than the Holy Grail and the Shroud of Turin to me would be some of the chairs and wares Jesus may have made engaging his earthly profession. Imagine there were some Hebrews of Galilee that could honestly say, Jesus, the carpenter's son made my physical house, my son and daughter's crib, and a cedar chest. Jesus, the Son of God made my spiritual house (Christianity) too, and according to Him, Jesus built me a mansion in Glory in the next world! What a great building. And Jesus builds all his houses on 'Rocks'. And it's one stop shopping because Jesus also insures whatever he builds, so you can get your insurance through Him and he runs a Moving Company that when it's time for you to go, they are coming to get you to move into your new home. Let them that have ears to hear, hear.

Part II

In a previous essay I discussed the role parents, aunts, uncles, cousins, and older siblings play in how children develop skills and talents. There has been an intergenerational shift in Black America and masculinity that has been shocking in its effects. We have generations of boys that don't know how to cut grass, rake leaves, take out trash and other common household chores. Then we look around and blame White racism when at 18 they are virtually unemployable, because not only have they no real skill or discipline, this is combined with a minimally competitive and barely on grade level high school diploma. They do not have the proper attitude to be a good dutiful employee or even pretend to be for any length of time. Many of our boys are filling up the jails not because they are inherent criminals, but because they literally don't know anything else to do, or have any skill to do it, other than having watched the hustlers on the bock run traps.

Our boys are missing valuable work and life skills experience like discipline, practice, and patience, because of family disruption, dysfunction and the poverty associated with that. The fact that they do not have adequate supervision makes them vulnerable to gangs and gang behavior. The lack of 'healthy care investment' by older men and boys is patent, because they have no family skills as well. That is to say, they have not seen how people who love each other diffuse tension and disagreement in a family setting. Had they gotten a chance to live in functional stable situations, they would observe in their nuclear families and extended families loved ones working cooperatively even when they disagree and have disagreements. This is important, for it is the root of the idea of contributing your all even when you didn't get your way. which is the basis in family life. It is also part of being a good citizen and contributing member of a democracy because of the loyal minority necessary to any functioning democracy. And we are failing as an American nation/polity precisely because we are failing in our families to model the behavior of love, trust, faith, and if needs be loyal opposition.

It is precisely just such a lack of experience in our children of watching functional, loving families diffuse conflict and disagreement that makes our youth (male and female) on the one hand be sullen and withdrawn, or fly off the handle all the time, refusing to tolerate anyone dissing or disrespecting them to the point of being willing to risk it all going to jail maiming or injuring someone because they 'felt' disrespected. They have no experience watching parents, aunts, uncles, cousins loved ones, who love each other, argue, disagree, and fuss vehemently, but politely and with an end towards eventual unity. Mama got pissed off at Grandma, and neither mama nor grandchild has a relationship with grandma. What lessons are we modeling for children in terms of conflict resolution?

It is those same forces of dysfunction that cause susceptibility to gangs, lack of academic and vocational skill development, and contribute towards the dysfunction in our schools because our children end up being undisciplined and thus, damn near unteachable. Recently on the news, a teacher tried to confiscate a young lady's cell phone. The young lady maced and pepper sprayed the teacher, the whole time yelling insanely like an enraged rabid feral raccoon for the teacher to 'give me, my phone back'! Does anyone, let alone her, believe the teacher's intent was to steal the phone or hack it for passwords and credit card numbers? Or perhaps the teacher wanted to use auto-pay pal info logged in her phone to buy school supplies for the classroom? No, the girl simply had no home training, self-control or self-respect, and those lessons are primarily taught first at home, long before you get to anybody' classroom (genius teacher or doofus). Such that if our homes aren't teaching those basic lessons there is nothing the schools or even the police can do with our children. When I was a kid, my older female cousins braided my hair and having reached sufficient age, I began cutting my grandfather's hair and my little male cousins' hair. Many a barber and beautician started out cutting or doing their little brothers, sisters, and relative's hair.

We are told over and over what a serious problem bullying and its corollary, school violence and gangs is, and yet the liberal geniuses ignore the very bulwark that stops nearly all bullying, strong families. Being in a family is good for self-esteem and is patently anti-bullying. First of all, kids pick on other kids for varieties of reasons, the easiest anecdotal targets are the fat kids, big nosed, little nosed, big lips, lips too skinny, big in the wrong places, little in 'wrong' places, being poor, being richer than your peers, too dark, too light, too dorky, etc. Well guess what, all the above could be true and if you are around your older brothers, sisters, cousins, aunts and uncles, guess what, the chances are very likely that nearly all y'all got the same big ass lips, big asses, bowlegs, slew footedness, pigeon toes, etc, that some kid might want to 'joan'.

The fact of being able to see qualities that may not be appreciated by your peers, reflected in your older siblings and relatives gives a kid strength (in numbers) and this naturally makes a child far less self-conscious about the fact he or she is not built, colored, or shaped like the other kids and can consequently be mocked. It is quite a blessing to a child to know that the buck teeth and the same lazy eye that runs in the family has not kept the family from being successful in business, getting married and experiencing the respect of the wider community. In addition to the fact that physical, mental, and emotional traits tend to run in families, the bully that makes the mistake of mishandling somebody's little brother, little sister or little cousin, is usually going to get their ass beat on the playground at 1 o'clock sharp as their older family members come to defend their honor at your bullying about their 'Jones family' big noses.

Is that not a better starter solution to bullying than police in the schools, metal detectors, and spending inordinate amounts of time monitoring kid's online activities. We send our kids to western therapy thinking that his will help our children. But all it is doing is making them think they are crazy, and giving them an excuse to act crazy. Thus this puts scars on their scholastic record and perhaps even law enforcement record they will never live down in the computer age. There are counselors and teachers with PHDS in child psychology and counseling, and education, but none of that shit seems to be working in urban schools. No, imma tell my older cousins that you're picking on me and guess what, their nose is even bigger than mine and you can tell them to their faces you don't like their noses, and I can tell that their response will be to beat yo muthafuckin ass for fuckin with me. But no, we live in a world where kids don't have brothers, sisters, cousins, aunts, uncles that they are around every day, to notice their similarity in unique characteristics and support and defend those characteristics in each other. That is why in post-modernity children are filled with anxiety, self-loathing, self-hating, wanting plastic surgery at 12, desperate for others to 'like' their pics on social media and then get so upset by disses, slights and perceived bullying that they bring a gun to school and shoot up the school.

Two

Crepuscule With Nellie

4Dances with my Fathers

The thought has recently occurred to me Negritude. Will we trust Government (any government), White benevolence, post-modern socialist-atheist techno-cyber-materialist-therapist-corporatepharmaceuticalcomplex to govern our lives or will we govern our lives ourselves, the old-fashioned way. Religion may not have fixed any of that in reality, except as a placebo, but I'll tell you one damn thing, it was certainly cheaper as a means of explaining and treating socio-psychological existential dysfunctions. This is no disrespect to my father, who even post-divorce played an important role in my life. His intelligence, his artistic interests and capabilities and the fact that he was a science teacher in the public school system very much influenced my ideas as a child. As a matter of fact, nearly all my relatives on my mother and father's side are in public service, teachers, social workers, and even law enforcement personnel. Quite often I left the school I attended and went to another school to wait on my mother or father or participate in their school events. So, I spent a lot of time around teachers, students, and administrators, at sports games and many other school performances.

As a matter of fact, these 'duties' were so ingrained and such a regularized feature of my life that I never remember complaining or feeling put upon, or like I was in school(s) too much. It was my reality. It was job enough to find something to do, oftentimes reading or finding some other kids to play with when available. Quite often they were the children of other teachers or administrators who were stuck there like I was, or other kids stuck there in general. Oddly enough I have no negative memories of kids saying anything negative to me or trying to 'get me' for some perceived slight done by my mother or any other teacher on the teacher's children. And yes, they taught in urban high schools. Neither do I remember many fights. My how things have changed.

Let me talk to the men right quick for a moment. Post-divorce my father went through a series of serial monogamy type relationships. In each case I observed his choice(s) wearily. Selfishly like a child, I'm trying to figure out why his own son, whom he's with only twice a month on weekends must play second fiddle to some woman he just met a few months ago? And now my father is fully domesticated, excepted with some other woman than my mother, which is a level of cognitive dissonance do we really want to ask 9-year-old male or female children to entertain? That was my dad's right, however. He had/has a right to 'live his truth' no matter how it made an 8-year-old kid feel. I'd take some appreciation for the fact that the women were usually cute or fine enough (even in my youthful eyes); the urge to judge at all probably motivated simply by the childish urge to compare her to my mother as I wondered what she 'has' over my mom, in being the symbol of the breaking up my home.

After the effects of years of cigarettes weakened his lungs, none of the women of those serial relationships that I remembered were around to help my father. Their children, whose braces he contributed to, and sports games he cheered them on at were not there to help him. In such a state, as his health worsened, my brother and I took on more caregiving duties but my brother by then was a city manager in another state and there was only so much he could do, or that my father felt comfortable asking him or anyone else to do. My older brother was a child of divorce, just as I was, probably feeling at first towards my mother the way I felt about my dad's other women in his life, but he went though it 10 years earlier than I did. And unfortunately, much as they try to make weekend daddy-ing, two different parent household daddy-ing, 2 weekends a month daddy-ing legitimate, it doesn't breed and build the kind of trust, confidences and affections that make a child or cousin drop everything and come take care of Daddy. No matter how much lawyers and parents try to make shared custody sound like a hip and a healthy ersatz version of live in dual parenting, it does not build those kinds of bonds between father and child that tend towards the necessary sacrifices towards the end of the father's life. Rugged as that sounds my brothers, take it to the bank.

Consequently, my father experienced depression. Ladies and gentlemen, there is no worse feeling for a 26-year-old than taking your father to the doctor for what you think is a routine physical. Then after longer than usual, the doctor sends a nurse to the waiting room to call you back at the end of the visit and in sober and dour terms, with your father sitting there looking childish not looking you in the eye, the doctor tells you that your father is depressed, and suffering the symptoms of clinical depression. On one level you hope your dad is working some kind of hustle to get more money out of the insurance, but then you look at him sitting there looking confused and childish and realize these muthafuckas are serious! My father is 72, what the fuck does that mean to diagnose him as depressed and tell me about it? My mind was blown. I didn't know what it meant, and I certainly did not know what to do about it. So immediately after and ever after, we both did what many families do when they are bewildered by the sufferings of their loved ones, we just pretend like it doesn't exist, it didn't happen and as long as no one talks about it, it doesn't matter. My father and I never had a single conversation from that moment to the day he died a few years later about his 'depression'. He never denied it, but never talked about it and neither did I. In hindsight, I know it must have been true on some level, but I didn't really accept it at any level and apparently neither did he, and the consequences of this leaves many unanswered questions.

And so 40 years after his twice a month parenting of my older brother and I, we are his only children, however minus the sense of duty that comes from the daily observation of your parents making sacrifices for you. That is to say, observing our parents living lives where they help you as a child find out and live your truth, rather than being out there in the world trying to find and live some truth when they have babies at home, or trying to find their truth with some other woman than my mother or my brother's mother, when she was 'the truth', your truth as a man 10 years ago you met, but now no longer is your truth.

So my father suggested, and my brother and I believed oh yes, better the government, personal care assistants, personal care aides, personal care facilities, they make up a lotta euphemisms and titles to stay un-licensed and unobserved and on the margins, getting older people to pay for their 'care' services. It will be no problem finding good care for dad. Clearly, all we must do is go the website 'whattodoaboutdad.com' and we'll be directed to excellent care where they play bridge every night, lawn tennis and croquet every day and socialize with convivial compan-ionship all day and night long. Only being away from home, around people you don't know, and dependent upon people who are only there for the check, oh yes, and the antiseptic smells and the sounds of people in the same facility or even room as you in emotional and physical pain, I am sure made my dad's depression worse and shaved months, if not years off his life.

In such circumstances, he never complained to me, but looking back I would have preferred it if he did. The effects of resigning himself to what I know he sensed as the effects of his fractured and failed relation-ships with his former wives/baby mamas and his sons, probably caused by the twice a month/2 weekend a month parenting that doesn't build family structures of reciprocal obligation, intensity, and strength (and intensity of love and dutifulness) weighed on him and contributed to his depression. Without enough glue and cement, the family structure created by twice a month fathering can look stable enough from the outside, but storms, winds and rains come, and it cannot stand. Broth-ers don't let that happen to you. You may think you will live forever in good health and strength, you may think 'living your truth' trumps all other human considerations (even your children), but go into the nursing homes and see all the men, who were playboys in their younger years and now their former lovers don't have any loyalty and neither do their children. And to add insult to injury they will all show up at your funeral wanting to talk in the mic during reflections, and 'lawyered' up in order to make sure they get what's 'coming to them', and 'rightfully theirs' out of your estate.

Brothers, let us not make the same mistakes many of our fathers made. Quit sacrificing Black women and your daughters to 'your truth', which far from being 'truth' is motivated by ego and low self-esteem such that taking advantage of women and girls makes you feel good about yourself. Dropping babies like Nick Cannon makes you feel good about yourself, and you're dumb enough and psychologically naïve enough to think that just sending money, birthday and Christmas gifts like Herschel Walker is enough to make you a father and a man. How did we get the idea life is about living 'your truth', your 'truth' is your family! You're dressed in high fashion, your kids scattered all over Atlanta get their clothes from Walmart and the Dollar Store. Do you think your kids don't notice that discrepancy and 'feel some type of way'? When they are young and dumb, they are impressed because their father dresses nicely, but when they get slightly older, they will resent you for dressing yourself up fancy while they dress from thrift stores. And we niggas and baby daddy' parade around with pride in our fancy car with the rims, the tint, and 'trues and vogues'. Your wife and your baby mamas are living vulnerable, and every 3-bit nigga is banging her out taking your kids to Chuck E Cheese more often than you do. Seeing all of this, nay even living with it, after a certain point, your son or daughter doesn't respect his mother because she disrespects herself and runs with every 4-bit nigga in the neighborhood. Then his mama is scared of him and begins calling the authorities on him. At the same time the folks at his school fear him (unless they are the police) and the only people that can console and control him are the gangs, the police and legal and illegal psychoactive drugs.

All this, so you as a man can go out and 'live your truth' as a thug rapper, pimp, hustler, and gangster. Your homies in the gang might ride with you on a 'hit' but they won't change your diapers once your colon gets blown out. The Crips, the Bloods, 42nd Street gangsters, hustlers, pimps, thugs, etc. don't have retirement plans and senior citizens facilities. As ubiquitous as thug and gangster imagery is, unlike the Italian, Jewish and Russian mafias, urban Black American gangsters are hardly ever shown living to an advanced age and dying of natural causes. Brothers we need to be there for our children and womenfolk. I recognize from personal experience that your baby mama, ex-wife may not desire your attentions and affections, and both sides, wives/baby mamas and adolescent and adult children may argue they don't need you in their lives and that it is too late. Hang in there, they may need a kidney one day and the only match is you, and then they and their mothers will develop a whole new appreciation for you. Initially you just donated sperm, but now a kidney, aha, what a great man you are!

5Mama is Butt Ass Naked on TV

In one stroke she has disrespected her fathers and mothers, any husband/boyfriend/baby daddy and her children and children's children. And the fact that she can disrespect either one of them means she can and is perfectly willing to disrespect them all. Your mother is prancing around on tv butt ass naked. You send them to private school only so they can have a mother that prances around butt ass naked. You live with your children in Buckhead, or an exclusive White neighborhood and your mother's Instagram and Facebook page are filled with pictures of her in varying states of undress, popin' her pussy and dropping it like it's hot. You buy them the latest iPhone, latest Nikes, latest Adidas and when it's time to get them a car they drive elite European and Japanese luxury automobiles, but you prance around naked and dress like a stripper or like she is looking for men to approach her and give her attention. Comedian Dave Chappelle had joke revolving around the idea that quite a few post-modern women prance around in near states of nakedness in clothes less than 40 years ago only strippers and prostitutes would wear. Then when men (quite often unfairly and in a demeaning way) approach them like the strippers and whores they are dressed like, they get offended and suggest they are dressing like that for themselves and not to get attention. Perhaps, but if a human being were really dressing up 100% for themselves, it would be perfectly acceptable, even likelier that would dress that way at home or in private settings. (Like Jesus admonished us to pray in secret in our closets at home)

Do you think a 14-year-old boy or girl (probably with no daddy) is old enough and emotionally intelligent enough to have a healthy attitude to these random dudes their mother is dating? What lessons are we giving our children when mama and daddy are out here having random sex with other people but cannot, could not and are not even trying to make it work for the sake of providing a stable environment for their children? Do you think kids really understand the difference between, yes, my mother is out here simply 'living her truth', and I applaud her for not spending time with me, and making sure I can read and do math on grade level, as she spends time in the largely Asian nail salons and beauty supply stores, clubs and posting on YouTube and Instagram? And... she's a full-blown social media whore, sacrificing her children to her whoredoms every day in the name of satisfying her pathetic need for attention, her trivial conception of her own sexual needs, and living her truth. And inevitably, this phrase 'living her truth', ends up becoming just a clever disguise for whatever whim and fancy she wants to do, and that pops into her head from moment to moment.

Your child gets up to go to the bathroom in the middle of the night at your baby mama house, or to brush her teeth before school and its some nigga she knows vaguely in there washing his nuts. Our boys and our girls are watching their mothers get disrespected and deceived, and crater their and their children's opportunities at a healthy psychological, academic, and professional life at the same time. Do not fool yourselves, if your mother is gay and its some butch woman in there washing her strap or her vibrating ding-a-ling at 6 am in the morning, it is not any better or any easier for the child to understand and may be worse. All these hookups and the hookup mentality is proof of our damaged psyches and egos, and the very means by which we are damaging future generations; condemning them to lives of instability, sexually, academically, familial and otherwise. And yes, unstable homes, makes unstable communities, make unstable schools, and make unstable economic environments, dependent on criminality to provide jobs instead of entrepreneurship and capitalist development (which require stable relatively safe communities that respect the rule of law). No one puts a business or office space in a high crime area except the police, fast food, people that sells ribs and shit on the street, those with mental health issues, loiterers, prostitutes and dope boys; all of which contribute to third world type environs in many urban areas and create a self-fulfilling prophecy in that no 'real' business would locate there. So no jobs come, and the only community members who are there are too poor to go anywhere else and take no pride in the community.

You don't have to be a criminologist, just a good brother, sister, cousin, aunt, uncle to know that step-fathers, step-mothers and folk just magically living with people, usually have negative impacts on the child. Quite often these persons have a criminal impact on the child that goes far beyond the simple neglect of the baby mama who is out dating while her children need to be learning how to read and play a musical instrument or sport... to step-live in folk actually abusing their stepchildren. But it happens so frequently that it is probably not a coincidence. As a matter of fact, police know that when there are reports of abuse, the first place they look is the stepmother or stepfather or live in boyfriend or girlfriend. This is all in the name of parents, who already (according to them) made bad decisions concerning mates, making even worse decisions in the name of living their sexual truth, and making sure they feel pleased and get enough attention. Apparently, they are guided by some ridiculous sensation we have in post-modern American culture that 'we deserve to be happy'. Bah humbug. Anything above your duty to God, family and education is a grace before God.

Part II

But this aspect of being butt ass naked is more than an issue of clothes or honor. The bible uses a somewhat strange, archaic, and vague phrase, nearly always in negative terms that is in some cases translated as 'uncovering someone's nakedness'. Sure, we can keep it in the literal or take strictly in terms of the physical act of sex, but for a moment lets go deeper. Perhaps we might understand it as knowing someone's inner, deepest darkest secrets and then exposing or presenting them publicly. Out of respect for his children Kanye should have never said anything negative about Kim Kardashian let alone showing or revealing home porn tapes you or someone else made with her. Yep, we should demand that paternity court(s) are removed from television because they include the mass 'uncovering of Black women's nakedness'. This is the Black woman with such little self-esteem that she is on paternity court for a trip to Chicago or Atlanta, and because she has had unprotected sex with six different men in one month's time or one ovarian cycle. Then in the neighborhood, when all the gentlemen claim it's not theirs, and they are going to need a paternity test, it is another level of what she has been doing in secret and its implications. That is to say the public 'uncovering of her nakedness'. These implications include assertions about her character (and the character of the men involved) being exposed as a joke in that community and by default the Black community writ large. Thus a complete uncovering of American Black men and women's nakedness and sexual licentiousness. It is presented to us and the wider public as entertainment. And what a dangerous joke at that. Every last one of the dudes and the young lady could have gotten a venereal disease or worse, and they'd all share more in common than a night on the town with Tremishia, and a trip to Atlanta or Chicago to go to paternity court with Lauren Lake, Judge Mathis or the Cutlers. Black people are just 'uncovering each other's nakedness' for shameless self-advantage and promotion. The young men took advantage of her when they fucked her, all in one month's span. The young lady in question probably ain't got no daddy, uncles or older brothers which explains the low sate of her self-esteem, so she comes from a long line of mothers who got taken advantage of by men. The neighborhood young men took advantage of her by calling her the neighborhood whore, and making a joke out of using her and using her as sexual entertainment. Lauren Lake and the production company took advantage of her to 'uncover Black people and women's nakedness' for profit and watch this. White people take advantage of such presentations as they show the world what 'problems' the Negroes are, and how sullied their morality and ethics at every level, and why they have all of this dysfunction in their schools and communities, and why they have all of this violence...i.e. 'see world it's not my White fault, you can see for yourselves how the Blacks are on Paternity Court, Steve Wilko, Jerry Springer, etc.,'. There the world can see the mothers and fathers of Black children and grandchildren and children as yet unborn, yelling at each other, calling each other the vilest of names, on television and the internet. This cruel memorial to future generations is a memorial in digital stone forever, as long as YouTube and Instagram and such things exist, your children and your grandchildren can see their grandparents in a video circa 2019 calling each other the worst names and assaulting each other's characters...what a foul legacy to leave our children.

The young lady and the litigants (young men), go on tv, she is screaming at them that none of them would step up (presumably even the ones she thought might), and them screaming back at her that she is nothing but a whore, it was a one-night stand and never meant anything (as if meaning something caused pregnancy). The men rip her character down on national television (uncover her nakedness), even though that is a sister from your community, and thus reflects your community and that went to your elementary schools, your churches and this how she turned out, and you get on tv and call her a whore and worthless in front of your and her potential children, White people, and the whole world. This shows the world, how apparently Black communities are filled with random casual sex and unstable families. Thus, 'uncovering the nakedness' of our entire community on national television for a trip to Atlanta and a few thousand dollars' worth of spending change, which you will promptly spend at Lenox mall and in Buckhead where they don't want you anyway, unless you are spending money.

Guess what, it is not a joke. It is not funny, and it is not entertainment for a Black woman to be on TV 'butt ass naked' (as it were), no one defending her honor (neither herself, nor her man). They should make the fathers get up there with her and testify about what they didn't do, why their daughter's self-esteem is so low she had sex with 6 men, none of which were her boyfriend or even in a boyfriend/girlfriend relationship with her, and needs the White man's science (DNA test) to determine who her child's father is. Can you imagine being a child witnessing your mother undergo that trial? No matter who the father ends up being, and whatever platitudes the man makes about taking care of the child and wanting to be a good father, it is highly unlikely because the nigga has 4 other kids, he's either not taking care of or taking care of minimally. As for spending quality time with the kids, how can he ensure his children know how to read before kindergarten, if he doesn't 'read good' at 19? And the young men always fall back on, well I buy pampers and send $100. OK but the li'l nigga and niggarette can't read when they get to school and are discipline problems. The pampers and money, in decisive terms, weren't worth as much as the time spent raising and bonding with the child (giving the kid some self-esteem). What kinds of lessons and values is he giving the child, when he does spend time with them, with his lifestyle of justifying random casual unprotected sex on television and nearly driving the child insane with the pounding bass when it is in your car?

How is he really going to be a stable and positive influence in the children's lives if he is in and out of jail, dropping babies all over the community and then trashing his baby mamas for how trashy they are, when the very reason he's with them is his poor judgement, poor life management skills and the fact he's attracted to trashy women, and the ONLY women that are attracted to him are trashier. Chances are the father doesn't know his father, or any of his relatives on his father's side intimately for that very reason. All his father's people were trashy too, and unconcerned about having produced the next generation of trashiness; contributing to further instability in his child's life. What kind of financial and emotional network can the child's father and his extended family provide? Chances are he and his whole family are financially unstable as well. When these men trash these women on national television (uncover their nakedness), it is like they don't under-stand they are saying the same things about themselves, their mothers, and their family situations. It is like Black men calling women bitches, hoes, tricks, and chicken heads, in laughing scorn, all the while we Black men are ignorant troglodytes, ogres, cavemen, and Cro-Magnon in not just appearance but behavior. That is to say, whatever you call a woman, reflects on us as men worse. I include my own derisive com-ments and invective about Black women's liberal LGBTQIA socialist, atheist, political leadership in my books in that regard too. But I already know I am an ignorant Black male conservative troglodyte, ogre and

Cro-Magnon and I am proud of it, which at least has the effect of saving me from being a hypocrite.

Ladies and gentlemen of niggerdom, in these simple and oftentimes portrayed by the media as humorous human 'baby mama, baby daddy drama' foibles, that require paternity tests, and insults back and forth, we are 'uncovering the nakedness' of our individual selves, our families, our religious traditions and institutions and our entire communities. Whether we should be 'ashamed' of it or not I won't speculate, but I can tell you that it is virtually destroying our children by destroying their scholastic and professional opportunities. This is because of the level of our family dysfunction and how casual we seem to be about it, in that we think it's funny and makes for good entertainment. Yet our youth are destroyed by this family instability. Teen boys with no fathers and/or compromised mothers go on to self-destruct in criminality and alcohol and drug abuse, nihilism, and nearly suicidal rages. All because we want to 'publicly uncover our nakedness' and run around butt ass naked like Lizzo, and have 'any old sex' we want to with 'any old body' we want to, damn the consequences to ourselves and the effects on our children and communities. Why not, the White man makes big pharma products that make you 'undetectable' and like you don't even have a sexually transmitted disease?

I'm beginning to wonder if this perhaps is the 'curse of Ham' circa 2023 in that we are being punished for the biblical accusation of 'uncovering our father's nakedness'? So now it has come full circle and 'Ham' in America uncovers 'its nakedness' and the shame of its women on national television for the amusement of all who would watch, and to the delight of our former enemies who use it to justify their conservative peccadillos and justifications for arguing Black people are taking advantage of the welfare system by just dropping babies willy-nilly, and kill the welfare system...and with abortion....problems solved. This post-modern 'passing our children through the fires of Molech', sacrificing them to the 'god' of sex, drugs, partying, good times, anti-intellectualism, anti-scholasticism, smart phones and video clips. We don't educate them as Black parents, we let the TV, radical liberal public-school curricula, Facebook, tik-tok and Instagram educate our children. We feed our children mass American fast food and fast pop values in ways affluent White people don't and certainly Asians and Latinos don't, even its just because of language issues. We feed them anything except the good ole values of God, Family, Education, and that is exactly why the Black community is getting the results it is getting on the 6 o'clock news, and in begging the government to give our children curfews. This has the unintended effect of making a target out of them at night and example out of them for their bad nigga behavior, blaming it on the kids instead of bad parenting, bad extended families, liberal radicalism, self-centered Negro politicians and celebrities who could care less about the difficulties of being a Black parent in America as long as they get paid and bask in the glow of White mainstream celebrity culture 'tacit' acceptance and equally tacit 'wealth'.

6How the Pursuit of Happiness Confused Post-Modernity

In America it is an illogical truism that it is somebody else's responsibility to make you happy. We send food back at restaurants that teenagers, former felons, alcoholics and drug addicts cooked with the general complaint that it is not 'something' enough. We assume stores have liberal return policies and the moment something isn't everything it said on the package, and doesn't make you happy, you are sending it back. We assume politicians are there to make us 'happy', instead of providing good governance. We think the government itself is supposed to make everybody happy. It cannot, and for being fooled for so long that it can, people are encouraged to have unreasonable expectations. The longer people go with their unreasonable demands and expectations, the greater their disappointment with the status quo. And then they start talking silliness like draining the swamp, throwing the bums out and revolution. Then 'a people' starts doing silly shit like following up conspiracy theories on both sides that drive the debates of the day more than actual policy or even international political considerations. Then people start hating the other side and calling all liberals stupid or all conservatives arrogant and hard hearted. A house divided cannot stand. A house where its teammates continually undermine and subvert one another cannot stand and makes itself vulnerable to outside enemies who often get invited in as leverage for one side or the other. Divided isn't the real problem; polarization is. Divided and polarized Houses of Representatives, divided and polarized political parties, divided, and polarized judiciaries. Each division accusing the other and the executive branch, each branch weaponizing itself against the other.

The situation on the Supreme court deserves special attention. A set of political activist conservative judges ignore precedent (for whatever reason it undermines the principle). Another set of political activist liberal judges, on the Supreme Court (no less), is accused of leaking documents, with the political end in mind of generating public support against the changes in the law. Because of the ideological machine politics involved in the whole process of selecting judges to go to the higher levels on the Democrat and Republican side, any judge that reaches the higher levels has already been long beholden to one position or the other. Trump needed no discretion, wisdom, historical knowledge, legal knowledge nor genius to select judges to appoint to the Supreme Court or any other Court he was responsible for during his tenure as president. All he needed was to know who the Federalist Society picked. It is also problematic that Supreme Court Justice Thomas (for one) having his children's or grandchildren's education paid for by family friends, who just happen to magically be major donors to Conservative organizations and the Republican Party. And this is a man who is patently anti-affirmative action in court rulings for general Americans and minorities, but he lets the political machine system affirm his children into action and foot the bill for trip, gifts and amenities.

Each side, Fox, CNN, MSNBC, trying to mock each other's on air personalities and catch them in lies and compromising positions. Political candidates don't argue policy anymore, they just dig up dirt on the opposing side and conveniently and selectively release it when it's most political effective and damaging. What have we got in America when two grown ass old men trying to lead the free world will get up on TV in a debate and one says, "You're a wild eyed MAGA Jan 6 totalitarian dictator in waiting and other says "Oh yea, go get Hunter's laptop because not only does it have connections to Chinese business and donors, not only does it have video of Hunter having sex with his stripper baby mama, not only does it have discussions with Ukrainian officials about laundering intelligence (magically pre-Ukraine-Russia War), not only does it have his cocaine and crack connections in it, not only does it have all the salacious details of Hunter's love child with the stripper that Hunter and Joe refused to even acknowledge or see, until legally forced to, if you look in between the keys on the keyboard part of the laptop, there is literally coronavirus and herpes in between the keys of Hunter Biden's laptop. Hunter brought coronavirus and herpes simplex 123.2b (the Chinese strain) over here in the laptop. Vote for me because the secrets of the universe lie in Hunter Biden's magic laptop and Hillary's magic emails. "Oh Yeah," Biden will say...to the tune of the jazz classic 'Stormy Weather', Joe Biden starts singing 'Stormy Daniels'.

Everyone reading the above words knows damn well that scenario is far more likely to occur in a 2024 Presidential election debate than a well thought out discussion of domestic and foreign policy challenges in the coming 8 to 20 years for America. And as it goes in post-modern American politics, so it is going in our homes. We are told, the idea behind relationship and marriage is to make you happy. We have developed excessive expectations for being made happy, and no sooner than the relationship was enjoined, it is disjoined because one or more partner didn't get made as happy by the whole situation as they thought they would get made.

While in seminary some years ago I took at class called 'Judaism since Jesus' from a man we called Rabbi Shapiro; who happened to be an ethnic Jew. One time Rabbi Shapiro opened the class with another thought-provoking question. He asked us to jot down or think of some ideas in answer to the question 'what was the worst thing to happen to marriage in the past 150 years'. As he went around the room listening to answers, people said stereotypical things like, tough economic times, the impact of alcohol and drugs, a couple self-professed conservatives said men not leading the family, a couple self-professed liberals and feminist-womanists saying men leading the family. When he got to me, I proudly announced 'post-enlightenment political and cultural liberalism'. After seeking further explanation what I 'meant by that', which I summed up as people and morals getting too free, he shrugged and announced to the class, that the worst thing to happen to marriage in the past 150 years is 'getting married for love'.

There were gasps, and 'shock and awe' in the classroom like George Bush wanting to impress the Iraqis with American firepower and the White man awesomeness. The more outspoken Black women in the class immediately objected and felt that would be a recipe for bad relationships, domestic violence, and women getting stuck with kids in bad relationships. Rabbi Shapiro gently reminded us that we get married for love now and the divorce rate is 70%. Very often a relationship that started in great love, amorousness and affection, ends up in a nasty, nasty, bitter, angry divorce. One has to really wonder, nay imagine and fantasize to believe that the couple ever could have thought they loved each other, the level of vitriol and hatred the couple spews at each other is so hateful and even violent. And yet, we must know that there were times in the now busted and asunder relationship that they held hands, cuddled, kissed and told each other their innermost secrets, aspirations and desires. If that were not so they wouldn't be accusing each other of betraying those trusts (as they always accusing the other of doing). Moreover, the couple betrays those trusts in court by weaponizing the inner most secrets, aspirations, and desires of their former spouse. All of this takes place in public and in court, as the once happy couple begins to insult each other in a court of law where the above-mentioned secrets, aspirations and desires can be weaponized so that they have legal, juridical and law enforcement consequences. As bad as that is, the entire process takes place in front of the children whose estimation of their parents cannot increase by witnessing such interactions as their parents publicly tearing down one another morally, and tearing down one another with legal and financial ramifications. The situation I'm describing has a better name, provided by African American postmodern social history; 'baby mama/baby daddy drama'.

Rabbi Shapiro went on to make something that resembles the following argument. Marriage is an institution. One's interaction with institutions is not governed or conditioned by how you feel. As a citizen in good standing, you don't pay taxes because you feel like it or this year was good financially. Whether the year was profitable or not one still has to pay taxes on what one earned. It is calculated the way it is and in order to remain in good standing with the IRS and Enforcement divisions, you pay every year (or are liable to) no matter how that year was for you financially or what government benefits or services you did or did not draw upon or from. No matter what financial stresses, problems on the job, stress with your children, health problems, or your overall emotional state, taxes are due. The IRS as an institution makes these demands irrespective of your personal problems or who died in your life, or who was born, or getting divorced, how you feel or how the individual IRS agent feels about your case. The institution of the IRS is backed and is a division of the Federal Government. We have obligations as citizens that transcend how we feel about foreign or domestic foreign policy or who we root for in the Olympics. Whether we are proud to be an American or the idea of it fills us with shame and disgust, it will not affect the sales tax when you buy your groceries. You cannot opt out by pleading ignorance or disapproval. Fair or not there are things in this world we give institutional weight and yes; obedience to the point of sacrifice. Marriage used to be one of them. But let me stay on citizenship a little longer. Moses didn't tell the ancient Hebrews the aim of his leadership was justified because he was trying to make his people 'happy'. Au contraire, mon frère, he was trying to make God happy and them Holy, and they were just coincidental to that process. This is evidenced by their longing for the cucumbers, onions and garlic of Egypt even if it meant slavery, a theme earlier reflected in the Esau and Jacob story. One would surely make the same assumption of the prophet of Islam, Muhammad. He might add, with all due respect, that getting people into right behavior and lifestyle to be worthy to inherit Jannah (heaven) does not come from a life of ease and only doing things that make you happy.

Perhaps this would be an opportune time to read a few of the Prophet of Islam's sayings about marriage in various collected sayings.

(Narrated Aisha) the Messenger of Allah said: "Marriage is part of my sunnah, and whoever does not follow my sunnah has nothing to do with me. Get married, for I will boast of your great numbers before the nations.

Of course, that is the Islamic counterpart to the physical imperative in Genesis to be 'fruitful and multiply'.

Furthermore

Anas ibn Malik reported: The Messenger of Allah, peace and blessings be upon him, said, "Whoever Allah provides with a righteous wife, Allah has assisted him in half of his religion. Let him fear Allah regarding the second half."

Recorded in the Hadith of Bukhari with additional notes by Adil Salahi

Hadith (214)

Ibn Umar reports that the Prophet said: 'All of you are shepherds and all of you are accountable for whatever is under your charge. A ruler who is in power is a shepherd and is accountable for his flock. A man is a shepherd of his household. A woman (wife) is the shepherd in her husband's household/home (writ large), and a servant is a shepherd of his master's property; adding that he (Umar) reckoned that the Prophet also said: 'And a man is a shepherd responsible for his father's (family) property.

"Highly significant in this hadith is the mutual responsibility of man and wife. The Prophet puts this mutuality of responsibility in the clearest of terms. They are both responsible for their family. The responsibility is total and includes all affairs. They discharge it by doing their best to provide their household with a comfortable living. Yet is not merely the material aspect of life that is meant here. It is the general welfare of the family and it's place in society. When parents work for the welfare of their families, they do not do it as a charity or (simply because it is court ordered). It is their responsibility, for which they are accountable. Pg. 172 (Imam Al-Bukhari: Al-Adab al-Mufrad with full commentary by Adil Salahi.

Nearly all of our religions told us marriage and family is an institution. Post-modern relativism, however, says it's whatever you say it is as long as it's making you happy. What a selfish screed. We know damn well what divorce and absenteeism does to kids, but mommy and daddy got to 'live their truths', which magically and coincidentally is 180 degrees different from what their 'truth' was 2 years ago when you got pregnant or got somebody pregnant. And who do we make pay for changing 'truths'...the children! The countless Black children that wonder (as I did) where their daddies are, and feel so vulnerable, they need gangs, become runaways, get sex trafficked, and/or need to tolerate abusive situations in order survive and feel as though they have some kind of shield against the vicissitudes and vagaries of the world. They are turning to gangs and running away because they're parents have made them orphans before their parents have even died.

7 Kangaroo Court

One day I was watching a documentary on kangaroos late one night on PBS. Mankind's impact on the outback of Australia has been disruptive. Between farms and man-made development, much habitat, ancient migratory routes, and shelter has been lost. Invariably in some areas, highway traffic and collisions with cars and trucks impact the population of native animals. Also, man has killed some of their natural predators so in many cases the population explodes in unnatural ways. Of course, this added migratory pressure during mating and other seasonal affectations, forces the kangaroos to come into contact with humans, farmers and their animals, cars and trucks, which brings us to our conversation today.

A White Australian lady that runs a wildlife sanctuary receives 'joeys' from all over Australia that have lost parents and extended family/ social groups and perhaps most importantly, lost their mothers. Sadly, many lost their mothers while they still dependent in the pouch and not experienced or mature enough for life outside the pouch. For a joey with their mum, there is the psychological strength necessary to explore outside the pouch (necessary for development), because of the reassuring knowledge that mama and the pouch are there, and in case of danger I can just run to the pouch. And of course, you know the developmental story because it is much like the advancement of human children. The joey wanders off slowly, slowly, always keeping an eye out for where mama is and an ear out for her distress call, until one day the joey stops needing the pouch so much, and magically, he's too big to get back in it anyway. But all too frequently in Australia, Mother gets hit by a truck; 'joey' survives but the mother dies. Many animals are designed, nay, even evolved to fend for themselves relatively early on in life, with little or no input from either parent. Ladies and gentlemen of Mammalia, advanced land mammals didn't in the main, evolve that way. We evolved with mothers and their extended families, nursing and 'educating' future generations. We evolved with fathers and mothers and extended family units, birthing young that at least initially require constant protection, nurturing and training until they get the lessons (social, edible, political) that are necessary for survival. Human babies stay with their parents/caregivers longer than any other species except in rare cases.

That is no surprise, but guess what happens when motherless (by kangaroo default fatherless) 'Joeys' come to the shelter before reaching age of being socialized by their mothers and extended family? The same damn thing that is happening in urban schools. The proprietor of the shelter said that when 'Joeys' come to the shelter without having spent enough time with mom (in the safety and shadow of the womb with confidence to explore), and the stability and nurturing of extended families socializing and forming bonds, she can tell. Motherless and without extended families, the Joey's are easily frightened, suspicious, and resentful and thus don't make friends or socialize easily. Either they are cowed down too easily and intimated too easily by other and even smaller animals (lack of confidence); or they overcompensate and become bullies. They don't know how to share food (even when it is in abundance), and fight all the damn time (my curse words not the rescue lady's). She has noticed over her years in rehabilitation, the negative consequences of 'joeys' that have been too isolated from social interaction without their mothers and extended family, and get too big to be able to deal with, too big have such a negative attitude and social influence. Black teens being charged as adults in the criminal justice system comes to mind here, they're just too big to be that negative, no matter why and what traumas they suffered that produced that level of negativity. Michael Jackson eventually had to get rid of Bubbles. Quite simply he got too big to be out of control. When the joeys relationship with their mothers is stunted and emotionally insufficient; it is almost too late and that kangaroo will be miserable himself and he will make the other kangaroos around him/her equally as miserable and condemning himself to a kind of perpetual outsider status.

And let us take this moment to question the issue many in the LGBTQIA community recently raised. In the long and growing list of things they want to cancel because it hurts their self-esteem, which couldn't have been too high in the first place because you cut your dick and your titties off trying to fix yourself, in which case, how bad you felt about your 'natural' self, stimulated your quest to fix something that for all intents and purposes wasn't broken. You thought it was broken. But similar to my thoughts on purely cosmetic plastic surgery, if you can breathe through your nose, it's attached to your face, with many thousands upon thousands of blood vessels going through it, it was the one your great grandma gave you, and that you will give your children if you dare to get in a traditional relationship and have some the old fashioned way; who am I to change my nose because of current post-modern social-media driven fashions of attractiveness? Really ladies and gentlemen, if you can breathe through your nose relatively easily, that oughta be enough for every human being alive not to be too gung-ho about getting a nose job. Anyway, recently, the LGBYTQIA community suggested that there should be no more mother's and Father's Day, just parents day. Tell that to a kangaroo mother.

She literally carries her joeys around in a specifically designed pouch for upwards of two years. I've seen Joeys try to get back in their pouch but they were literally too big and their feet stuck out and their mothers labored and toiled greatly to carry them, looking like a Hebrew or Mississippi delta slave trying to lug him around, which she does at great inconvenience to her, but her maternal instincts tell her to have an attitude like if my Joey is 3 years old and 150 pounds he/she can always try to nurse and/or come jump into mommy's pouch for a sense of comfort and to feel safe. No male kangaroo is physically designed for the pouch thing, and their paternal instincts (similar to some of their human male cousins) tend to be somewhat less than what females put into the childbirth and early raising and parenting. Let us just look at some issues, while we play games with human sexuality.

Ladies and gentlemen, at the risk of stating the obvious unnecessarily, only Female Kangaroos have a pouch. They are not born with a pouch; the pouch develops over time and after puberty the pouch is fully capable. Is this pouch a social construct, by defaulting making whatever a male is, a social construct as well? No, because we find in the literature that "A male kangaroo hasn't got a pouch. He can't incubate and deliver a child so there is no need to have a pouch because he couldn't raise a joey. Joeys not only need a place where they are protected, but they also need milk with nutrition based on their age to become a grown-up kangaroo. Male kangaroos could provide shelter and warm body temperature, but they cannot produce milk and therefore cannot feed their young." My fellow Americans, how can we put this up on a website devoted to children learning factual information about animals (kangaroos), but we act confused and loath to argue the very same point in human terms relative to our Kangaroo and other mammal cousins?

No male kangaroo is physically designed for the whole pouch thing, however let us assume that 300,000 years of evolving mental capacity and biological knowledge and retention in the medical arts, kangaroo scientists 300,000 years from now can cut pouches into male kangaroos that sense themselves female. As the quote from the children's website said, a male could provide shelter and warm body temperature with a pouch cut in him by surgical means, but they could not produce milk, and not feed young. Thus to even make the argument they with their cut in surgically placed pouch, so well installed that it could fool males, females, and even young for a while...but the no milk situation proves (does it not) that equating the two would be illogical unless we argue magically, sex and the physical machinery of it, isn't for child birth and rearing at all. Perhaps all that equipment down there in our crotches is simply to have fun and use the restroom or whatever else real social constructs human beings come up with to do with their sexual organs besides their (for all intents and purposes) natural function. If the fun and the sex construct was more important than the biological/reproductive function, then it would be as that Republican senator idiotically said that time, 'women can't get pregnant if they get raped' (his argument was some magical way their body would reject the implantation of the man's sperm). Just as that is blatant idiocy, we know damn well that the actual reproductive function of sex, trumps any other consideration. How many children have human beings made from rape and forced (if not arranged) relationships and marriages? How many children are the product of getting drunk at the club and a random sexual encounters? If men and women have physical sex to the point of male orgasm (and in quite a few cases not even to that point in the example of pre-cum), the sheer biological weight of what a man and woman represent as biological mammalian entities is of more importance than any other consideration...political, cultural, religious, whether or not the woman wants to be there, whether or not the man wants to be there; the sheer born physicality of it, and born physical characteristics and potential trump everything socially, politically or religiously construed or constructed by the LGBTQIA community. Two post-puberty male/female adults, engaged in the sheer physicality, completely absent any other considerations will do something no same sex couple can do (make a child) no matter how much they love each other.

But back to the difficulties of really being a female in the mammalian, marsupial and human world. We know from human history that carrying and birthing a child is dangerous and for most of human existence, the leading cause of death for women. No it was not male patriarchy and abuse but dying in childbirth. As a matter of fact, in such circumstances, it proves quite the opposite of the 'patriarchal/ paternal disregard myth' held by feminists in that with women dying so regularly, it would seem to necessitate that the best and fittest of women were certainly held in high regard, desired and valued. We might even go on to argue as evolutionary biologists do that patriarchy and the sexualizing women are not the sole or even primary cause for the evolutionary pressures on women's tendency to wider and fuller hips. Any evolutionary biologist will tell you that patriarchy has nothing to do with it.

Evolutionary pressures were on the development in women of wider, fuller hips because the wider hips helped to facilitate safe childbirth and the extra fat was not only a resource for a developing child and a nursing child, but the woman herself in the struggles of our ancestors to get enough to eat for survival's sake, especially when they were migrating. But hey, feminists and the 'alphabet soup committee' can spin history however they want and to whatever contemporary political and cultural ends they want. Can a transwoman (biological male) in 2023 really understand, what women before 150 years or so ago and many women in non-western medicine societies had to go through? Namely, that if you get pregnant, no matter how much fun you had making it happen, and how proud you are of being fertile and pregnant, there is a 50% chance that you die in childbirth. Can cutting your dick off and taking $2500 worth of hormones a month enable a biological male to understand that? Sometimes the death rate was even higher for women. Can a man really understand that? Do Dylan Mulvaney, Lia Thomas or Katlin Jenner really understand that and would their commitment to being a woman extend that far if it were 'necessary' and possible for Kaitlin, Dylan, and Lia to birth children? Would their commitment extend far enough that they would birth a child like a woman from prior to 100 or so years ago, with a 50% or higher probability of dying in the process of childbirth? Maybe, but I hardly believing cutting your dick off and saying you feel like a woman, automatically means you understand it at that level. My childbirth example should have been enough but let me give you some of the other rigors of Kangaroo maternity and why the shit Americanized and Europeanized women be talking about as post-birth depression is trivial compared to the real life of hominid females.

Ladies and gentlemen (and my brothers and sisters who consider themselves misgendered by God or fate), why do Kangaroos need a pouch? Let us cull some materials from a children's website. Children love kangaroos right. I am almost sure that if kangaroos could read and had story time hours, children would much prefer 'kangaroo reading time' to mom, dad or drag queens reading them books. Kangaroos need a pouch for reproduction. Although kangaroos are not born in the pouch, they still need the pouch to raise their young. A kangaroo's pouch is the home of their young for the first few months of their lives. It is the place where the young are kept warm and get the food they need to develop into a grown-up adult.

Even when their young leave the pouch, they continue to drink milk for a few months. They just pop their heads back into the pouch and suckle milk whenever they like.

Do Baby Kangaroos mess in the pouch and mom has to clean it?

Do Baby Kangaroos Poop in The Pouch? **Baby kangaroos do poop in the pouch**. They also pee in the pouch because they cannot go anywhere else in the first few months of their lives. When young kangaroos are a few months old they begin to leave the pouch from time to time. But they continue to go back to the pouch but that brings in even more dirt, for example, when the kangaroo played in the dirt or hopped on the beach.

The pouch is an almost entirely enclosed area where dirt collects easily. Dirt can't fall out of the pouch because the pouch is only opened upward. Kangaroos aren't the only animals that have pouches where they raise their young. Other animals with pouches may have the opening to the rear, for example, if they are digging in the dirt and that would fill up the pouch.

A kangaroo's pouch opens upward but dirt still comes into it. The pouch is also the place where kangaroos raise their joeys

A female kangaroo cleans her pouch by licking it out. She puts her long snout into the pouch and simply licks it out. A female kangaroo can easily clean around a joey which is still attached to a teat in the pouch.

It's that simple.

I think Ru Paul, Billy Porter and the afore mentioned 'alphabet soup community' like the drag, the makeup, the dresses, the shoes, the disco, 'sashay Shante' and all that shit, but if they had to magically go back in time and live how women, or for that matter kangaroo women or any other mammal women had to live, I'm not sure they'd be so gung ho about it. Perhaps a few, some or even many would. I just think the number of men supposing themselves to be women would go down if they literally had to go back in time and live as our human mothers, gorilla mothers, or lionesses, or mammal females in general etc., had to live, with or without the physical and hormonal literal differences that make nubile females, nubile females. Would they really choose to be everything it meant and means to be a full fledged woman biologically and get pregnant if they knew there was a 50-65% chance they die in childbirth? I'm not sure taping your dick under your legs with masking tape and cutting your dick off and taking hormones automatically proves that a man has that kind of female dedication or the level of dedication it would take to be a female in those circumstances.

But let us get back to these badass misbehaving Joeys that didn't have good parenting and thus were not socialized properly (and our kids). This rehabilitation specialist has told us of the difficulties when Joeys come into the sanctuary, with too little socialization from mother and extended family, and too old to be taught something different. They either become cowed and traumatized, or become bullies. They don't know how to share. Everything makes them feel uncomfortable and neurotic. They become unsociable, disaffected, dejected, which intensifies the feelings of isolation and yes, makes them even crazier. They're not bad joeys. There is not a 'culture' problem or genetic component in a slew of badass Joey's suddenly (post-European contact). It is that because of the demands of human encroachment and environmental degradation, kangaroo and kangaroo culture(s) live lives where the old means of transmitting kangaroo culture and stability are not getting done. Ladies and gentlemen, we of negritude have had 3 or 4 generations now, post-war on poverty where we have done a tremendous social experiment raising our joeys as single parents (most often mothers), and without the reliable support and influence of fathers and extended families. Ladies and gentlemen, the results of this experiment in our urban communities is in, and we must begin to re-invest in our families (nuclear and extended). Ladies and gentlemen of Mammalia, the socialist atheist LGBTQIA great society welfare experiment has failed, we failed our children, we failed our religious traditions, we failed our communities socio-economically.

The socio-cultural and political effects of failed relationships, marriages and families may be convenient to we adults living our 'truths', but we have enslaved and penalized our children because we want to be out there running the streets and dropping babies; thinking it's some kind of human right not only to have babies but to kill them at will.

*****Lady in the news killed her1 year old or so baby******

I made the argument earlier (I'm fully pro-Choice), what message are we really sending our children. They are not stupid. What moral, ethical, theological, and technological choices and rationales, do you think make a giant difference between killing a baby at 3 months gestation or 3 years post-womb? How is post-birth a different moral question? Really? The only way it would make a moral difference, was if women (and men) did not know or could not tell they were pregnant until after gestation and birth. When a woman or man have sex at all, they cannot plead ignorance as to what the possibilities might be. When a woman misses her period, she (or he) cannot plead ignorance, thinking what's in her womb may just happen to be a wombat and have nothing at all to do with a human baby. No, if you kill a baby in utero or you wait until he or she is 2 or 3 and just dash him or her off the side of mountainous gorge because it is no longer convenient, there is no fundamental difference except in the vanity of liberal Feminist/Womanist LGBTQIA human being's minds. Here again, I support 'Abortion Rights' because sending women back to the dirty back alley side street doctors, root doctors, witch doctors, herbalists, witches, warlocks, etc., would be worse than the present situation.

In conclusion, let us get back to our cousins in the kangaroo community. Joeys that didn't spend enough time with mama or socializing with related cousins, older siblings, etc., learn slower or not at all, because nearly all learning is social to some extent. Furthermore, the lack of being able to socialize with their peers at the Rehabilitation Center means that they are lonely and unhappy. That is hardly an environment that promotes the kind of emotional healing necessary after the loss of a mother, nor is the rehabilitation center at that point a 'safe' environment for the young 'troubled joey', despite the food and shelter. Under the psychological circumstances of the joey not adjusting well, the 'care' environment itself at the rehabilitation center, for all the good it does, ends up not only damaging them more in the short term, but traumatizing them in the name of trying to save them, and they carry that for the rest of their oftentimes lonely, unhappy, and shorter lives. They carry that trauma with them forever and it affects every relationship the joeys have thereafter, with other kangaroos and with human beings (who Joey's see as their sole providers, not nature, not being taught what to eat by older adult roos and older roos). More importantly, socializing with other kangaroos means knowing what it's like to be a kangaroo and be out there in the wild foraging for yourself. Imagine the feeling of looking in a baby kangaroo's eyes as he ensconces himself in his fake pouch made for him by human rescuers, which is just a woman's scarf tied at the end and hung, designed to resemble (you guessed it) the size and shape of his mother's pouch. This the joey would needs be prefer, to being outside of the pouch socializing with other joeys his age and older adult kangaroos. These are skills he will need in the future, when if possible he is released back out into the wild. But he hasn't had enough experience doing socializing because he or she was neglected as a youth and didn't form the bonds necessary with the mother and her extended family to promote confidence in the stability of their environment, and potential for growth based on the trying of new skills and confidences in exploratory situations. Instead for the joey deprived of a stable family, these opportunities to socialize cause fear and anxiety. The only thing he knows however is the fake pouch to resort to. And it is fake. A crude imitation, but in the absence of the real thing, a crude imitation oftentimes, ersatz, must suffice. But like the Jewish people (absolutely no disrespect intended to them, the Palestinians or Ugandans) realized in the debate wondering whether a 'homeland' in Uganda was just as good for the time being as one in Palestine. It's just a crude, cruel substitute.

The Other conclusion, if you think my usage of the kangaroo theme is overwrought, Google Kangaroo parenting and more shit will pop up about human parenting than kangaroos. Let them that have ears to hear, hear.

8Imma Call Your Daddy and other post-modern myths, urban legends, and fairytales

This essay includes a discussion of its counterpart, 'Imma tell your mama'. Ladies and gentlemen, what does it mean to live in a culture where both statements have less and less meaning, and for all intents and purposes have lost all meaning in Black culture? It means to live with the kind of chaos and violence we find in our urban schools and communities today. That is what it means!

You have some that argue 'freedom' demands children not be overly concerned with pleasing their parents. We are told by post-modern intellectuals, therapists, and 'social-media lifestyle influencers' that children have their own lives, and need to spend a lot of time out there 'finding themselves', not submitting to the dictates of parents and family. Of course, the pendulum can swing too far in the other direction of dictatorial parents and family. Yet as wonderful as children 'finding themselves' sounds to human agency, the power of secular human rationalism, and blind post-big bang atheistic aesthetic evolution, it means that 'children finding themselves' is often the prelude to and the combinative effects of parental neglect and the complete ignorance of the child. It becomes a vicious circle and cycle of intergenerational trauma because quite often while today's parents and grandparents should be parenting, they are somewhere at 35, 45, 55 and 65 trying to 'find themselves' and 'live their truth too'. Meanwhile, in the name of being allowed to 'find themselves', our youth end up never 'finding themselves' and on a perpetual search, mostly as the country song said, 'in all the wrong places and faces' (gangs). Yep, you had no curfew, and your parents didn't give a shit, who you hung out with or how you did in school, in the name of you 'finding yourself' and 'your own way'. But how can you competitively 'find yourself' reading 3 grade levels behind, and going to school when you want to? What kinds of options in 'finding yourself' will you really have crippled by ignorance and little or no job experience, because your parents never even required chores of you, let alone a little teen appropriate job.

Let us argue for the time being that biological fathers are unnecessary and completely replaceable by any socio-sexual LGBTQIA panoramic construct. Well, if we accept that as true, then we must view fatherhood as one gigantic global mammal experiment in a gigantic placebo effect. If fathers are unnecessary, irrelevant, and replaceable then any success(es) fathers have ever had, is the result of a placebo effect. Well, before we fathers start getting depressed and feeling bad about ourselves, there are many, many occasions where the placebo effect not only works, but is safer and a better alternative than medical or pharmaceutical intervention. Furthermore, there are worse placebos women/mothers submit to earnestly in the name of disciplining their children.

I'd be curious to know what percentage of American mothers has ever told a child to reprimand them, or to promote good behavior, "I am going to tell Santa Claus on you'? The obvious implication made to the child in the statement is that Santa won't bring you any presents or toys for Christmas. Whether it works or not, presuming it does, it is quite a placebo effect inasmuch as the mother is Santa Claus and/or Santa Claus is a fictitious person. Of course, if you don't celebrate Christmas or have never given the child any gifts in 'the name of Santa Claus', the threat is less meaningful. What does it mean when Black culture is such that to tell our children 'Imma tell Santa Claus on you' is more often stated than 'imma tell your daddy on you'? Teachers used the same placebo effect to great effect (in the old days). In the old days it was enough to threaten a child with 'Imma tell your momma/daddy/grandma/caregiver on you. Usually that would be enough to get a kid to straighten up. Now we have so weakened the bonds of family, familial responsibility, and paternal responsibility, that 'imma tell your momma/daddy etc.,' means nothing to our children. This is to the point that teachers now know it's best not to even make the threat. They may be greeted with the response 'I ain't got no mamma or daddy', or 'tell them'. 'Tell my momma/daddy'! The kid doesn't give a shit because the kid knows the parent doesn't have time to give a fuck because the parent is out there 'finding themselves' when they should be checking homework, and checking out their child's friends and associates. Quite often because of parental drug use and the kid's early childhood experiences of neglect and deprivation, the parent doesn't have enough authority (moral or experiential), for the child to assume the parents 'critiques' and 'opinions' are even worth listening to, let alone actually implementing the corrections to or adjusting the child's behavior to. It is thus as if every child in such circumstances as a drug addicted and drug addled parent, says to his parent the same thing the the thief on the cross said to Jesus, if thou are the Son of God (so smart, so powerful, so all knowing) take yourself down from this cross of drug addiction. Now consider that the teacher in societal terms (at best) is a symbol of the parental relationship, and you see why urban public school systems have such a high teacher turn over rate and teachers feel abused by students and administrators. The students are abusive because they come to school and transform their anger and resentment at their parents (or lack thereof), into anger and resentment against their ersatz parent, the teacher, who is obligated by law and professionalism not to argue back, cuss back or fight back. That is why the turnover rate amongst teachers is so high ladies and gentlemen. Teachers are abused by administrators because from the principal to the school board, to the parental public, they are expected to turn lumps of coal into diamonds in a semester or two. Do you know the length of time and the pressures involved in turning lumps of coal into diamonds in the natural world? Teachers are expected and even held accountable for taking a child that is reading and doing math three grade levels behind when the children got to that teacher's class, and magically by the end of the year 'White man test taking time", transforming that same child that was three grade levels behind when the teacher got him, into reading and doing math on grade level! To add insult to injury, this magical transformation is supposed to happen in an atmosphere of poor student discipline, student apathy, students fights every day, metal detectors, x-ray scans and real trained official duty police whose other duties when not patrolling the hallways of our urban schools, is hunting down real criminals; murderers, thieves, drug dealers, gangs, and all the most violent criminal elements in society.

And this is not just parents and teachers that have no leverage with many young Blacks today. Remember the days when the postman, your older neighbors, the folk that work at the local grocery store or the shop at the mall could say to our children 'Imma tell your mama/daddy on you' (or even the preacher) in response to bad behavior and it actually meant something? And the very fact that we cannot do that today signifies the very failure in African American civilization and the reason it is so confused and socio-economically dysfunctional. This failure is the very reason urban environments are quite often plagued with criminality, violence, greed, deprivations, and trivial materialism of the crassest sort. This failure is the reason Mayor Dickens and the Black liberal political and religious establishment, has no response to 'out of control youth violence' except more police, government sponsored policing programs and curfews....and shipping excess prisoners to southern rural Georgia and Mississippi to private incarceration facilities and work camps? Is that not some kind of disgrace before the God of the Black man? Sons and Daughters of Ham! That is what the Black Liberal Political class here in Atlanta would rather sell Black Atlanta as a rational approach to the proliferation of crime and its byproduct, incarceration, definitely not the old fashion solution of 'Imma tell your muthafuckin /mama/daddy on you'. That phrase has lost all meaning in contemporary Black urban culture.

Black urban culture has been bought off by, and thus defined by, a 'bread and circuses' welfare state, and coliseum massive entertainment industrial complex. We of negritude apparently have resigned ourselves to utter dysfunctionality in our homes and communities, with the only consolation being social media, vapid celebrity culture, streaming and binging movies, sports, eating out, buying luxury items and this massive 'entertainment industrial complex' America has created in order to distract citizens from the very real civilizational scale problems America has (not just Black people). For instance, how the fuck is it sane to blame Kia and Hyundai for America's theft problem? The problem is not that Kia's and Hyundai's are too easy to steal! In watching documentaries on Japanese culture, masses of people regularly leave their bikes at the train station without locks and cameras. If the ease of theft, breeds theft, Japan should have a serious bike theft problem, but it doesn't. A statement was also made that if you left your bike on the curb in Japan, other than someone mistaking it for litter or being inappropriate, no one would touch it, quite simply because it is not theirs, and they come from a culture where property rights are respected and youth are taught at a very young age to respect the property rights of others and to expect that their property rights will be respected. It is reciprocal and that is what makes a society and culture 'stable' enough for high levels of academic, technological, religious, cultural, and economic development historically. A society and culture like that could not look in the mirror, let alone in the face of humanity and make the argument that the fact there are high numbers of car thefts in Black America is because Hyundai's and Kia's are 'too easy to steal' and our adults and even children and youth can't help themselves from stealing them. This is as though the tendency to thievery, like the tendency to a particular hair color, skin color, hair texture, facial features, etc., is just something all Americans are born with and if you make anything around us, 'easy to steal', we Americans can't keep ourselves from stealing...so the onus is on you corporations and government to make commercial and other products that are ever harder and harder to steal. What the fuck kind of argument is that? Don't worry, it gets worse. The police themselves here in Atlanta and Dekalb County have taken to giving out Kia and Hyundai steering wheel locks as a public service...that is to say, as opposed to encouraging the largely Negro citizens of Atlanta and Dekalb Counties to encourage get some religion and religious values and morals that de-emphasize perceived 'property crimes of sheer opportunity'. Even if the thefts are the result of virally idiotic Tik-Tok trends, is the problem social media (a technology) and not the hearts and minds of our children? The problem is not inherent in the technology or any technology (including nuclear), you can kill someone with a steak knife, is the solution thus to create 'safer and safer' knives, which by default ends up completely defeating the purpose for desiring a knife)? Is African American political and cultural leadership so poor, that we blame Hyundai and Kia for crime, instead of looking in the mirror and at our families? You see which strategy the 'liberal socialist atheist LGTBQIA Black elected officials' are taking, because it's easier to blame Kia and Hyundai than to say, let alone fix the socio-cultural and familial problems that are draining African American culture of stability, viability, and vitality.

This American massive entertainment industrial complex, our version of Rome's 'bread and circuses' make the entertainment of the Roman coliseum look like 'Romper Room'. A worldwide ChatGPT Bot driven world where students get immediate answers instead of doing research, where job applicants give the details of their life to ChatGPT Bot AI, and it does their resumes for them. In this new America, marriage and sexuality have gone from respected institutions, too anything goes bazaars, carnivals, and techno-markets. The assumption is often made that porn and liberal sexuality definitions would make sex more exciting, more pleasurable and more prolific, but we find in America just the opposite, and birthrates tank and fall like acid rains, harbingers of death and foul emanations from the lakes and streams charged with giving life in the original scheme of things; for agriculture, the propagation of flora and fauna and the animal life that depend upon it. This is the new America, an America where 'zombie' and 'flesh eating' drugs circulate in major urban centers, and fentanyl and crystal meth ravage rural areas. Quite frankly, if half your citizens are getting 'doped up', 'liquored up', and 'entertainment upped', damn near 'zombified' out of their minds every day, obviously they spend far less time on social, political or cultural criticism and related activities. This is why as rough as it sounds, America's White mainstream socio-economic elites are relatively content behind their gated communities, private schools, and affluent social organizations to let urban and rural

America fend for itself and destroy itself in the process of a weird attrition that is perpetually trying to 'find themselves' and 'speak their truth'. They have no problem with Honey Boo Boo on tv. Honey Boo, nor her mulatto love child, will go to their schools for long and not pass the tests. It's all just entertainment for the masses.

And what does it mean to not have a mother/father/aunt/uncle/grandma/caregiver? To not have protectors, and guides, 1st teachers and windows into your culture and the sexual roles that historically define your culture (and advocates in your assimilation of that culture)? It means our children seek to reproduce that relationship in gangs, with weird hand signals and handshakes (gang signs), and these depraved 'cultural artifacts' have replaced things we learned from older relatives, siblings, and cousins in our nuclear and extended families. Gang initiations require stealing, violence and getting jumped and beaten into the gang. In Black American culture this has replaced baptisms, confirmation classes, bar and bat mitzvahs (relatively), age-appropriate activities and classes at the mosque, pick-up games at family barbecues and get togethers. The 'family' is the 'original gang', and the mentality extends so much wider. Some families are into motorcycles, cars, real estate, the factory, the plant, the theatre, the academy, the polytechnic, the brokerage house, etc. And yes, some muthafuckin families will tear everybody a new asshole in card games.

Glory to God, families are powerhouses and engines of community, civic, country, state, national and international prosperity...ergo I can't figure out why we niggas don't seem to give a shit in these areas (family etc.,) in post-modernity. Ergo, how can any sane society neglect families? And therein lies the problem in post-modern America and more specifically post-modern Black liberalism. This is not because there is anything necessarily wrong with liberalism or its adherents, but because the effects of weak family structures are so transcendent across multiple categories of socio-economic, cultural, and political inquiry, it seems to me even Black liberals would not shoot themselves or the Black community in the foot by being anti-traditional family and overtly and vehemently pro-LGBTQIA socialist atheism. This family instability of course not only affects internal Black community relations but also negatively impacts our interactions with and relationship to White mainstream America. As a matter of fact, family dysfunction in the Black community has now become a political trope, as has the idea of fatherless homes in the Black community. Now, mass fatherlessness in Black America is assumed to be the rule and not the exception. Furthermore, complicating our political position in America is that White people conveniently use the 'war on poverty' welfare policies and affirmative action, to imply that those policies themselves were the problem and deflect from themselves, any political, economic or cultural liability or responsibility to earnestly and sincerely invest African America as fellow Christian American citizens and not portraying 'helping' African America as some kind of charity case or entitlement for undeserving Negroes. Quite importantly, that is to say that 'aid' to Black America in the wake of the 'so called War on Poverty' and 'The Civil Rights Movement' should have looked more like a post-World War II Marshall Plan for African America, like America did for Germany and Japan; and like it did for China in the wake of post-Sino-Soviet breakup and after Nixon and Kissinger's famous 'opening up' of China politically. Can you blame Black America in such circumstances as wondering aloud to mainstream White America, if that is how White people treat their former enemies, it would have been far better for us to be their enemies, than to be their friends and brothers in Christ. It's rough, but it's true. 'Let them that have ears, hear'.

9I'm in love with a Black woman that doesn't need me

The recent passing of Diva legend Tina Turner, alerted me to the fact perhaps there is no greater symbolism of the post-modern dynamics between Black men and women and the Black individual as an existential reality than Tina Turner. Born into poverty in Nutbush, TN, she had childhood experience picking cotton. Tina stayed behind in Nutbush when her parents moved to Knoxville to work in the industries that sprang up prior to and during World War II. During this time, she lived with her strict grandparents who were Deacon and Deaconess at Woodlawn Missionary Baptist Church and she sang in the choir at Spring Hill Baptist Church. Perhaps in a bizarre foreshadowing of the future, Tina's mother ran off to avoid an abusive relationship with Tina's father and Tina moved to live with her grandmother in Brownsville, TN. When her grandmother died, she moved to St. Louis where her mother was. Her father remarried and moved to Detroit. It was in St. Louis that she met Ike. The church played a significant role in so many Black entertainers lives that it is almost a truism. The early experience singing in the church gave Tina a 'leg up' (bad um dum cymbal crash) when she got around musicians playing Blues and R&B on the club scene in St. Louis. She paid her dues on the chitlin circuit with Ike (literally and figuratively) in the Black Blues/R&B experience/ early rock n' roll music and Black entertainment variety shows.

But a funny thing happened on the way to the forum. Trivialized and marginalized as 'race music' here in America, that same Gospel/Blues/ R&B sound and aesthetic was now embraced by the White angelic heralds of the British beat; people like the Rolling Stones, Eric Clapton, etc., that idolized Blues/Soul/Gospel/R&B legends like Howlin Wolf, Muddy Waters, et. al. This paved the way for more acceptance in White mainstream America. This put Tina and many other Black musicians in a unique position. Had they plied their craft only 20 years earlier they would have died broke, penniless and all but ignored as artists. But growing White acceptance meant that Black artists were no longer relegated to the 'chitlin circuit' (with Ike and the other niggers). With a little talent, the support of established White British bands and singers, a little mainstream appeal, White pop-rock flair, and White mainstream management and Tina could now play bigger integrated audiences and venues under the auspices of the White music industry champions pushing you.

A whole new world opened to Tina, including the shedding of the Black Christianity of her youth, and embracing Buddhism. The Black Christianity of her youth had too many negative memories, too much baggage, she needed a clean break from her past. She of course kept the training and disciplines it gave her as a singer and in terms of that grounding in the blues and spiritual aesthetic, but Tina wanted to start over literally and figuratively with a new career, a new religion, new life, new White pop-rock n' roll infused soul music, and sooner or later, new man. Tina left Ike and blossomed. As she blossomed, she towered over Ike, towered over the nigger shit like the chitlin circuit and an all-Black audience, towered over 'the ignorance' and 'backwardness' of nigger Christian religion and the nigga musical culture of her youth, outgrowing it, outstripping it and putting Ike and all the other little niggers in the shade.

Without the benefit of extensive therapy with me or anyone else, we might even suppose that the little nigga girl from Nutbush, TN blossomed so much, she left all her nigga shit behind her, even her nigga kids with Ike. Tina Turner, like Operatic singers Jessye Norman and Leontyne Price spoke in a very dramatic almost punctilious way. Their Negro relatives did not and in Tina's case, her son's did not have any of the advantages that should have accrued to them academically (if nothing else) by being the child of Tina Turner. Tina's nigger sons were not raised in the rarefied environs of Europe and hanging out with rich White East Coast and West Coast elites, or the London and continental elites that Tina circulated around. They were raised with Ike, fully ensconced in nigga shit, except when he sent all the kids to live with her during the divorce. Apparently however, the kids were not socialized and educated with the children of her rich White friends. They grew up looking like, acting like, and thinking like typical lower working-class American niggas just like their father. Thus, I was not surprised that she buried two sons (one committing suicide), whose deaths were most probably caused by the kinds of lifestyle choices that afflicted Ike and unfortunately, many, many young Black men. She could not take them out of all that with her continental jet setting and elite White friends and associates. Tina, however, got out. She escaped niggerdom, even if her children as they escaped Sodom and Gomorrah were forced to look back out of fear and admiration (bizarre and contradictory but powerful nonetheless) for their father and were turned into pillars of salt (or perhaps Cocaine), not making it out. Tina on the other hand, traumatized as she was from what must have been early childhood, ran from niggerdom and never looked back.

How far did she run? All the way to Germany and a German prince. Clearly, she unlike the 'woke left' of today, was not looking for reasons to cancel people. Her husband's wealth and relative comfort(s) during the Nazi era Tina saw as no hinderance to a relationship and good thing she didn't. For I can only argue that what we are told Ike put her through was (at least somewhat) alleviated by the love, care, support, and affection her German prince showed her as he doted on her and made nearly his entire life about her.

We are told in the wake of her many later health challenges, that he bought her a 27-million-dollar home in a picturesque area of Switzerland. If that were not enough, when she needed a kidney or some other organ transplant he provided his own. We can only imagine what Ike would have said, had Tina asked him for a kidney at any point in their relationship, except when he was broke and would have gladly sold her one of his kidneys. "Ike, I need a kidney or imma die." Anna Mae, you must be out yo' muthafuckin mind, bitch you crazy. You don't want my kidney no way, it's filled with liquor and cocaine. The White doctor told me I did enough liquor, cocaine and amphetamines', to damage a horse's liver. Could any Black man have given her that assorted marital gift bag as the German prince making her life almost a fairytale?

It's always strange when we Blacks are forced by the unpleasant realities of our present, to look back towards our Jim Crow past. We then lament how some things seemed to be better in our internal relationships before we had all this access to the 'big wide White mainstream world'. Then we could not afford the splintering and division that comes from 'some of us' being creamed off the top and allowed to take advantage of the 'big wide White mainstream world' and the myriad of opportunities the big, wide integrated White mainstream world provides, and some of us not being 'allowed' to take advantage of those opportunities. But unfortunately enough, because it is still a White mainstream system, only as Black individuals 'creamed off the top', can we advance in the White mainstream world, not as a group.

Tina became a princess (before Meghan) and every material fantasy and dream she ever had as a child in Nutbush, TN was met or exceeded by her post-Ike Turner integrated life. But the Black community in Nutbush, and the old Baptist, CME and AME, AME Zion, Methodist Episcopal church other than having signs up that proudly say 'birthplace of Tina Turner and Tina Turner sang here as a child' haven't changed much in 75 years except that they have weakened dramatically as cultural and religious influences on Black children's lives in the Black community that produced Tina. And yet we must be happy for her that she found Buddhism, which saved her life; but for that matter, she didn't open a Buddhist temple in Nutbush, TN, or anywhere else in Niggerdom either if she thought it was that great. Tina died a princess in a chateau in Switzerland under the best doctor's care and with every convenience. Can a little Black girl born in Nutbush today dream so grandly, when the Black churches aren't what they used to be, and Black families aren't what they used to be in that as Tina's nuclear family ebbed and flowed and finally failed, her grandparents and other relatives took up the slack, along with the churches they attended?

Even simply from a musical perspective and what Tina learned in the church, if the children aren't going to church are they getting less opportunities to sing and learn the roots and rudiments of Black music that have made it so successful? Are we to assume the public schools in Nutbush are any better today than they were when Tina was there? Clearly, Tina must have been a bright girl whether this was believed by her teachers or her parents, or whether demonstrated in terms of standardized tests by Tina, or not. I'm sure there are many bright little Black girls in Nutbush and similar places to it in rural and urban African America. Are we to assume her chances of finding and marrying a stable Black man are better than Tina's chances when she came out of Nutbush and went to St. Louis via Detroit (if I'm not mistaken). Is it any better for Black women in 2023 than it was for Black women in 1950. If not, even with all Tina accomplished as a Black woman, human being, artist and businessperson, we have to wonder.

Here again had Tina been born 50 years earlier, she would have died playing the chitlin circuit not in a chateau in Switzerland. Let's go even deeper, had Tina been born 45 or 50 years later than 1940 she might be Nikki Minage, Kardi B, Black China or Glo-Rilla. Or just a stripper in Magic City, with the nickname 'legs'. No disrespect intended, but just in terms of the music, I'm not sure our community (in terms of the artists that represent us) have gained much. Yeah, yeah, I doubt Tina could read music, knew music theory or knew the academic difference between the ionic scale, Phrygian scale, pentatonic scale or the one Indian musicians use in the complex formulations of Raga and Carnatic music. But ear training would have been better learning music in the old days because there were no technological means of correction. If the piano at the gig was so out of tune it sounded down a half step, you as singer and the other musicians had to switch keys or adjust your ears to the sound and make it work as best you can. Where can Black children go in contemporary American society to learn to make music the way we once did in churches. The tradition of choral singing, church singing, and churches being places young musicians, singers and praise dancers could learn the ropes, going around to the different churches and talent shows on Sundays' filled with performances, food and socializing at different churches. Where is the secular equivalent to those opportunities for our children in the world the Black elected officials liberal socialist LGBTQIA like Stacy Abrams are trying to create?

And yet. Tina Mae Bulloch is not the real reason for this essay. Indeed, I am in love with a Black woman, and she doesn't love me. I do not say this to illicit support or sympathy, nor as some sort of dig or critique of her. To be frank, it is the same advice I tell my male and female friends of a certain age and my dear respected family, and dear readers. I merely repeat the best advice I ever got on marriage. I asked a friend I had known since childhood, a policeman no less, if he had any advice for someone about to get married. He looked me straight in the eye, as seriously, and as clearly as if he were giving testimony at a murder trial. He said 'don't do it'. That was his advice. Don't get married.

In my natural mind (absent the commands of God), he was exactly right. My first marriage ended in divorce, my second marriage (the other one I was seeking advice from him on) ended in divorce. And both were the kind of divorces that feel like they set you back in life 10 years because of all the emotional, financial, and relational strains and issues that must be assuaged and sorted out that require much, much time, prayer, hashing, rehashing, opportunities for anger and resentments on both sides and yes, lawyers and their expense.

And yet as a Christian and considering Islam and Judaism there is no way to have sex without being in a covenant and socio-legal-religiously sanctioned marriage with exclusivity as the assumptive assumption; with another human being of the opposite sex. For some strange reason that's what God told us, some oh, 3500 years or so ago at Sinai. Apparently, he provided little or no caveats to this basic assumption.

Forgive me for presuming a window into, nay a spare windowpane of inquiry into the mind(set(s)) of God, but supposing God made such a thing as covenant marriage for only legitimate disbursal of sex, simply because he wanted to keep us from embarrassing ourselves on paternity court? What if it's as simple as that. As a general rule, its best to know your father and not wonder who he is. What if God just wanted to save kids the potential trauma.

***Presuming for the sake of argument, and the realm of the sheer indeed possibility of the thing, a woman God, a Female God, a great Mother figure, were she really a benevolent God, would have to 'invent' the same law for humans, for the exact same reason the current patriarchal Father God created laws of marriage for the purposes of non-bastardization. Anybody ever wondered why the books of Genesis, Numbers and Chronicles, and Kings et al, include genealogy. Why is it so important to God for us to know who our fathers and mothers were? Why is it so important to God for us to know Christ's genealogy as it opens the New Testament or for that matter who and what the names were of the Apostles and early Christians. Which ones were brothers. Why does Islam exalt not just the prophet of Islam but his 'noble' companions as well. Their names are registered, and their biographies are long read and lifted as models. First of all, to know that Your father's God, is your God and his father's fathers and so on is lesson number one to a child that his God is the God of his fathers and that God is transcendent; intergenerationally powerful. Being able to call on the God of your fathers provides intergenerational psychological stability. God the creator, the beginning, and the end. We weren't there for either, but we can as extant individuals bear witness to what that God has done for us during our time of living on earthy circa whatever time. There is a record in my DNA (and in Heaven with the Mother of the Book) of which I am in a long line and tradition. Acknowledging that means by default acknowledging that I owe my ancestors to reproduce as effectively and as efficiently as possible and do my utmost to ensure not just the survival of my offspring but their thriving as well. And if we overpopulate the earth that is ok, because we are destined to colonize the moon, and what ever other orbs we might encounter as we explore space the way our ancestors explored the seas, and left Africa on foot to explore the land masses and continents that could sustain us and our families.

Memory being 85% of operative and physiological consciousness, the memory of parents, home, local geography, give children early formulations of parents, physical and emotional warmth, food satisfaction, and stability in early care giving and that stability is extremely important. This is fundamental to stability and the emotional and psychological health of a child; or a Chimpanzee baby, or a Kangaroo Joey or a baby wombat. Parental and caregiver attachment consistency is crucial. It is fundamental to home training. Send children to school without home training and they are not only damn near uneducable, if it's too late and too far gone, they end up making the educational environment damn near unbearable for other students who perhaps want to apply themselves, and the teacher that would like to teach them if not for being distracted by the 'bad kids'. So, these children with no home training, great statisticians of the type Schools systems hire when they spin their test score results, use these children and their poverty rates to look more successful. But it is a horrible trade off, because for every 3-5 of these children with no home training in class making a nuisance of themselves distracting the teacher and other students, they bring test scores down 3% to 5% in every class they are in!

Surely a female God would recognize this and institute the same rules of paternity and maternity that are currently extant, even if for no other reason than if it's not particular broken, why in God's name (male or female) would anybody want to fix it. If it is a good idea and more or less all around conducive to a stable environment for a child to know who their daddy is and for him to be covenanted to support your love and support your mother, you as a child and your siblings; that there be no confusion in such matters, it is a good idea and from a female God to just a wise secular society, surely they would encourage that children know who their fathers are and have extended families to draw from.

Even if a 'Woman God' instituted matriarchy, if she had any love for her children, she would not impose undue hardships, trauma, and stress on them by having them wonder who in the hell their fathers were and why their fathers don't matter, especially the boys. Would a woman God in full power, still be so angry at maleness, men, and patriarchy that She says and legislates that children don't need fathers, just sperm donors, so that willing women can have children or not depending on their sole preference as women and whether or not they want to have an abortion? Why would it take two, to not have to take two my feminist womanist friends? Isn't that counterproductive in the extreme. Would a woman God tell women that their children don't need a father at all, his help, his presence, his voice, his care, to play with them, to rock them to sleep when sometimes you as a 'super woman' are tired and/or might just not feel like it. Would a Woman God say this, and not create a helpmate for her daughters at all? Would a female God tell women this, and that they can do it all by themselves and should do precisely what they want to do with 'their sexuality and family ways'. At least the male God, patriarchal or not, was kind and considerate enough o say he was creating a 'help mate', would a woman God not create a helpmate for women? There is a Rabbi I watch on YouTube, who is nearly unsparing in his critique of Christianity and Islam. I am thankful because, absent that, I would be inclined to think him of a way higher grade sadiki than I would because he's so insulting when he gets it in his mind to critique Christianity and Islam. He makes the argument that somebody (that is to say Christianity or Islam) created a God that hates them. Notwithstanding his argument, I'm stealing his argument to make slightly different point. Have feminists and womanist created a God that hates them? Your Woman God didn't create you a help mate that you could depend on and rely on and expects you to do it all by yourself, that is to say raise children, be religious, have a profession, etc. and considers your obligation to prove your freedom from patriarchy and men and maleness that you do it all precisely by yourself. That doesn't sound like a kind God. And look how your female God is treating men, calling them completely disposable, calling them unnecessary, either a slave to women or some kind of automaton functioning with the sole intent of serving his spouse (the same exact thing women rebel against in their perception of the patriarchal system and its history)? Can this female God love children, and tell them, if their mother doesn't feel like playing with them, they are dead in the water because their absentee dad, because he's meaningless, irrelevant and superfluous is not around for you to play with? Whatever he knows of skills and attributes doesn't matter because only what a woman can give is important, as though a child might not ever want some skill or trade his father has that his mother doesn't? Does that type of feminist/womanist God sound like they love anybody? What if this female God hated the idea of the need for men so much that they abolished mammals because mammals have two different sexes. Does that sound like a loving, notwithstanding one's conception of the patriarchal God or not. The patriarchal God was jealous, this feminist/womanist one is just pissed off and angry all the time, whether she has a reason to be angry or not.

What if our Woman God was like current womanists and feminists in that her children don't matter much to her because this female God is out here 'living her truth' and that doesn't include maternal instinct things like caring for her children or what her children think of her? Would a woman God say for that matter she doesn't need the love and admiration of those who seek her. A woman God that doesn't need her children because she's liberated and has many other things she'd just as well could be doing besides being maternal over some flock of humans. Just like a woman having an abortion, she doesn't owe her children anything; damn sure not to keep them alive. What kind of Mother God would that be, were she just like today's feminists, womanists and LGBTQIA warriors. This type of feminist/womanist Mother God would just drop her children off at Grandmas or get a babysitter, or maybe invent smartphones to entertain her children when She doesn't feel like it. Does that sound like a loving mother God? Would not such a Mother God traumatize us just as much, if not more than our so-called patriarchal equivalent, or were she really loving would she not legislate something that resembles what we have today, imperfections and all, but the idea that men and women create children together as equals, work in families with their children and extended families to propagate the genetic line.

Based on the trauma, stress and emotional instability that comes from entrenched feelings of abandonment, family drama and criminal dysfunction that requires state intervention; it almost serves the purposes of crippling a child in their adulthood, stunting and disabling the child, the adolescent and the adult, absent intensive and consistent intervention and strategic support if that child doesn't know his father and his father's family. Don't take my word for it. Nearly all the adults that appear on Family Court, Paternity Court, the People's Court, have some drama/trauma (they are twins dressed up and disguised as one another) in their past. To a person, they nearly all feel their lives would have been better or more stable if they had their fathers in their lives. Listen to their stories and how this lack made them feel vulnerable and they overcompensated for it in sometimes pathological ways.

No sane female deity would put that on her own children let alone the children she was a Goddess of. And we would not call such a convenient thing Patriarchal. It would be matriarchal by default to know who your daddy was and for him to be involved in your life for the exact same reason the children of the dominant male (and his close male allies) have more social and food advantages than orphan children or children with no extended family. Even supposing a matriarchy would make the argument fathers don't matter, even males aren't that mean spirited. How could a matriarchal God be less just than a patriarchal God in depriving children of their fathers? That would defeat the whole purpose of a loving, benevolent, Mother God.

Assuming only the Holy Ghost could impregnate a Mother God in the same way it is take for doctrine Mary was impregnated. She would still need it to be known for doctrinal purposes that she was not a whore. Thus, any version of feminism, that determined necessarily a Female Matriarchal Mother God, she would by default institute the same exact system the current patriarchal system created, and not devalue fatherhood within a context where it can clearly be devalued because of the clear hard rationality of the anecdotal phrase 'mama's baby, daddy's maybe'. No female deity would announce her own whoredoms, when so clearly the effects of whoredom on her children's children are so on display in the universal paternity court. Testimony is being taken from both sides...well one side. The mother God and all her the potential (for legal purposes 'entities') that could be the father(s) of her creation. Do you know how long that testimony would take. Mother God isn't a whore she's just sexually liberated? Does she get wasted at the club and go home with 'some entities' and end up pregnant and birthing bastard civilizations on bastard planets no one has ever heard of until it is exposed on the intergalactic version of paternity court? Tune in and see in the next episode. Hot damn, Von Gneisenau, that's why you get paid the big bucks... "Intergalactic Paternity Court" that does DNA tests that go back 57 generations, to 57,000 years or 13 million years, or 13 billion years. Imagine the galactic scale 'back child support' would be imposed on whoever or whatever aka 'some potential entities' (for legal purposes only) that accrued over 57 million years of child support payments. No wonder God the father stays hidden!

Three

New Orleans Suite

10God and Family in the Marketplace

A virtue which should distinguish moral life is integrity in business dealings, and this is reflected in all our monotheistic faith traditions. According to tradition, 'If thou wilt do that which is right in His eyes" (Exod. Vx. 26) – this refers to commercial dealings and teaches that he who acts honestly is popular with his fellow creatures, and it is imputed to him as though he had fulfilled the whole of the 'Torah' (Mech. Ad loc.; 46a). The disastrous consequence of dishonesty in the life of the community is taught in the dictum: 'Jerusalem was destroyed because honest men ceased therein'. (Shab. 119b)

Every damn time I turn around Kanye et al are getting kicks from accusing the Jews of being behind all sorts of wild plots to dominate...well, I'm not even sure. I just know every two-bit religious and racial hack and their imitators like Kyrie and Kanye, spend an inordinate time talking about the 'crimes' of the Jews, implying that their financial success is problematic, and a result of duplicitousness and villainy. Sure you can blame their success on wild conspiracy theories but I'd like in this article to examine some Talmudic conceptions of labor and its value, and then afterwards ask the question if their success might not be due so much to cabals and dastardly schemes, but instead, to a long ingrained theological, ethical and moral system of values that emphasized work, the dignity of labor, family, charity, and academic achievement. Perhaps most important, their 3500 year old system of life emphases unity and a theme that this unity is important because it is the means by which they are responsible for themselves and their own development as a people, and not dependent upon others. This is whether the dependency is on former oppressors or not (presumably even friends, admirers and lovers). Might these factors be somewhat more important than Kanye's psycho-conspiracy theory rantings about why some people (the Jews for example), have more than others and why we do not seem to be doing as well. Can we even speak of such a thing as core values when we talk about Black American values.

Even as a Black intellectual do you want to live in a mysterious universe where you blame your 'despoiling' on the cabals and treacheries of other peoples? Does it not take agency and control out of our lives to think such a thing? Is the totality of the future for Niggerdom not controlled or determined by our intelligence, industriousness, unity, family values, community values and economic zeal, or is it controlled by a group of hidden illuminati and assorted groups (I assume in my unfamiliarity with these presumptions to include the Jews and even the Boule), who work day and night and spend enormous amounts of money and resources to 'hold us back' (as it were). Ladies and gentlemen of Negritude, the choice is ours and the answers we come up with to those questions today, will in great wise determine the quality of lives for our children and their children's children. Let us briefly examine some of these Talmudic thoughts on work and labor. Of course at a certain point Christian Protestant Work Ethic Renderings will be Superimposed on Torah and Rabbinic Tradition. Some of them will be allowed to speak for themselves and others I will offer some sort of commentary on.

1. It is a man's duty to work, not only to earn his livelihood but likewise to contribute his quota to the maintenance of the social order. (Everyman's Talmud p 192)

2. Greater is he who enjoys the fruit of his labor than the fearer of Heaven; for with regard to the fearer of Heaven it is written, "Happy is the man that feareth the Lord" (Ps. Cxii. I), but with regard to him who enjoys the fruit of his labor it is written, "When thou eatest the labor of they hands, happy shalt thou be, and it shall be well with thee. "Happy shalt thou be" in this world, and it "shall be well with thee" in the World to Come. It is not written, "and it shall be well with thee," about the fearer of Heaven' (Ber. 8a)

3. The dignity of labor is upheld throughout the Talmudic literature. 'Great is work for it honors the workmen' (Ned. 49b) It must be so, because work is an important part of the Divine scheme for man.

4. 'Love work' (Aboth I. 10) Even Adam did not taste food until he had done work; as it is said, "the Lord God took the man and put him into the Garden of Eden to till it and keep it" (Gen. ii. 15), after which He said, "Of every tree of the garden thou mayest eat" Even the Holy One, blessed be He, did not cause his Shechinah to alight upon Israel until they had done work; as it is said, "Let them make for Me a sanctuary that I may dwell among them" (Exod. Xxv. 8)

5. If one is unemployed, what should he do? If he has a courtyard or a field in a state of decay, let him busy himself with it, as it is said, "Six days shalt thou labor and do all thy work'. For what purpose were the words "and do all thy work" added? It is to include a person who has a courtyard or a field in a state of decay , that he should go and busy himself with them. A man only dies through idleness' (ARN x1)

6. A legend tells that 'at the time the Holy One, blessed be He, informed Adam, "Thorns and thistles shall it bring forth to thee' his eyes ran with tears. He said before Him "Sovereign of the Universe! Am I and my ass to feed in the same manger?" When however, He added, "In the sweat of thy face shalt thou

eat bread", his mind immediately calmed down, (Pes. 118a) The moral is that by his labor man raises himself about the rest of the animal kingdom.

7. Indeed, work is the very foundation of man's existence "Therefore choose life" (Deut. Xxx. 19) i.e. a handicraft' (p. Peah 15c). A Blessing only alights upon the work of a man's hands' (Tosifta Ber. VIII. 8) is another utterance indicating that work is the path to happiness. The law enacts that even if a man provides his wife with a hundred servants, she must do some of the housework herself, because 'idleness leads to lewdness, and it also leads to mental instability' (Keth. V. 5)

8. The important place which work occupies in the scheme of the Universe is further pointed out in the treatment of the following passage: 'God came to Laban in a dream by night, and said to him, Take heed that thou speak not to Jacob either good or bad'. 'Hence we learn that the merit of labor holds a position which is unattainable by the merit of ancestors; as it is said, "Except the God of my father, the God of Abraham and the Fear of Isaac, had been with me, surely thou hadst sent me away now empty". If so, the merit of his ancestors only availed for the protection of his weal. "God has seen mine affliction and the **labor of my hands and rebuked thee yester night";** this shows that He warned Laban against harming Jacob through the merit of the labor of his hands. In this way He taught that a man should not say, I will eat and drink and see prosperity without troubling myself, since heaven will have compassion upon me. Therefore it is stated, "Thou has blessed the work of his hands' (Job); a man should toil with both his hands and then the Holy One, blessed be He, will grant his blessing' (Tanchuma Vayetz 13)

9. A popular saying ran: 'Who has not worked shall not eat' (Gen. R. xiv. 10) Moreover, one should not think of his personal requirements as the motive of his labor. This is exemplified in an anecdote. The Emperor Hadrian was passing along the lanes near

Tiberias and saw an old man breaking up the soil to plant trees. He said to him, "Old man, if you had worked early there would have been no need for you to work so late in your life." The Old man replied, "I have toiled both early and late, and what was pleasing to the Lord of Heaven has He done with me." Hadrian asked him how old he was, and the answer was a hundred; Emperor Hadrian exclaimed, You're a hundred years old and you stand there breaking up the soil to plant trees! Do you expect to eat of their fruit?" The old man replied, "If I am worthy I shall eat; but if not, as my fathers labored for me, so I labor for my children".

Protestantism and Post-Catholic Christianity has it's own version of the value of labor and the importance of work. The following information was culled directly from Wikipedia and is simply about 25% of the entry for "Protestant Work Ethic":

From Wikipedia, the free encyclopedia

The Protestant work ethic, also known as the Calvinist work ethic or the Puritan work ethic, is a work ethic concept in scholarly sociology, economics, and historiography. It emphasizes that diligence, discipline, and frugality are a result of a person's subscription to the values espoused by the Protestant faith, particularly Calvinism.

The phrase was initially coined in 1905 by Max Weber in his book The Protestant Ethic and the Spirit of Capitalism. Weber asserted that Protestant ethics and values, along with the Calvinist doctrines of asceticism and predestination, enabled the rise and spread of capitalism. It is one of the most influential and cited books in sociology, although the thesis presented has been controversial since its release. In opposition to Weber, historians such as Fernand Braudel and Hugh Trever-Roper assert that the Protestant work ethic did not create capitalism and that capitalism developed in pre-Reformation Catholic communities. Just as priests and caring professionals are deemed to have a vocation (or "calling" from God) for their work, according to the Protestant work ethic the "lowly" workman also has a noble vocation which he can fulfill through dedication to his work.

The concept is often credited with helping to define the societies of Northern, Central and Northwestern Europe as well as the United States of America.

Basis in Protestant theology

Protestants, beginning with Martin Luther, conceptualized worldly work as a duty which benefits both the individual and society as a whole. Thus, the Catholic idea of good works was transformed into an obligation to consistently work diligently as a sign of grace. Whereas Catholicism teaches that good works are required of Catholics as a necessary manifestation of the faith they received, and that faith apart from works is dead and barren, the Calvinist theologians taught that only those who were predestined to be saved would be saved.

For Protestants, salvation is a gift from God; this is the Protestant distinction of sola gratia. In light of salvation being a gift of grace, Protestants viewed work as stewardship given to them. Thus Protestants were not working in order to achieve salvation but viewed work as the means by which they could be a blessing to others. Hard work and frugality were thought to be two important applications of being a steward of what God had given them. Protestants were thus attracted to these qualities and strove to reach them.

There are many specific theological examples in the Bible that support Protestant theology. Old Testament examples abound, such as God's command in Exodus 20:8–10 to "Remember the Sabbath day, to keep it holy. Six days you shall labor, and do all your work, but the seventh day is a Sabbath to the Lord your God." Another passage from the Book of Proverbs in the Old Testament provides an example: "A little sleep, a little slumber, a little folding of the hands to rest, and poverty will come upon you like a robber, and want like an armed man."

The New Testament also provides many examples, such as the Parable of the Ten Minas in the Book of Luke.

Luke 19:11-27

King James Version

¹¹ And as they heard these things, he added and spake a parable, because he was nigh to Jerusalem, and because they thought that the kingdom of God should immediately appear.

¹² He said therefore, A certain nobleman went into a far country to receive for himself a kingdom, and to return.

¹³ And he called his ten servants, and delivered them ten pounds, and said unto them, Occupy till I come.

¹⁴ But his citizens hated him, and sent a message after him, saying, We will not have this man to reign over us.

¹⁵ And it came to pass, that when he was returned, having received the kingdom, then he commanded these servants to be called unto him, to whom he had given the money, that he might know how much every man had gained by trading.

¹⁶ Then came the first, saying, Lord, thy pound hath gained ten pounds.

¹⁷ And he said unto him, Well, thou good servant: because thou hast been faithful in a very little, have thou authority over ten cities.

¹⁸ And the second came, saying, Lord, thy pound hath gained five pounds.

¹⁹ And he said likewise to him, Be thou also over five cities.

²⁰ And another came, saying, Lord, behold, here is thy pound, which I have kept laid up in a napkin:

²¹ For I feared thee, because thou art an austere man: thou takest up that thou layedst not down, and reapest that thou didst not sow.

²² And he saith unto him, Out of thine own mouth will I judge thee, thou wicked servant. Thou knewest that I was an austere man, taking up that I laid not down, and reaping that I did not sow:

²³ Wherefore then gavest not thou my money into the bank, that at my coming I might have required mine own with usury?

²⁴ And he said unto them that stood by, Take from him the pound, and give it to him that hath ten pounds.

[25] (And they said unto him, Lord, he hath ten pounds.)

[26] For I say unto you, That unto every one which hath shall be given; and from him that hath not, even that he hath shall be taken away from him.

[27] But those mine enemies, which would not that I should reign over them, bring hither, and slay them before me.

The Apostle Paul in 2 Thessalonians said "If anyone is not willing to work, let him not eat."

Protestant theology shares its origins with other and older Judeo-Christian theologies, if for no other reason than it shares some of the same source documents.

So, if White people have been teaching these values for five or six hundred years religiously, and Jews from the Talmudic period, at least a few hundred years BC and in the Talmudic period AD, is it necessarily the result of hocus pocus, illuminati treacherous cabals and White villainy that the economy they evolved has driven the dynamism and wealth their culture(s) have enjoyed? Is Black economic dysfunction solely attributed to all these people who hate us and are planning and plotting against us and/or are wicked?

Or, does teaching these values and virtues, of education, dutifulness, and hard work to you children over generations produce results? Does making sure your children have educations and trades, work for any group of people that emphasizes it generation after generation? Does making sure your children and people are encouraged academically and encouraged in commerce, finance, and industry generation after generation produce results? Or do some 'special races' of people have superhuman strength from cabals, witches, warlocks, superstitions and the Black arts, God Forbid. It is not rational to believe something like that in an era of science, the global economy, technology, AI and the internet. Black people should be enthused about the future and what 500 years of that kind of mentality as a people can produce in the way of prosperity and power. Or will we follow behind the ignorant and the superstitious that nominate themselves our leaders, with no vote taken, just White mainstream corporate and government sponsorship, who believe our problems have more to do with the cabals and superhuman capacities of others, and not the sweat of our brow and the excellencies of our own flowering and development. Ladies and gentlemen, if any people thinks that way, teaches that way, encourages that way, invests in its children's, brothers, and cousin's ideas, that way, any group of people will see a dramatic rise and increase in their productivity, economic activity and quality of life.

Many will see in my remarks that I 'm saying Black people don't know how to work or have good work ethics. Far from it. Pre-Civil Rights and War on Poverty era (that is to say, Jim Crow and prior), that protestant work ethic and Judeo-Christian approach to work and labor was our main thing. In the wake of the post-Civil Rights era, it became fashionable and current in Black circles however to talk about what White people/America owes us; presumably for labor and works already done by our ancestors.

In the wake of the post- Civil Rights era, the seat at the White man's table, being affirmed into action and being appointed to boards and executive staff of White mainstream fortune 500 companies and the highest levels of government was seen as more important than the work it takes to build those competencies and structures independently, organically, and holistically. This is how you create institutions that survive. But for so long unfortunately, the Negro has fought in America only for the opportunity to integrate (in existing White mainstream society), instead of and rather than, creating opportunity (that is to say auto-executed global economic institutions). It is hard to be angry and resentful and make the kind of connections with varying races and peoples necessary to global economic development. It is part and parcel of demanding reparations and that somebody owes you something to be angry and resentful in your tone and this we find in the BLM movement and the Post-Civil Rights Woke era. Everyone is angry and resentful, yelling and screaming and peeing in water bottles and throwing them at police but compared to what the real Civil Rights era personages went through, the BLM crowd ain't experienced racism. Micro-insults are on a completely different scale from police batons, attack dogs and fire hoses at full blast! Motived by religion, in their suits singing hymns and 'kum by ya', and ain't no body gonna turn me round' the civil rights era generation primarily didn't seem angry. They were focused and dedicated. Not a thing is keeping the woke crowd and BLM crowd from anywhere in White mainstream colleges and universities except their test scores and their attitudes. But they want to blame the White man for that and say we are owed something. We find this culminating in the idea that Black people need reparations or are owed reparations.... here again, for work our ancestors did. I do not raise the issue to argue that we do not deserve reparations, I raise the issue to argue we do not need reparations. We can develop and thrive without them if we develop proper economic models, values, and work hard towards achieving those ends.

Society's current critiques of Black work ethics, usually of the conservative variety are met with niggas must know how to work, we did so much of it for free during slavery. Ok. But your children know damn well they are on camera at 8 gas stations and shitty ass post-modern fashion stores, all with pants sagging just walking out of the store with armfuls of merchandise in a flash mob and still do it? Even today in the rap game the primary way to be that nigga is through your vocal defense and exposition of the lifestyle of drug dealing, pimping, thugging, hustling, poppin pills, poppin bottles, smoking, casual sex, driving fancy cars and ballin! Not na'an where in any of that are the values I cited earlier of the value of labor and the value of hard work, education etc., let alone sobriety, marriage, and family.

Interruptions, oh my. I'm sick of people saying how talented Alicia Keys is. She trots out 3 or 4 piano licks, sings half as good as Whitney, Aretha, and even Mary J, and does like most rich successful Black women when they date, and go slumming. Is it because she's a mulatto and that's her debt of service to Negritude? Is she somehow doing us poor peons of negritude a favor? Lead us oh mulatto nigga princess, but never princess of the niggas, lead us!

11You are Here: Notes on African America and Afro-aboriginal Australia

When one goes to huge malls, amusement parks and municipalities there is a map showing varying stores or locations of interest. Theoretically you could wander aimlessly and mentally map it out through traversing it backwards and forward. Children are limited that way. If they can't read and/or don't know what the symbols mean, they must spend the time walking the streets, alleys, and walkways to get a mental map of their surroundings. But if you know how to read and you understand the symbols, you can read the map and go straight to a desired priority destination. The map usually will use a big red star symbolizing where you are presently on the map relative to other locations. There will be a big red star and immediately next to it, you will find emblazoned the words, more often than not in all caps, **YOU ARE HERE**.

At this point in the essay, I'd like to insert some euphemisms culled from the internet for being lost.

Euphemisms for being lost:
1. "Geographically Challenged" Marty Wicks

1. "Location Disadvantaged" Damien O'Toole
2. "Occasionally Misplaced" Damien O'Toole
3. "Unexpectedly Relocated" Scott Marshall
4. "Positionally Challenged" Scott Marshall
5. "Situationally Naïve" Scott Marshall
6. "I'm never lost. I'm just "exploring".

7.1 I'm never "Lost" either. (As in we are all lost)

1. "I always know where I am - Right here. I always know where I want to be." Occasionally I have problems equating the two, but I'm never "Lost"

8, I always know where I am. I'm here. Everybody else goes away sometime but I'm always here!

1. Virtually displaced?
2. Spatially displaced?
3. I've never been lost, though I have sometimes engaged in Zen Navigation.
4. 'Stream of consciousness navigation'
5. Locationally heuristic

Ladies and gentlemen, it can be amusing to think of all the ways to describe being lost. Yet make no mistake about it, it can be very disorienting, frustrating, and dangerous as well. As I speak an elderly veteran with Alzheimer is lost and presumably wandering the streets of Atlanta. Let us pray he and others in similar condition(s) are not victimized and find their way back to their loved ones and caregivers as quickly as possible. Awful as it is to be lost oneself, (that is to say thanks to grammar check, lose oneself), those who have ever experienced losing a child at the arcade or park know this feeling of helplessness, in our loved one being lost to ourselves, and that feeling as a parent is painful and emotionally traumatic. Children who are 'lost' or 'lost' from their parents and caregivers are vulnerable. Every parent knows, the more time that goes by with the child 'lost' running the streets, the more likely it is something negative has happened, or the likelihood they never will come back increases exponentially. God forbid.

That it's worse for children, it is damn near just as bad for adults. When one is lost one feels vulnerable. Have you dear readers ever 'got lost' in a bad neighborhood? Tex McKiver (disgraced White southern aristocratic lawyer with the high fallutin wife from a historic southern family and southern horse breeding socialite), claimed that while driving through downtown Atlanta, he, his wife, and another occupant of his car got 'lost', and felt so vulnerable seeing all the homeless niggers, beggars, and hookers, that he put a gun on his lap. As his wife was driving, quite unexpectedly, she hit a bump and the 'Tex' gun acciden-tally went off killing her. Apparently, that's one of the negative things that can happen to you simply from getting lost at the wrong time and in the wrong place. Thus, you are vulnerable. Overcompensating for feelings of vulnerability can make you make mistakes.

Thus, you are vulnerable by being in unfamiliar surroundings, and then as bad as that is, it doesn't take a scientist or a logistician of great merit to realize that if you don't know where you are, getting where you thought you wanted to go is damn near impossible, subject to luck, or subject to the 'sheer will o' God'. I have spoken earlier about our chil-dren's sense of vulnerability in our weakened family structures causing much or even most of the pathologies we see in our communities like academic underperformance, drugs, crime, and violence. Ladies and gentlemen, our children are lost within the post-modern ersatz version of family structure(s) where the family is anything people say it is, two men, two women, etc.. Do not misunderstand, I am not arguing that those forms aren't 'better than nothing', but to promote it as normative and thus 'ideal' is a disservice to future generations psychological health. And the abandonment of the traditional family as normative and ideal, is precisely the reason today's youth feel insecurities and lash out, en-gage in antisocial behaviors to the point of joining gangs and engaging in criminal activity. Why? Ladies and gentlemen of Negritude we are not teaching them 'where they are' and 'who they are' on the map. The problem is not an issue of freedom of choice, the problem is that gangs and internet social groups are a bad ersatz version of the family and will give our children their own skewed versions of who our children are and can be.

Can you make an argument to a child he or she should aspire to college. Yes. But if they don't know where 'here' is on a map, finding an education at the end of a 12-year journey from Pre-K through high school graduation seems daunting and impossible. Our children don't know where they are or who they are. These things they do not know because they don't know 'whose they are'! Who you are and where you belong is nearly 100% determined by 'whose' you are. Who is claiming you? Who is claiming you will give you a very strong sense (or not) of where you belong and a sense of a safe space necessary for they healthy psychological development of children. Reciprocity and the child usually claims his inheritance back in debt and obligation to older generations? You think the people around you are claiming you, as in some gang, or some trumped up 'family' created in the minds of the LGBTQIA community as an ersatz version of the standard mammalian family. But they are merely 'around you' and are unstable themselves, and use your instability to feed their own lusts and needs for a sense of ersatz family, and ersatz community. Our children don't know where they are because there is a family crisis in the Black community of our children not knowing 'whose' they are and not knowing who they belong to (or having thereby a safe space where they belong). So they miss that stability and sense of protection and seek to get an ersatz version of it in gangs and the communities created by alternative lifestyles. Who they are with (gangs and internet fetish subgroups) is not stable. Who you are is nearly 100% completely determined by 'whose' you are. That is to say, family and the God of your family. Wild as I was as a kid and completely ambivalent about what I perceived to be standard education at the time, I always felt I could be academically successful. Why? DNA of course. My father was a college graduate and teacher, my mother has a master's degree and taught, and my older brother got two degrees from Georgia tech. I grew up with these examples and assumptions around me, whether I graduated with a 2.0 GPA or not. Nearly all my cousins had post-high school degrees and training of some sort. At the time I didn't know 'where I was' but I knew who I belonged to and the people I came up with. I knew 'where they were', whether I knew exactly where I was and where I was going or not. But by default I must be destined for something similar to my kith and kin whether I am trying or not, or whether I know 'where the fuck I am' personally or not. I know who I'm with and they know me, and if I get lost, I have every confidence they will come look for me. Absent that, join gangs and go out and embrace an alternative lifestyle and get you an ersatz alternative family.

Let us be frank, from Colonial American days to post-colonial life, Antebellum life, Reconstruction life, Jim Crow/Black Codes Life and the Civil Rights era life was and now the Post-Civil Rights/Post-Modern Era, life is and has been disorienting for African America. How can you know where you are if you sailed on a ship 3 months to get to the Caribbean, and South and North America, absent open ocean navigation techniques. Similarly, how can you know where you are if British settlers take your land, and ship you all over the place in Australia, supposedly relocating you, but just in a sense making you move, and thus more confused about 'where you are, who you belong to, and where you belong'? The feelings of familial and cultural dislocation and alienation; the feelings of the future being completely out of your hands and the sheer will of God, blind fate, or the will of your colonial slave masters. This heightened sense of vulnerability and loss of agency engenders much of what today we call distinctly African American and indigenous Australian psycho-social pathologies. If I believe in intergenerational trauma, I believe in it in that sense, more so than a deterministic sense. And yet making the argument I tear it down because as I just demonstrated about orphans and children and adolescents raised on the streets, one generation can cause your sense of where you are to be very distorted as happens to runaways, drug addled and addicted children and adolescents and sexually trafficked children and adolescents. So in that sense, the issue of not knowing where you are, or that there is map, can come to a person or race for geopolitical, economic, and cultural reasons. Loss of agency, loss of pride, loss of self-esteem, and not knowing where you are, who you belong to, and thus having no where to belong and feel safe. Quite often adolescents in these circumstances do not feel any purpose, that is parents and family haven't exposed you to their purposes of helped you define a purpose for yourself, so the hustlers, and the exploiters, and then the criminal justice system designs a purpose and a place for you (on the map), and a purpose for you while you are there...all because you did not know 'where you were' and 'whose you were'. Is the violence in the Black community sane, are our busted-up families and 70% out of wedlock birthrates sane, is sending our children to schools we know damn well will have them graduating reading and doing math 2 or 3 grade levels behind sane? And lastly is thinking White people's therapy can fix us, and depending solely upon White people's therapy and pay per view mental health schemes sane? Were we all insane before European culture and specifically Freud built the psychological tradition? Oddly enough to me, knowing Freud was for all intents an atheist, it is amazing to me that I sense his work is like the Talmud with absolutely no reference to God...that is to say, interpretations and traditions and technics of mental exegesis to arrive at a secular oral Torah of the human mind if you will. This is not to dismiss his work or therapy at all. In college and its immediate aftermath, I was in an Erich Fromm phase, and though hardly well read, nor would I argue I understand everything about his concepts I find that I benefited from them greatly in the development of my own thought.

But I need to drill down here for a moment. Is it sane for Black people to think White people's therapy and therapists can fix us or our children? If they can't fix themselves how the fuck can they fix us, and if you trusted White folk's ability to fix you anyway despite that fact, is that sane? Dr. Amos Wilson had a big impact on the development of my thinking on psychology, Black psychology in America and the diaspora. His understanding of the White European and American psychological tradition and/or their use of it as regards Black people was informative, challenging, and entertaining. Black psychologists like Amos Wilson and Frances Cress Welsing, agree with them or not, were of the first to question whether or not we as descendants of Africa in America can always assume White mainstream psychology relative to us, is being used to benign and therapeutic ends. If mainstream educational psychologists trained in the European tradition are using psychological techniques in high school interactions with Black boys to send 40% of all the Black boys to remedial classes, are we to simply assume this is the way it is…40% of every grade level group of Black boy needs remedial classes? Superimpose on that the fact that these are our former slave masters that used to own us, and still consider themselves superior to us, if for no other reason that they don't want to live with you or send their children to school with ours. Of course my psychology includes you little Negro boy and girl, now sing me some songs of Zion, run me a lilac, chamomile and lavender bath Oprah, entertain me Tyler Perry, and run and shoot them balls and make tackles, and while you're at it, li'l niggers, my Negro psychological wards, make me some grits and be Vice President Aunt Jemima, excuse me, Kamala, I'm old uncle Joe getting old and confusing the two and nibbling on 8 year old girl's ears). Anyway, I shall indeed quote Amos Wilson in saying 'is expecting your former slave master to educate your children to the same standard he educates his, when he doesn't even want to live around you sane? Look in the mirror Black man and Black woman! Is any of that sane?

Which is to say, expecting your former slave master to tell you 'where you are' and 'who you are' (that is to say affirming you) is fucking insane. This is not to say they all or that they always had/have bad intentions, far from it. It is just hard to ignore the problematic nature of such an idea. Uh, he thought you were slaves and that you didn't belong to yourself, your people, your family, or your God, you belonged to him, to do with as he pleases. And the discomfort you feel in 2023, Whitey is going to fix, with therapy, his pills instead of nigger shit like weed and cocaine, affirmative action, sexual freedom, abortion rights, and reparations? That shit is muthafuckin insane, but Black liberals believe that shit like the kingdom was coming…and it is. So Black liberals willingly subject themselves to White rule because there is a prize dangling out for the one who acts like White people can fill their every need by affirmations or reparations. Thus, they position themselves under White people, and lick White folk's mouths the way a mother or father cliff warbler comes back from the sea, or a wolf mother or father comes back from a hunt and the pups and baby warblers and pups, lick their parent's mouths to stimulate them to regurgitate the prey, and then they eat. Black Democrats and Black Republicans engage in this disgusting behavior.

And thus, when White folks want to affirm us, want themselves to look welcoming and post-racial, they say to Black females, come join the club and we'll give you a great position, and niggas compete like crabs in a barrel to kiss White ass, even if it's socialist-atheist LGBTQIA ass just get those positions in Hollywood, the woke corporate world and the Democrat Party. White folks will pay you to run them balls up and down the basketball courts and football fields of America for his entertainment. If he wants to cast you as 'Ariel' in a remake of a cheesy Disney movie, your former slave master does as he pleases, and you lick his mouth so he can vomit up more roles and positions for you. He does with you as he pleases. If you fit the role in his narrative the White man will use you whether you are Tim Scott, Raphael Warnock, or Stacy Abrams. You have not determined 'who you are and where you are going, you just walk the mall, window shopping, going in the arcade or the movie theatre and accepting the invitation to spend money any-where and to anyone that bids your tired feet welcome (for their own purposes mind you).

And yet how does one take this thesis? Is the map your former slave master and colonizer gave you, the one he uses, or is the one he gave you different, reflecting his sense of your limitations, vulnerabilities and thus areas you aren't qualified to go. Oh, yes nigger aboriginal and nigger, the football pitches and fields and entertainment stages are open to you and on the map. Other places where the real power lies, not so much. And so, we must ask the question, is the map they have given us, telling us where 'here is' and that we are 'here' accurate and without hidden meanings and intent(s).

So, if you're looking at a problematic 'you are here' map can you get a second opinion? Can you compare it to anything, in order to verify it, or simply make it more accurate. Ladies and gentlemen of diaspora negritude, you cannot depend on your former slave master, or any other human to tell you 'where you are', 'who you are', 'whose you are' or where you belong. Such a thing necessitates your indebtedness to your colonizer and slave master that he in no wise deserves. In that regard I would urge us to let God and indigenous religious underpinnings tell us 'where we are', independent of yes, where the White man tells us we are. Don't get me wrong however, in many regards the Europeans and Americans have designed a 'map' that is for all intents and purposes, when read properly, objective and science driven. The proof of this level of White objectivity is in the fact that Japan, Germany, Singapore, Malaysia, China and for lack of a better phrase, even the Arab world off oil, have figured out a way to leverage the 'map' Western Europeans, Americans, and Australians use to describe and edify their own development, as a basis for much of their own competitive development. Let we African America and Aboriginal Australia do the same.

12 The Apparently Big Black mermaid/merman in the room

Everybody's pissed off at Disney and I agree with everyone completely. Afro-centrists and Black nationalists are pissed off because the idea of little Black girls crying because they see themselves in a warmed over thrice White Hans Christian Anderson tale, is anathema, and the idea of Black people once again seeking White affirmation is insidious and disrespectful. Thespians, screenwriters, writers, pitchers, show runners and developers are angry that Disney, instead of developing new original content and material, is content to rehash old, nay even ancient material by today's standards, and call it modern because of CGI choices, woke feminism, LGBTQIA, and leftist ideology.

The White right is pissed off because of the 'woke' themes in Hollywood generally, culminating in Ariel being Black. That is the cartoon manifestation of every anti-affirmative action trope you can trot out or put on celluloid. This of course leads back to the vintage 'Tiki Torch', KKK/Alt-Right/Neo-Nazi frat boys march a few years back in Virginia when a young lady got ran over. They were chanting with a straight face a 'we will not be replaced'. How disrespectful? The feminists and womanists on the other hand are pissed off because apparently, it's the same ancient theme of a woman sacrificing her 'voice', her 'talent', her 'girl power' for the love of a man (and by default family). To feminists, womanists and the LGBTQIA community that is insulting and anathema to them.

Meanwhile, sea creatures everywhere are pissed off that mankind is so vain and arrogant as to portray Ariel and her father as some kind of nominal King and princess of the sea. This is to favor an impossible humanoid merman and merwoman instead of the real kings of the sea...maybe Orcas and Sharks. Naw, it's a Merman and Mermaid, slowest thing in the sea and with the smallest teeth. At most there can only be three or four thousand mer-people, who we are to presume rule over the entire domain of the sea, which covers 75% of the surface of the earth. 3 or 4 thousand mer-people are King, Princess and elites of the ocean, and rule over all the indigenous seagoing animal life? What kind of shit is that? So of course, sea creatures are pissed off with Disney at their unfair and shallow portrayal.

Men are pissed off at the emasculated performance of both one-dimensional male characters, father and boyfriend. This is not to say (we) can't understand that the young female is the lead and thus the entire shebang must be about Ariel. Fine. Why is everyone so revolted by the idea that she would give up her 'voice' or whatever it is, (I am unfamiliar with the entire production) in order to be with a man and of course make a deal with a transvestite witch. Which brings us to the fact that the LGBTQIA community is pissed off because for some reason they feel the witch should have looked much more like a drag queen, than an actual woman, wearing way too much make up. The LGBTQIA community is pissed off because they think that instead of Disney casting Melissa McCarthy as the witch, they should have cast an actual transvestite or transwoman with way too much make up on, or real drag queen (which automatically means they have way too much make up on). They are already coming off victories. Cinderella's 'Fairy Godmother' was I suppose a literal 'fairy'; and was portrayed by Billy Porter. I suppose the LGBTQIA community thought the reimagining of nigger Ariel should have included a trans-sea-witch.

Historians, science fiction nerds and marine biologists are pissed the fuck off because there is no 'back story', no creation story, no prequels to how and why the fuck mermen and merwomen got started and why the fuck don't they communicate more often with the human terrestrial world, and perhaps even unite with their legged cousins on land? Especially if Ariel finds herself prone to such imaginations as falling in love with a 2-legged human, who is no good in her water kingdom because even if he swims like Michael Phelps (with or without weed and therapy), he is no good to her in her watery domain because he would be so slow, and it would be impossible for him to 'keep up'. Maybe that is the point feminists should concentrate on, Ariel went out and got a '3-legged man' (I couldn't resist), who is by default inferior to her in the water. To say she 'could swim circles around him' would be an understatement. But hell, that is what some psychologically insecure women want, an effeminate or weak man, whom is so obviously inferior to her, that she can swim circles around him and boss him around. This is like the proverbial successful woman, who goes out and gets a working-class man, and then she's disappointed and treats him like shit because not only does she think she married beneath her, but complains daily that his working class job sea legs, are not good enough to provide her with the lifestyle she deserves. How could she not deserve it, her father has given her that luxurious lifestyle as a princess, every day of her natural life up until that point. Her consolation is fussing at her '3-legged' husband every day for the rest of his life, which is what I expect for Ariel's husband as he makes his life with her in her watery SeaWorld. If she lives on land, legs or not, she will complain to him about how she misses the sea, her family, the pretty coral reefs, and pearls so numerous the children play with them like marbles. She left a watery, Edenic paradise, where her father is king, she his sole princess and heir, and she will inherit his kingdom (as it were), in order to live with a common '3-legged man'? Is there a creation story? Are Ariel and her father the only (read Aristocratic) important ones of the mermen and the mermaids? Where is the lumpen proletariat? Does every little mermaid girl have the opportunities Ariel does and if not, is that 'woke' or fair or are 'mer-people' societies content for the aristocracy (like Ariel and her father) to dominate the working class mer-people and all the rest of the animals of the sea? Are only the aristocratic stories like Ariel and her father worth telling? Is there no Meghan Markle telling the mer-people of the mer-world to 'live their truth' and defy the aristocracy? What ironies present themselves in that; a fake nigger princess, telling another fake nigger princess of the sea that she needs to live her truth.

Are all the ruling mer-men and mer-women mulatto and/or Hispanic like Hailey and Javier or White. There are no straight nigger mermen and merwomen that look like Hutus and Tutsis and perhaps even fight like them? Is there a reason for that? Are there racial/species problems in this land/water world where Ariel and her father dominate the political and cultural 'landscape'? Just how are Ariel and her father down there with no gills, competing with the gilled. How absurd is that? I will happily tell you; it is as absurd as a fish with fins and tails and no legs beating Usain Bolt in his prime in the 100-meter sprint. It is as absurd as Usain Bolt or Michael Phelps beating a 165-pound Tuna in a swimming race. It is like having a whale scale Olympic swim meet and entering a human, which is to say long distance swimming like from the South Atlantic coast by Florida and Georgia's whale calving grounds to the North Atlantic feeding grounds in the coastal Northeastern United States. Naturally this would be a range of some 5000 or so nautical miles. A sprint in such circumstances might be the 300-mile dash in whale sprinters, and entering a human to race 300 miles against an Orca, dolphin or Whale in the open ocean is ridiculous and ludicrous...as ludicrous as Disney's latest reboot.

13 Its Halloween Every day and night for Black Youth

I am sure you know that there is a whole genre of teen horror and slasher films. In these movies somebody, something, some monster, some evil, and/or some demonic force is killing children and adolescents, or body swapping teens and turning them into ruthless killers. Do not take my word for it that a whole genre of films is based on these premises. From Friday the 13th to Slumber party Massacre, Halloween, Sorority House Massacre, Scream, My Bloody Valentine, Final Destination, Fright Night, M3Gan, Nightmare on Elm St., Freddy Vs. Jason, Texas Chainsaw Massacre, Carrie, Lost Boys, The Baby Sitter, Christine, It, Hostel, Blair Witch Project, Buffy the Vampire, Pet Cemetery, I knew what you did last summer, House of Wax, Urban Legend, Gremlins, Children of the Corn, etc. ad infinitum.

Clearly there is a big market in scaring the shit out of children. This is precipitated in no small way by the fact that apparently, youthful folly enjoys such diversions and Hollywood is more than capable of providing them. There is more to that however, than one would assume. Teens believe (in the sense we are interested in what teens believe to be worth being interested in), that they inhabit a malevolent world where they can't trust adults, for quite often adults are the killers and manipulators of evil, and the youth must rebel, not give up, fight against the force and rely solely upon themselves because the adults are either the source of the evil, or the teen saviors have to save the adults in a reversal of roles. Post-Modern realism and dystopian fiction finds that theme nearly inexhaustible in teen books and film. In addition to the teen horror genre cited above, post-modernity has also brought us and our teens the dystopian future novel, premised on the idea that children can't trust adults or adult 'teachings' (Hunger Games, Divergent, The Giver, The Maze Runner etc.). Thus, the malevolent forces in children's and adolescent's lives can be adults or teens compromised by, and working with adults who oftentimes either represent weird religious forces, or dehumanizing corporate forces. They can be spirits with powers, and thus it takes 'special' teens, nay even 'chosen' teens to confront the evil, and ultimately triumph in the end; not only saving themselves but all humanity and the natural order. Presumably these 'special', 'chosen' and 'gifted' teens are saving the world from 'adults' and the failures of adult religious, moral, religious, and political teachings.

Part II

All the above cited films usually revolve around White children and teens, but Black children and youth are playing out their own macabre version of houses of horrors and dystopian film noir, and what is altogether worse is that these are not movies scattered throughout three of four score years of film noir and cinematic history. For Black American youth and teens this happens every day all over urban America! Every day here in Atlanta teens get shot and the headlines are worse than teen slasher movies titles; "Sweet 16 Party gets shot up," "Graduation Party gets shot up" and "High School football game team supporters' brawl and shots ring out". Those are all too real. Fights at our urban high schools are on the six o'clock news every other day, even when school is out! Recently in the local news here in Atlanta a young man got stabbed repeatedly in a fight and none of the student or teacher onlookers, cameras in hand intervened at any point. How's that for dystopian? I guess it's just part of the daily 'academic purge'.

As per White teen slasher films, our children and teens can't trust adults either. Abandoned by their fathers, they are even more vulnerable and susceptible to demonic spirits and forces, and yes gangs. Absent being rooted in strong family, religious and community traditions our youth can as it were, be 'body snatched' becoming fodder for sexual traffickers, predators, and groomers. 'Body snatched' little boys that just wanted to be patted on the back, being turned by gangs into heartless cold killers, robbing and knocking down old ladies. So angry are these body snatched boys that they are willing to shoot up Hollywood Beach in Florida surrounded by innocent men, women, and children, because they had a beef with a gang led by rival demonic spirits and forces. Body snatched little girls with no fathers to treat them like princesses, get groomed and body snatched by peer pressure and social media to think they don't feel like princesses because they are 'actually' boys trapped in girls bodies and clothes.

The literal form of body snatching is being sex trafficked which happens most often to fatherless and motherless children isolated from their birth families and communities. Runaways find themselves fodder for being sex trafficked. One of the first terrible lessons adolescent sex workers learn, or any other sex worker learns is disassociation. That is the only way to survive. Rabbi YY Jacobson has a video on YouTube called 'The soul cannot be raped'. I haven't looked at it but the title itself implies one level of the kind of disassociation I'm speaking of. The act of sex and sexual activity is just the act, and their minds are 'disassociated', i.e., somewhere else. I am reminded of that vacuity and emptiness I have noticed when I have had occasion to be in or see representations of the goings on in Strip Clubs. The dancers stare off into space or stare into the ubiquitous mirrors found all over strip clubs. While staring at themselves in the mirrors and not looking in the 'customer's' eyes, the exotic dancers and strippers are focused on themselves shaking and grinding to the beat, looking at nothing in particular, just going through the routines of shakings, gyrations, dropping it like it's hot, shaking it like a salt shaker, butterflying, poppin that pussy, etc. The entire time, their minds are really anyplace but there, and so the vacuous stare into space and the mirror. The stripper pole here becomes an infinite phallic symbol; from the roof to the floor that the stripper dances on, grates and gyrates on, pretending to worshiping it, pretending to desire to sacrifice herself and her body to it, climbing and writhing on it, pretending (as it were) to ride on it, to swing on it and every man fantasizing about his wood being as consistently erect as the stripper pole wood (or whatever presumably it is made of). Body snatched as well, is the stripper that dibbles and dabbles in stripping and exotic dancing's evil twin...prostitution. The irony is, emotionally speaking, what is the use of engaging in sexual activity of any sort and it requires the mind to be completely somewhere else, lest other weirder feelings creep into the mind because it is not exactly romantic and loving for a woman to be butt assed naked on stage surrounded by 40 or 50 obviously sexually stimulated men with nothing but security and 911 standing between her and a gang rape. Or similarly being paid to have sex with a man you've never met before and therefore have absolutely no real feelings for, requires a level of disassociated minds to be capable of the act the level it takes to get paid to have sex. If the mental abuse involved in exotic dancing and prostitution was not enough, ladies it is one of the most dangerous jobs in the world that a woman can have! Sexually disguised 500 shades of gray assaults, other sorts of physical abuses and even death can be the result of prostitution for women. Yet it never fails that some liberals and liberal cities try to rationalize the behavior as a legitimate source of income for women when it is actually psychological and physical trauma(s) being repeatedly perpetuated on more of than not younger women and adolescent girls. Thus, her mind must be somewhere else as her body goes through those motions of stripping and the sex industry. Let us go one step further and give her the W E B Dubois' 'dual consciousness'. We also find this in soldiers and others that have experienced traumatic situations. They survived the trauma in the immediacy of the danger, by disassociation, but then inevitably have problems adjusting back to normal society because the disassociation has them doing things inappropriately.

Don't believe in the slasher demonic forces and the liberal socialist atheist LGBTQIA adolescent and teen agenda? Technology has often been used in the slasher mythology. There was a movie about TVs and radios that would blink out or on regardless of ac/dc and act as portals and windows to other realms. Remember the car that had a mind of its own, Christine. How far is that from the reality of AI, but it can't be called demonic, or can it? There is myriad crazy stalker, hacker, emailer stories, who steal your identity like Mr. Ripley, and you end up broke, in jail and the world thinks some other person is you. And yes, Tick Tock challenges making teens and youth do everything from OD on drinking challenges, to stealing Kia's and Hyundai's, to taking the soap dispensers off the bathroom walls at school and posting yourself doing it on Tik Tok. Teen Body snatching? Putting Mentos in a coke bottle and watching it explode. All because electronic signals of code, programming, and algorithms felt your child is dumb enough to be interested in doing such a thing and kept feeding it to him or her like milk.

This horror film Black youth inhabit was only reinforced by the mayor of Atlanta's recent comments on the death of a teenage high school student. For 2 or 3 years now, I have censored myself and not called Atlanta Mayor 'Dickens', 'dumb ass Dickens'. But in this case, I can refrain no longer. In the wake of the post-graduation celebration party at B E Mays high school, where 2 youths got shot, one killed, the mayor implored teens to make better choices. In every other race and community, parents make choices for their children and teens, only relinquishing the responsibility at the age of 18, 21 or graduation from college, or…. But for Black youth we assume they have no parents or significant caregivers that can either provide adequate supervised educational, recreational, and cultural activities or can discipline the children or youth; that is to say, make them 'stay out of the streets' and dangerous situations. We get so 'woke' we want to 'defund the police' and then when our kids get out of control the first thing we want is government police sponsored programs like midnight basketball and curfews; all enforced by the police. The same people you are trying to defund, and complaining when they try to build training facilities is your first and only line of defense against the unceasing criminality of our own children! What a contradiction, theoretically Black liberals should want the police to get more training, more cameras, more means of accountability. But simple ass niggas get they minds turned out by White socialist atheist LGBTQIA liberals who end up not only controlling you by shaping what you choose to get mad at (the police, traditional sexual values, religion, education), but shaping you by pulling the trigger on your behalf when you get mad like you're a puppet or toy. You can't tell me niggas cared about the APD/Fire Department training facility in DeKalb County until White liberals started coming down here educating us about it. Not na'an nigga selling dope, thought to himself, oh shit I better stop selling dope and sell my guns because 'the man', 'them White folks', the 'capitalist pig enforcers' are building a multi-million-dollar training and whatever else facility on some land in Dekalb County...but White socialist atheist LGBTQIA liberals from all over the country got enraged on our behalf???? What the fuck my niggas? How can we keep falling for this shit? When I sold dope in South Carolina, the biggest most productive 'trap' in the town was right down the street from the law enforcement complex. One of the biggest open air dope and flesh markets in Atlanta is within easy walking distance of the City Jail and Rice St. County jails. Some of the highest crime rates in South Dekalb are in areas not far from the jail and law enforcement complex off 285. So clearly, niggers have no reason to believe (absent White liberals) that when a police facility moves in you area it automatically becomes a 'police city' and under some kind of lockdown. We better stop letting White liberals and the socialist-atheist-LGBTQIA driven Democrat Black elected officials they prop up fool us.

14 My Problem with Intergenerational Black Trauma

...is not a question of whether or not it exists. My problem with is using it as an excuse, in order to excuse post-modern bad Black behavior. Logically speaking, the people (generations) closest to the trauma would suffer it the most, but crime, ignorance, violence, out of wedlock births, are worse now than during Jim Crow, the Civil Rights era and in the aftermath of the Civil Rights era. We can't blame White people and racism for our busted families if as late as 1955-60 the marriage rate for Blacks was nearly the same as Whites. Similarly, we can't (shouldn't) blame poor Black academic performance on the lack of integration, White mainstream government educational policies and funding issues pre and post slavery and racist Shakespeare and White math, if prior to the Jim Crow era and in the Jim Crow era and the immediate post-civil rights era, Black children had no problems assimilating and accumulating standard White mainstream curriculum in addition to Afrocentric and religious curriculum; here again closer to the actual trauma than present generations of urban students. How is it that we excuse poor academic performance when by any definition, at least the fundamentals of public education is within reach of every Black child in America. Our post-modern children are not taking advantage of it, even after the many Black lives that scrimped, saved, and died trying to make education, public or not, a reality for Black people. The early post-Civil Rights era children (me), had one foot in Jim Crow with grandparents and great grandparents, who could literally tell us what Black lives were like during slavery and the height of Jim Crow/Black Codes/Lynching in first person terms. How in the hell can we as Blacks be doing worse further removed from actual slavery (the supposed source of the trauma) than any other generation of Blacks 450 or so years ago, counting from the mass introduction of Africans into North America?

Ladies and gentlemen, that is not logical. So if common sense tells us that the generation(s) closest to the trauma should suffer its effects the most, compared to future generations, how in the hell are Black rates of Black on Black violence, economic dysfunction and educational competence worse? The Jim Crow Black economy may have been underdeveloped and unintegrated but there were no boarded-up storefronts on MLK, Ashby, in Tulsa, Harlem, and other pre-integration Black communities and towns. They were not people selling dope and pussy on the corner etc. And here in Atlanta on MLK and Ashby you had Le Carousel Lounge where nearly all the greats of jazz and R&B performed back when the Chitlin circuit was all Black entertainers could depend on. Booker T Washington and David Howard, 100% segregated schools were graduating future scholars, mayors, doctors, businesspeople capable of successfully navigating the supposed best White mainstream American and European Universities and Schools. We weren't just producing rappers, strippers, and hustlers then.

Of course, the Black community in the Jim Crow era experienced White on Black crime and Black on Black crime, but no person above the age of 40, let alone older would argue crime in our communities was worse than it is now. Again, I will not sit here and write naively that Black on Black violence didn't exist in the Jim Crow or Slavery eras and other highly segregated eras, but no one over 40 remembers it being this bad or this seemingly random, even if we adjust for higher powered guns and weapons. Here again the question must be begged, how can some psycho-social dysfunction be worse further out from the actual trauma that presumably caused it? How can White people and the White mainstream government be treating us legally better, and in terms of political correctness better, but we feel worse about it (racism in America) and feel ourselves to be suffering racism's self-destructive psycho-social effects worse than our Jim Crow era and even slavery era ancestors would feel a sense of traumatic suffering in our present circumstances?

So how did we get here? That is to say, believing something patently absurd. How did we get to be the #1 complainers about racist lack of opportunity when other races of people, including Africans and those from the Caribbean who more often than not, are patently Blacker than us (literally and figuratively), are damn near swimming over here for opportunities...and end up taking advantage of them in ways we don't and sometimes find incredible. But it is not incredible. It is simply from them trying when we quite simply weren't trying because we wanted White people to affirm us (first), and give us a seat at the table we helped build. We were waiting and protesting for White affirmation and a seat at their table, when we should have been out buying, selling, and manufacturing things for distribution all over the world (from real estate, businesses of varying sizes, land, industry, etc.). Again, logically speaking, if Black Americans experienced crippling racism and it was indeed endemic to and a part of institutional racism, African and Caribbean immigrants would catch it worse or at least just as much because they are Blacker than us and have language issues. But all of them swear damn near everything is better here in America...except American born indigenous niggers and indigenous nigger behavior.

Note that I did not reflect the experience of Asians (Indians/Chinese/Korean/Japanese/etc.,). Asians in America often come here from the poorest countries and situations, hardly knowing English and end up damn near owning all the businesses in the communities of we African American former slaves. My mother taught at Tri Cities High School in Fulton County and there was a Vietnamese dude that came in the 9th grade barely knowing English and ended up Valedictorian or Salutatorian. Furthermore, how often do you hear Latinos (the foreign ones) bitching about how Texas and damn near the whole Southwest and far West was stolen from them. No, they don't complain about the White man's rule, they are just so desperate to get here for the opportunities their former enemy's land can provide that they literally will physically throw their children over the border fence, literally abandoning them to the White man, the White mainstream government of the United States of America, and trust them to border patrol and public services as a first step in their children having the benefits of life in America.

And yet we of niggerdom are so filled with anger and resentments that we sit by idle and paralyzed with paranoia about how White people, the man, the machine, the system, the new world order, the mafia, the illuminati, Kyrie and Kanye's favorite target, and everything else that looks, smells or feels White is oppressing us. How then did we get from the chutzpah of Jim Crow-Civil Rights era Blacks to the stagnation of present-day Black America? The answer is in the triumph, ascendency and rule of a post-civil rights era Black liberalism that told us that there would always be something to protest and thus we should stay woke. It is like China's experience with Mao and Maoism. He sparked a revolution, the central premise of which being that when there is a dictatorship of the proletariat (him), everything will be alright and we'll live in a socialist utopia that is so wonderful we don't need religion and shit like heaven and afterlives, etc. Human frailty being what it is, it was soon evident, even to Mao, that killing one group of leaders (Capitalists and Nationalists) and putting others in their place doesn't magically solve problems. But instead of Mao taking personal responsibility for the failure, he did what he was best at (revolution), and decided he needed another revolution, this time a cultural revolution. He believed this to the point that he envisioned a perpetual or permanent revolution against what he felt were bourgeois capitalist values and forces entrenched in society that were just waiting to take over, and that must be the cause of China's post-Communist takeover economy. This is why totalitarian states like China, Russia, etc., always have huge security/police/Investigative forces with far, far reaching powers. After the Civil Rights movement, while it didn't bring the promised land MLK JR. spoke of, some Black people were able to take advantage of new opportunities and openings in White mainstream culture, but for a lot of us, just the fact we could go to White schools, live in White neighborhoods, shop at White malls, etc., was not sufficiently motivating to feel motivated to take advantage of the opportunities that were around. So like Mao, liberal post-Civil Rights era check cashers and talkers, said the problem is not our assumptions or that perhaps integration and affirmation have limits, nay God forbid, or even that we may have oversimplified and thus been wrong by being naïve about what Civil Rights and the promise of integration could do. No, Black Post-Civil Rights era liberals did no such self-reflection and soul searching. Like Mao they replied, "we need a new revolution, a permanent revolution, a cultural revolution". That is to say, that we have to be perpetually be pushing for integration, affirmation, inclusion, diversity, socialism, LGBTQIA, etc...perpetually. It is Mao's permanent cultural revolution in Black American terms. In Mao's cultural revolution there were placards, billboards and signs against bourgeois morals and values everywhere in favor of revolutionary ideals and language of the proletariat, equality, socialism, communism. In today's woke American permanent cultural revolution, there are gay flags and parades, every month (like the old Red Mayday and Labor flags), challenging and tearing down symbols of bourgeois cultural imperialism like Christmas Manger displays on State property and erasing references to God and male and female. Instead, they promote the ideas of social justice, LGBTQIA freedom, abortion, and that Women have been oppressed since the dawn of man and the time for retribution and to make things right is NOW etc.! So Black elected political liberal elites and the woke mob they've inspired, do not miss any opportunities to complain, bitch and protest against White mainstream culture and institutions because we are on our nigga MSNBC Black female liberal version of Mao's cultural revolution. That is to say a 'permanent' revolution. A permanent revolution requires wokeness and being vigilant in order to eliminate supposed bourgeois cultural values everywhere you find them (and they are everywhere like micro-insults). It requires cutting out the 'bourgeois White male devil' every time he uses the 'N' word, every time his behaviors or comments can be construed as racist, sexist or anti-LGBTQIA, they have to go after them every time and cut off the heads of the bourgeois devils like their friends in Hamas do. Like Mao going after people in China during the cultural revolution that were said to have opinions against the catechism of the communist party and Mao's power particularly, the woke, socialist atheist, abortion, LGBTQIA elite has to go after the perceived 'elites' of the old bourgeois order, and their dangerous bourgeois values like going to church and knowing what a man and a woman are. If you harbor such anti-woke opinions then you will never get a job, don't deserve the job you have and will be made to suffer by the harassment of the LGBTQIA followers harassing your email and phone. The bourgeois White male devil doesn't even deserve a seat at the table to these liberals, at his own table, because he brings his institutional bias, like the aforementioned institutional racism and institutional bias. Joe Biden has realized the only way to placate this liberal culturally revolutionary, permanent revolutionary mob is to damn near only hire Blacks and minorities, the LGBTQIA community, feminists, people with developmental disabilities etc. These same people and the communities they come from view these placements as a victory for the movement. Yet it is only a victory in much the same way Mao looked at it, like a victory for the cultural revolution every time he saw a body hang out of his window in the public square for being accused of being a counter-revolutionary (that is to say anti-LGBTQIA, anti-feminist, anti-inclusion, or the general category of critical statements against that which woke pronounces as Holy). What these liberals and the communities they claim to represent didn't see coming was that there is a backlash and blowback to that 'victory'; hallow though it might be. That is because every time you catch one company counting Black jellybeans there are a thousand others you must put under the strictest forms of surveillance to get at the insidious root of bourgeois values that the woke crowd is against. This breeds the kind of surveillance that if a White person or bourgeois valued person has job, but a tape of a private conversation is produced wherein the person used language deemed offensive to the woke crowd, that person will be harrassed and fired. That is the whole purpose of being 'woke' and staying vigilant, because you must always, and every time root out the bourgeois elitist racist church values when they rise and be ready to protest? That is to say, assuming the primacy of being ever vigilant; a permanent LGBTQIA socialist atheist revolution. It is here and it will not weaken on its own. They are perfectly willing to tear down Judeo-Christian idol(s) and capitalist idols, just to raise their own and make you submit to them instead. Ladies and gentlemen, that is neither liberation, nor freedom; especially hen it is being peddled to the American public by hustlers and charlatans of 'freedom', whose only definition of freedom is the absence of any rules, your society is hellfire bound if it doesn't repent.

Part II

In a previous essay, I used the example of little boys and girls rightfully being afraid of wolves. But there are wolves howling in the distance, and then there are wolves that represent an immediate and imminent threat. If little boys and girls cry wolf every time they hear one in the distance, it weakens their witness and people's belief in the veracity of the claim. We are entering that stage, rightly or not, regarding racism in America. I think it is more Nigerian doctors than it is Black American doctors in America. Why? Can that even possibly be due to White mainstream American racism? Of course not.

Post-Modern, post-Civil Rights era Black liberalism has trained our children to believe that things aren't fair and can never be fair, so whatever they must do to hustle and survive is better than actually trying to navigate the system through God, Family, education, hard work and industriousness. I don't have any problem with Black English, but assuming the White mainstream or business world should be enthused about it, is a completely different matter, and accusing them of racism because they are not so enamored of it representing their business professionals is their choice. It is not inherently racist, and how did we get a definition of the inherency of American racism that only rises to the height of justifying our inadequacies and shortcomings. Dammit, even if it were true that we are still traumatized by slavery, there is oftentimes a palpable difference between being traumatized and paralyzed. Black people seem paralyzed and thus impotent. Many historical people have used their trauma and suffering as motivational principles. We seem to use it for paralyzation principles.

I am not minimizing the extreme psycho-social issues involved in oppression and slavery. In an earlier essay I spoke of the effects of 'being lost' and getting a map for the 'You are here' moment of clarity. Black people here in America have not had our 'You are here' moment and consequently, we wander aimlessly, no plan, no leadership, randomly wandering the aisles and streets of life, simply looking for opportunities where we find them (as opposed to creating them). The twin of finding opportunities where you can has a dark side, and that is committing crimes of opportunity as well. Beloved of Negritude if you have a real 'You are Here' moment, you can realize that not only can you know how the mall or city is organized and where 'you are' but you can enquire at the management offices (provided you know where their offices are and their procedures, and perhaps arrange to open you own store in the mall or the city, you initially came to not knowing where the fuck you are or having to navigate by map and not instinct or knowledge. But somewhere along the line you got a 'map' (received an education in interpreting symbols) and now not only can you navigate the mall/city effectively, but you received the potential in the thing and figured out how to get your own store go for your own productive purposes and ends.

But beloved brothers and sisters, you got to have your 'you are here moment'. You can't refuse to read the site map because it's the White man's map and system, and it is automatically against you and oppresses you. You can't ignore the map because the White man made it. If it's objectively consistent, it will suffice. Keynote! Not that it is perfect, but it will suffice. If it is objective it will suffice. As long as the map is consistent it doesn't matter who invented it, and we can use it to our own ends, vis a vis White mainstream culture and the rest of the world. But what if you are told by a significant group of liberal LGBTQIA socialist atheist segments of a minority of Black people, but a powerful minority of Black people (note they are the ones in power), that the White man owes you something because it's his fault your life is fucked up with the effects of poverty and underdevelopment. And instead of using 'the map' (proven consistent because Jews can use it, Africans can use it, Asians can use it, Arabs, Puerto Ricans, and Dominicans can use it, that quite often look just as Black as you and have so called 'weird' languages, religions, and habits) to develop your own excellencies and ends, you protest what the White man owes you (reparations). All of the above-mentioned people come over here and make their dreams come true (using the map), and knowing from Ellis Island their 'You are Here' moment. We on the other hands have been told by our Black liberal overseers that White people owe us something, and instead of using the map and the accumulated technological, commercial, and industrial advantages White folk have earned in their international activities in the world, we sit around creating whole industries, literal industries off telling niggers what White people and the White mainstream system owe them. Attorney Ben Crump is one of the richest niggers in America. You can see the lifestyle Al Sharpton leads because he has a podcast where he is doing his morning exercises and eating organic and hanging out with his nubile young wife who I think is about the same age as his oldest daughter. And what is their claim to fame, telling niggers what White people owe them, instead of leading Black people's engagement with the 'You are Here' moment, and your 'hereness' is not dependent upon any others. The NAACP, The Urban League, Congressional Black Caucus. Not na'an one of them has had an original idea in 125 years but every one of them can tell you what White people and the government owe niggers, and how they're fighting to make sure niggers get what they are owed by the White man. This we call leadership in our ignorance.

And let's briefly talk about reparations, the piece de resistance of what radical Black socialist LGBTQIA liberalism has told us White people and the White mainstream government owe us. First of all, if you own something and you're a part of the owners, you cannot be on the dole and be a leader in that organization. Black people can't claim we're American, 100% through and through, and share in its leadership and the stringent responsibilities of being good leaders and citizens, and then ask for money when the national debt is what it is, when foreign military obligations (Russia, China, Saudi Arabia et al.) reflect upon American Honor and prosperity, and the American Civilization which we are a part of. You can't be on the dole from it and lead it at the same time. You dig. If indeed 'I too am America', I am responsible for America and sinking gazillions into niggers when it could just as easily and more responsibly go to the debt, tax credits and to strengthen families and increase the quality of schools and decrease crime, I think is more important than somehow putting Black people on a massive dole type arrangement. As America fights Russian, Chinese, and other international aggression, we gotta spend money on satisfying nigga's head games and rationalizing their failures by consistently making the argument....'but look what White people did to us'?

Anyone that automatically thinks we niggers would do the right thing(s) with reparations money should look at the lives and experiences of average Black professional athletes and entertainers. Anyone that thinks we niggas know what to do with lump sums of money should listen to rap music and watch the videos; as a nigga from the hood is in his house flashing wads of money and half-naked women in bathing suits dancing around his house like expensive fairies...I suppose he bought out the strip club to film his video (then film with the same strippers at a fancy house in a White neighborhood they rented out to film the video). They pop bottles and pills all night and the girls dance and a video was done. This is what niggas are doing circa 2023 when they get 'surplus' money; oh yeah and 'make it rain in the club'. Uh, huh. Think we'd do the right thing with the money. Anyone who thinks that should listen as we make odes and hymns to cars that depreciate 25% upon being driven off the lot and only more increasingly with age. Big Gipp is middle class from ATL (I know T MO), and Gipp said that when he got his first real check off a 'Goodie Mob' show or album the first thing he did was buy a $30,000 pair of gold and diamond encrusted teeth. I think little John bought a pair of $80,000 gold teeth. No disrespect intended, but people with MBAs don't do that kinda shit. Have you ever seen a White, Asian, Indian, Pakistani or Arabic doctor, run out when he gets his first check buy an $80,000 set of gold and platinum to wear on his job at the hospital or clinic? Just us, huh? These are the types of choices we have chosen to make. White racism didn't cause Gipp and Lil John to make that choice, just the perfidy of nigga shit values.

Because your ancestors were enslaved, you want a check for simply being alive? Ladies and gents of Negritude, I am sorry. I do not know anyone that can look God in the face and say You owe me, let alone say that to any former oppressor race. Healing, wholeness, stasis, self-esteem etc., come from God not the reparations or affirmations of your former slave master and oppressor. Those things are not White peoples to give. White folks do not own them to dole them out, so by merely writing you a check, you cannot get what you are owed in terms of those things i.e. healing, wholeness, stasis, self-esteem. Do you want those things niggas, or do you just want money so you can 'consume it upon your lusts'? Would you build schools or strip clubs, barbecue joints, imaginary fish places like TI and Killa Mike (please surprise me)? Would you take care of your children and your baby mama or would you truck in White and foreign models to adorn your videos.

Your own initiative, will, sense of power and mastery are not anyone's to 'give' you. They cannot have stolen it from you, took it from you and thus they cannot return it to you. How can someone give you back what they never took? Indeed Rabbi YY Jacobson, 'they can't rape your soul'. Slavery didn't take away our ancestors' self-esteem; in the midst of slavery, they loved themselves and carried themselves with dignity and grace to meet the needs of the times. You cannot take a man's dignity and self-respect simply by physically enslaving him. His or her mind is free, even if survival makes demands. So if White folk never took our dignity, pride, or our ingenuity as children of God, how can they 'give it back' in the form of reparations and affirmative actions or anything else. It is not theirs to give and they never could have taken it in the first place. Black little mermaids and Black jedis is recompense? It was a disgrace before God to take Black pre-k girls to see the new update of the little mermaid, interview them afterwards for Disney commercials where some are in tears, and even grown ass Black women are in tears saying how wonderful it feels to be 'represented' by a White mainstream LGBTQIA socialist atheist company with an old princess to reboot? How does sticking another curly head mulatto in front of little Black girls and calling her beautiful improve the quality of life for little Black dark skinned 'nappy headed' girls and boys that in the main can't swim, and nothing about a Black Little Mermaid is going to encourage them in or give the opportunity to swim? Oh, to see a Black princess? To get acknowledged by a big White corporate structure, that invests in us and believes in is, this is portrayed by the Black liberal LGBTQIA crowd as successful imagery for Black girls. Yet it is actually destructive and almost mutilating Black girl's self-esteem to act like these little strong beautiful dark skinned Black girls should be happy and celebrate a White mainstream corporate entity sticking a little light skinned curly haired mulatto in front of them, and saying 'this is your new heroine'. Now cry and weep as though you are having a religious experience and bow down to your new gods. There is something sick, dark, and sinister about that. I thought we had Meghan and then I think there is a chick of African descent that is a 'princess' in Denmark or somewhere that married to a European Royal. And of course, we had Tina Turner.

And therein lies the muthafuckin problem with all that 'represen-tation' shit. It would be better to be a princess of the niggers, than to be a nigger princess. Get my drift niggerdom. Meghan Markle and the current little mermaid are just nigger princesses, but there is not reign-ing 'Princess of the Niggers' and to be such a thing would be far, far greater and with far greater impact than simply being some White man's nigger princess. A 'princess of the niggers' would imply 'the niggers' had collected ourselves and our ideas to the point that we nominated and ordained a woman or group of women to represent us and thus we call them 'Princess(es) of the Niggers'. It's hard to believe we niggers could even agree upon such a thing in a vote. Would we nominate Oprah, Michelle Obama, Meg tha Stallion, Cardi B, Angela Bassett, Whitney Houston honorary, . I would nominate Cardi B, because of that speech she did on women's health care when she seemed to endorse Bernie

Sanders when he ran for president. She'd never resort to socialized medicine, because clearly any sane nationalized healthcare plan would reject claims for unnecessary surgery, which among other things, would naturally include bigger booties, titties and harder, longer, and longer lasting dicks. For that matter plastic surgeons must be paid for with private insurance and resources. Anyway, Cardi B said with a straight face, 'women need health care, to go to the gynecologist and get they pussies checked out'. Cardi was right. Women do need health care to go get their pussies checked out, but how did she came to the conclusion Bernie Sanders has the answer, when it is not the answer she uses for her health care and plastic surgery, I do not know. I suppose that is some of that 'offset' logic. Maybe we'd nominate Berniece King, Jr.

You know what, ain't no sister running for Princess of the niggers, and no nigga from the transgender or drag community is running for 'princess of the niggers' either, prance though they might. Billy Porter, Ru Paul and Tyler Perry ain't even looking for that smoke, even though let them tell it, they are that smoke, fog and mirrors. Don't nobody wanna be that. They wanna be princesses in white people's shit, and in Switzerland, New York, LA, and all the toniest spots and shit. Don't nobody wanna be 'princess of the niggas'. Even Ru Paul and all the contestants in the Drag Race don't want to be princess of the niggas. They are happy to dress up as nigger princesses, literal, nigger princesses, but none has ever said she/he wants to be 'princess of the niggers' (to represent the political, economic, and cultural development of niggas). Is that because they feel they would be mocked (more than they already are as transgender and drag queens with huge hands, feet and Adam's apples). Which is more absurd and invites mockery most, to think you are really a woman, or that you want to be princess of the niggers? Yeah, imma sit here and call your chick Michaela (said with a luxurious Spanish accent); but she still has hands and feet like Dikembe Mutombo, and even with all the makeup she looks like Dennis Rodman. I'm using the correct gender pronouns too! Really. These are the new princesses the socialist atheist LGBTQIA Democrat Black elected officials and

Black cultural elites want for us, inviting the cruel mockery of a mainstream world that thinks taking Black men dressed as women seriously is easier and more rational than taking the notion of a Princess(es) of the Niggers seriously.

Believe it or not these are fundamental existential questions. Who is going to take responsibility for niggerdom? Who will stand up with the nigger equivalent of a crown of thorns that says mockingly and ironically 'King of the Jews', Crown Princess of the Jews? Is there one? Is there one? No, not even trans Black women and drag queens? Lots and lots of 'Nigger Princesses', no 'Princess(es) of the Niggers'? Can a people survive without princes and princesses (even of the niggers)? Did not slavery's first victims constitute the failure of African political and religious authority to protect us from the White man? The African Kings and Queens we had invested with the power of life and death, in near religious obligations, couldn't save us from the European White man; and for lack of a better phrase 'the witch doctor' couldn't save us. And thus the first casualty of slavery and colonization was the Prince(s) and Princess(es) of the Niggers. Individual 'Nigger princes and princesses' were allowed to survive and perhaps even thrive. But there was no Prince or Princess of the Niggers. 450 (or so) years later there still is not. There are many 'nigger princesses' and queens of this or that be it soul, reggae, art culture etc., but nary and na'aan "Princess of the Niggers'. There are many 'nigger princesses, as in Meghan, but no 'Princesses of the Niggers'.

15 Philanthropy dependence is not an economic or political strategy

Sunday May 28th, 2023 an article in the Atlanta Journal Constitution was called 'Auntie Angie's maternity home for unwed mothers, pregnant struggling financially unstable, facing homelessness women or in violent relationships'. Alveda King is one of her supporters and benefactors. No disrespect to the participants, the article is a prime directive of everything fucked up, futile and fatalistic about Black families and Black people.

On the strength, philanthropy is not a strategy. How old is the 'if you give a man a fish vs. giving him a rod and reel anecdote? Surely as old as there have ever been parents. The current crop of Black politicians and liberal thinkers have come to have a 'give me a fish' mentality rather than a loan or sell me a rod and reel mentality. You know what, better yet, show me, let me pay you to teach me, and let me observe you making a rod and reel. Let them that have ears to hear, hear. Give me fish, give me reparations, you owe me fish and reparations. Do you see what the Chinese did with the Post-Nixon/Kissinger Chinese strategy? For that matter, do you see what Japan and Germany did economically with Post-WW II White rebuilding strategies as Cold War hedges against the rise of Soviet Communism. Look at Singapore, S. Korea, now even Malaysia and other economies that have capitalized on their exposure to western development models, strategies, and capitalization, to develop their own indigenous economies, to the point that these places are now (or at least in good times are called) called 'Tiger Economies'. Of course, they are maturing, but they all at one time or another made the 'economic miracle' happen (or seem to happen). South Korea has (at the time of writing), the 10th largest economy in the world. It is 96% of the size of Kentucky. The path to economic viability for any people is neither impossible nor even illogical. These nations and places suffered under varying forms of colonization, both Japanese, Chinese, and European over the centuries and yet now they are little Asian economic powerhouses. Do you know what else I find interesting, the relationship of ethnic Koreans with White mainstream American culture and people, White European culture and the White international power structure is not antagonistic. Note to self niggerdom, maybe that's how you 'get back at them'; by your own communities living in aesthetically good, safe for families, subject to the rule of law, and peaceful and prosperous communities with good fiscal, administrative, and legal governance. We seem to be so angry and resentful we're doing the opposite of that, and reaping those sour fruits of unnecessarily strained racial relationships because we're trying to prove to White people that they 'owe' us to 'fix' us.

The Japanese don't 'complain' about Hiroshima and Nagasaki in overt ways, they just are real competitive, have a lot of memorials, and be heavy off into peace and anti-nuclear activity. They don't plank out and chant 'Japanese Lives Matter', and protest in front of the UN or the White house. You do not see Japanese young people in America pissing in water bottles and throwing them at the police in front of the Pentagon. Remember the pictures from the 1960's of the Vietnamese men, women and children running down the street, literally on fire, flames bursting from their bodies, butt assed naked as their clothes had been burned off them because of American firebombs? The Vietnamese aint' over here protesting Vietnamese Lives Matter in front of the UN and the White House and Senate. No, they are over here trying to sell Vietnamese industry and production capability and cheap labor to Western corporations and the Vietnamese market as outlets for (their own version of politically correct) western products that they want to make available to their citizens as a sign of rising prosperity like China. And it is even in our American interest to support Vietnam (former enemy that for all intents and purposes defeated us in battle), because strategically speaking, they don't like China dominating the "South China Sea" either, to the point that they don't call it the South China Sea, they call it the Vietnamese Sea. And thus even Vietnam, with all the negative history that came with French and American colonization/intervention in the past, understands quite clearly that it is in their interest to piggyback on the naval and aerial dominance of the Americans and Europe. This is because the quid pro quo with America and Europe is better than the one with China. A Vietnamese quid pro quo with China the Vietnamese know by default, means the Chinese doing whatever they fuck they wanna do, marking off whatever borders they wanna border, leaving South Korea, Vietnam, even Japan et al completely out of the picture. With all the anger and resentment the Vietnamese could manifest at the gringos and resentment about what has transpired historically, they still realize damn well where their strategic interests lie currently. That is the bare minimum of 'real politque' and presently construed Black people seem incapable of it, preferring to focus on strategies of anger, resentment and what other people owe you. For that matter, even with all that negative history, many Vietnamese immigrants and what used to be termed 'boat people' to America opened businesses in Black communities, taking advantage of the American dreams their former enemies could provide. But we have not...to the point that now it is unmistakable and ridiculous. We've got to develop before it's too late because unfortunately, there are many reasons to believe this whole American experiment is a sinking ship. Slowly or quickly, it will sink, and it will be wise to have come up with other means of flotation or at least think that it is in every American's interest to help to keep the damn thing afloat. But there is some binging, bilging, and purging to do.

But more specifically as regards post-Civil Rights era liberal socialist atheist LGBTQIA politics, upon which philanthropy dependency is based; quite frankly Black women have built an empire and a kingdom off White mainstream philanthropy. Anyway. So Auntie Angie runs a women's shelter....anything but the traditional family and the church to solve problems...anything. This is also why Alveda King's brand of anti-abortion philanthropy-conservatism is a one trick pony. Instead of supporting the conditions that support families. She supports the single female broken families, just the women and children at that, which sounds logical, but can Alveda and Angie provide support to a child or children as long as their father? Are Alveda and Angie's input more important than a father's input?

16 Representation and a Seat at the Table: 'What are they good for absolutely nothing' Say it again'

Why do White people think our goal in life is to imitate them. Were Black people sitting around the cosmic effluvia waiting to be born and then said to themselves and God, I want to be a 'Black Little Mermaid' or a "Black Jedi' or a 'Black James Bond' or yes Jada, 'Nigger Cleopatra'? I gives a fuck what race she is. If some African woman, creole woman, or mulatto woman singlehandedly unified Africa and the diaspora, turned it into an economic powerhouse ushering in an age for humanity of peace, love and rock and roll, that's the bitch to make a movie about not some mixed Greco-Roman wench from 1900 years ago. Kamala. Do Black people still sit around wanting to (as it were) be White or inhabit Whiteness. Said differently, a lotta niggas are willing to take affirmative action jobs and be diversity and set aside hires. Every time I see a nigga with the job title VP of Diversity I feel like the monkey at the zoo throwing his shit at patrons. VP of Diversity. Do we need professional corporate help? Is that easier and cheaper than purchasing, starting and strengthening the diversity and reach of Black business? Well, yes. That is why there are many VP's of Diversity, and no Black people with PHD's in Economics or not, rich or not, standing up to take responsibility for making the Black urban economy work. Our Negro leaders make the responsibility for Black economic development White people's and the government's responsibility, and then give themselves a fancy, good for nothing title title like VP of Diversity, making $250,000 a year as some corporations token of proof that they are concerned about diversity and inclusion.

Some of this stems from the ridiculous notion White people or America owes us something. Our ancestors struggled for the exact opposite. They struggled to be treated equal under the law, not live in a world where we treat America and White people like they owe us something or where they are the standard culturally and politically. If we treat them like White mainstream culture is the standard, then our survival is dependent on integration and imitation, or is dependent on forcing Whites and White mainstream culture's tacit and silent acceptance and agree with our 'wokeness' the way the LGBTQIA community demands mainstream culture accept and agree with their lifestyle choices. Their agreement and approval is not necessary. We make it necessary by trying to force them to pay for our development. They can't. They don't own 'development' to dole it out to whom they wish. These 'woke' Black liberals make the argument we deserve a seat at the table, a face in the boardroom and representation. Nonsense, never in the history of the world has a real artist ever consigned himself to painting and copying the same works other artists have done. To do so make you a hack. Sure, there is money in an artist copying other people's famous works, and selling them at discount, but that is not art, and you cannot call yourself an artist. No real musician worth his weight in salt really wants to be in a 'cover band' for the rest of his life, no matter how lucrative it might be. No real poet simply reads the works of others and establishes his or her reputation, he must write, live, and die by his own shit.

I was so humiliated for Black people when the issue came out about Sally Hemmings and Thomas Jefferson and what the exact nature of their relationship was. Perhaps her descendants are descendants of Thomas Jefferson. The Hemmings family's current scions go to family reunions and discuss those matters and seem to take pride in their White Jeffersonian possible ancestor. But similar to my argument to Meghan that it's better to be 'Princess of the Niggers' than simply a 'Nigger Princess', and affirmed into action. What would be impressive was if one of the Hemmings nigger descendants was as politically gifted, well educated, as talented a thinker, writer, and orator, and endowed with leadership skills to do the same thing for Black people, that Thomas Jefferson did for American Whites. That would be an act worthy of your 'ancestor'; Apparently we need not expect any such thing from the current Hemmings clan as I believe their present 'battle' is to be buried in the historic cemetery with their White Jeffersonian 'family' relatives. Too much 'George Jefferson' (The Jefferson's tv sitcom) in the Hemmings gene pool and not enough 'Thomas Jefferson'.

Furthermore, in addition to the 'we just want to be substitutes in the White man's world' argument as a political and economic program, Black socialist atheist LGBTQIA liberalism has saddled Black people with the necessary by product of that thinking, which is that White people represent some kind of end, in themselves. It is as though one of our goals (in life no less), is to be like them, able to be substituted in and out unnoticeably. I'm sure nigger defense secretary Lloyd Austin is a great man. But is he a hero to Niggerdom and even Africa simply because White people employ him as a substitute? Does integrating something and being the first Black to do something automatically make you a hero? Other than she's the 1st nigger Vice President, what else can we say about Kamala? What has she done for niggerdom? She's married to a White man. She's really just a few steps above, nay, she's the twin of Rachael Dolezal in a parallel universe, just more tanned. Joe Biden fell the fuck over yesterday handing out diplomas to graduates; Kamala might end up through no skill, means, talent or fault of her own in the most powerful White man's job in the world. Even then, her highest claim to fame is to be the first nigga female substitute for the American President, Obama being the first male substitute for the American President of the United States.

The idea that niggers should or would be proud of such a thing, simply because she is the first nigga wench that White man allowed to do it is humiliating in the extreme. I can imagine, little school age nigger pickinnies missing valuable class time so they can watch and celebrate Kamala's swearing in. It is supposed to make them feel really proud. It is supposed to make us proud and believe in the future for little Black pickinnies, like the first nigga in space, Guy Bluford. That was supposed have revolutionized little Black boys and girls and made them interested in science in 1983 but 30 years later 'urban education' is damn near a contradiction in terms and oxymoron. The first nigga to do some shit doesn't make you a hero and it has the unintended effect of always placing the 'integrating institution' (who, surprise magically is your former slave master) on a pedestal. No more nigger children go to MIT, CalTech, etc., than before the first niggas started going in space.

If you really want to see something impressive, consider the nigga astrophysicists or collection of them like Neil DeGrasse Tyson who parade around on TV being interviewed by White mainstream media and operate within White mainstream colleges, universities, and research centers. They didn't get together and start a nigger space program tentatively called 'niggers in space'. They didn't start programs in urban elementary, middle, and high schools for gifted Black children in math and science. They didn't put scholarships into urban students majoring in math and science degrees in college and higher learning. They are however, very eloquent in describing why there ought to be niggers in space and taking checks from White TV networks, NASA, and science programs that wouldn't have touched them with 10ft pole back in the beginnings of the post-civil rights era. Nor did these obviously bright ass niggas start taking up money from Oprah, Creflo Dollar, The NOI, the Urban League, the NAACP, et al, in the cause of putting niggers in space. They also didn't take that money and purchase airlines, and aeronautical engineering firms, and utilized their efficiencies and industrial products to fuel the nascent nigger aeronautical industry. Don't tell me it can't be done (Elon, Richard Branson, Jeff Bezos and big ass Michael Strahan went to space mind you), so I know niggers in space is more than theoretically possible. And what shames me is that Neil DeGrasse Tyson and his fellow astrophysicists of African descent believe more in the possibility of alien extraterrestrial life, than they believe that there should be a program to put niggers in space. If you really want to know what the illuminati is doing, they are sabotaging the nigger space program, that is what they are doing. All jokes aside, Nigger astrophysicists creating a 'niggers in space program' (instead of NASA, NISA) would be impressive, way more impressive than the first nigger in space or the first nigga with some kind of science degree from an elite White mainstream university or the first nigga to head NASA. The first nigga to head 'Niggas in Space Agency' will be my hero and the hero of future descendants of Africa that will indeed go to space in the name of niggerdom and make all sorts of nigger discoveries. That would be truly impressive, and 700 years from now when niggers meet our first aliens independent of White people and whoever else has gone to space first, those niggas 700 years from now will thank God some niggas in 2023 took the time create and fund 'the niggas in space: Space Program'.

I love it. Think NISA (Niggers in Space) it not possible? Fie on you! Broke and isolated as Russia is, to the point they have toilets in major cities wherein you can't flush standard toilet paper down the toilet even, in the flagship city of Sochi during the 2014 Olympics; they have a quite advanced and somewhat flourishing space program. Iran and North Korea have space programs and are not exactly economic or technological powerhouses. Saudi Arabia has a Space Program, China of course has a space program, and we've already mentioned the 'Musky', Branson, Bezos space programs, etc. We niggers can have our own space program up and running complete with our own nigger space station(s) orbiting earth and our own colony on the muthafuckin moon. Get it done Tyler Perry, get it done Oprah, get it done Obama! That muthafucka Neil Degrasse Tyson doesn't give a damn however about the niggers in space program and not the least of which reason is that he's married to a White woman. But I digress. The fact that many nations and even splinter groups and peoples have a space program, means that apparently it does not take a great, great nation, well organized, wealthy, excellent in practical and theoretical science and economic power and the socio-political ability to justify the mighty expenditure in resources (and quite often lives) it takes to do a hell of lot of damage in space or in the atmosphere terrestrially. The truth is that any two-bit dictatorship and banana republic, provided it has enough resources to buy the components and get training can have a space program...if they want one. But some of us, would rather play 2nd mates on White mainstream spaceships, the first Black captain in Star Fleet, Black jelly bean Jedi, liberal overweight Lizzo in space running a fake Utopia (The Mandalorian cameo) and anywhere else White people want to pay us to be their friends, associates and lovers in space.

Part II

Black ass Ariel in the White mainstream Disney Ocean SeaWorld? What message are we sending our children: that a Black girl can't be a princess of her own realm and her nigga father's realm, she must get her an affirmative action realm, provided by Disney Corp. That is the only way little Black girls or her own people think she is going to get a dominion; by getting affirmed into action in a realm that used to belong to a little White girl, until the little White girl went on to bigger and better things, and you little nigga wench took over her realm (excuse me franchise). The White man must give the little nigga princess realms and dominions. Little Black Princesses must be affirmed into action by their Prince Harry's Meghan, and you tell the world you are empowering little Black girls? Little Black princesses and their Black fathers apparently, are incapable of getting realms, dominions and kingdoms of their own the old-fashioned way before affirmative action...that is to say by kicking ass (not always literally or physically, quite often professional, commercially, industrially) and taking a realm or two of dominion.

How can we be so cool and comfortable with our daughters being 2nd class citizen princesses, only an afterthought after White girls have exhausted the role? But the humiliation for Black women and Black girls won't stop there, next in line to be Ariel and other princes and princesses is transgender boys and girls. They don't respect you niggerdom, when you get these jobs kamala and Obama, it is the principle of the thing in 'representation'! And more often than not, it is not our Oprah's, Tyler's, Kamala's and Obama's that are the best of us, those are simply are the ones 'talented', 'intelligent' and 'well spoken' enough to be useful (but rarely creative). Like a good thoroughbred, or hunting dog, their usefulness makes them master's favorites. They are docile and affectionate and either live in the proverbial 'big house' with master and sleep at the foot of his bed, or live in the master's neighborhood of big houses. In a complete abandonment of self-esteem, this situation is what we niggers call success in America, being talented enough to leave 'Blackness' behind and go 'shake and bake' amongst White mainstream elites who will never invite your child to the sleepover and think you are ignorant and got in their neighborhood by affirmative action or being an athlete or entertainer. Run them balls nigga!

Ergo this notion of 'representation'. 1) The White man owes it to us, that is to say, owes us a seat at 'his' table on the premise that just because our ancestors labored to build it, automatically means we deserve a seat at 'his table'. 2) We need 'representation' in terms of integration because we are emotionally dependent, economically dependent, and professionally dependent on the White mainstream. Both assumptions are the horrible by products of the Post-Civil Rights era Socialist-Atheist-LGBTQIA, Black Liberal agenda. Something that 'exists' represents itself; it does not need anyone or anything to 'represent' it. We yield White folks too much power even in assuming that they can 'represent' us (correctly), or represent us better than what we might think to 'represent' ourselves. His (the White man's) approval is more important than our own or our God's, I'm sorry to say. That is the most psychologically damaging thing the Black liberal socialist atheist LGBTQIA political elite has done to Black self-esteem in post-modernity.

Thus we niggas get in this political and economic mindset where instead of being creative, we want to integrate or be 'represented' in one of the White mainstream existing government, corporate or cultural productions that is already going on and was doing quite well before they started feeling it necessary to 'represent' us or any other people like Hispanics, Asians, East Indians (Mindy Kaling). It is a contradiction in terms. There is the "thing in itself," and then there is its representation. Recently Blacks got 'represented' in space on an episode of the Mandalorian. It was humiliating. Apparently Grogu loves 'Black women' and women in general and just jumps into their arms like a muthafuckin lap dog? Are you fucking kidding me? Baby Yoda? You got the 'force', been trained by Luke Skywalker, and Ashoka who was Anakin aka Dearth Vader's Padawan, and been exposed to other Jedi manifestations in all their infinite variety and arrays and Grogu just jumps up in 'big fat liberal half-naked Space Lizzo's arms'...in a world and galaxy far, far away, mind you? Get the fuck outa here.

'Space Lizzo' (it turns out) is not that much different at all than terrestrial Lizzo. A fat Black liberal hypocrite. I can say she is a hypocrite because in the latest news prior to publishing, Lizzo is being sued by many of her overweight dancers who allege that they were body shamed and hazed. Really? Anyway, Lizzo in space on the Mandalorian is married to a White man (Jack Black) who has impressed her by his intense liberalism (which comes off for both characters more like irresponsibility than it does motives of wisdom, peace or something religious, philosophical, and thoughtful). 'As it is in the heavens, so it is on earth'? Cue Florida Evans...damn, damn, damn! The little girl from 'Bad Batch' Star Wars series likes nigger women too, being attached to a character played by...wait for it, wait for it...Wanda Sykes...in space. The weirder part about that ('representing' in space), is that the character Sykes plays chases ancient artifacts, some to sell, some reminiscent of an old universe, more peaceful one, that is to say, a fantasy universe without empires (or the people that fight them) and that somehow reflect 'her own people's struggles' in the midst of all that. Her character is a typical Black woman, that is to say, she 'shoots from the hip', fast talking, spirited...takes a lotta risks...Black women 'represented' in Space and guess what, she is gay? They represented a 'gay woman' in space, which is to say a liberal Black woman in space, long before they represented any, any other type of Black woman in space, notwithstanding the possibility that Black women in space could love their Black husbands and be devoted to their Black families....why the fuck would a Black woman do that when they could be gay in space and run around with far more successful and gifted White people...in space. No disrespect or ill will intended, but I could not help wondering, considering Sykes sexual orientation, if there may be some implication of grooming 'in space' and Sykes character is (as it were) grooming 'Omega' (the female clone Child). Sexual allusions or not, clearly 'Omega' is fascinated by Sykes' character, her character's independence, strength, intelligence, and sense of daring/fun/humor/enjoyment. All these are usually considered the opposite of what traditional 'domesticity' brings girls, young ladies and women; at least that is the way it has been spun in the Post-Civil Rights, Post-Women's Rights, Post-Trans-Rights eras.

I am not the nigger or conservative sitting around speculating about sinister Disney Motives. But it seems patently obvious to me that at least as presently construed by Disney 'Star Wars Representation' in space, it includes Black women as stereotypically fat, outspoken and independent on earth, and Lizzo is fat and outspoken in space 'representing' what White people think 'niggers in space' would be like. They would be entitled, having dared romantic adventures with powerful White men in the Republic and empire, married White men, and their Black and White multi-cultural 'subjects and citizens' would love them because who wouldn't love a 'big fat sassy Queen' (or even a man dressed up as a big fat sassy Queen' Tyler). Liberals talk all the time about abolishing the upper classes, and reining in the power of the elites. then they wage a political and moral war against elitism which they win. The only problem is that when they win, and have torn down the old traditional upper classes, all they have done is replace the old traditional upper classes with themselves...in space and the future...the new Black liberal socialist atheist LGBTQIA elites! Yep, space niggers would not have a self-conscious bone in their bodies. There would be no 'nigger Republic' somewhere, even though that would be the most logical development. As big as the universe and the outer rim must be there is no 'nigger Republic'? Even though Lupito Nyongo, Lizzo, Carl Weathers, Samuel Jackson and Billy Dee Williams are out there, there is no 'nigger republic' or planet. What the fuck? Or maybe that was what 'Billy Dee's Lando Calrissian inspired 'Cloud City' was. Of course, it makes perfect sense that White people would think that if Black people were millions, trillions, billions of miles of light years from earth and the United States, the first thing on our minds would be opening planets and satellite moons, filled with Casinos, strip clubs, dancing music halls, pornography, prostitution and a haven for the intergalactic pimps, thugs, hustlers, bounty killers, scoundrels and thugs. Yes, Han Solo was a scoundrel, but he redeems himself and thus even White scoundrels are decisively important to the fate of the universe.... but not very many niggers are, unless they know some White scoundrels from having been scoundrels together.

No 'Nigger Federation of Planets' exists in White science fiction, even though presumably any planet that got a lotta sun would make niggers out of humanity or any other beings that happened to be there and used pigmentation as a biological defense. Of course, the reverse would be true where planets resided where there was not a lot of sun, they would develop the opposite physical characteristics. Shall we even go so far as to say that with no sun, they'd be albinos in the sense that naked mole rats are and many, many other animals have genetic markers for albinism. Not coincidentally, though the only familiarity I have is coincidental, scientists say naked mole rats are nearly unique in their ability to withstand disease and not get sick from parasites and environmental toxins. Those speculations make more sense than when Disney and highly paid Star Wars writers and executives make arguments about what Black people would be like in space! There ain't a damn thing wrong with them assumptions. But magically in space, you find large groups of White people that run themselves, but no damn independent niggers who run themselves? Magically in space, 50,000 fucking years from now, no nigger has ever gotten self-conscious enough to speculate on such matters? 50,000 damn years working for either the Republic, the Empire, and or the resurgent republic, the resurgent empire aka the 1st order, aka whatever manifestation its going to make when the Ashoka series comes out. How the fuck are there nigger or 'brown' Jedis but they don't procreate and lead celibate lives...unless accidentally and quietly they fall in love, sin and become sith lords. Great logic, George. Great logic. Niggers in space never run shit for themselves. They run shit for the empire, they run shit for the 121st order, they run shit for the republic, and the rebellion...but space niggas don't run shit for themselves anywhere, at any time. There is no niggerdom in space? There is no niggerdom, except what is 'represented' of us in space in the entire galaxy by White science fiction writers and entertainment corporations? Even though there is a planet of Ewoks, cute little furry panda like bears (minus the coloring) who are nationalists, even though there is a planet of wild sand people on Tatooine who are nationalists and hold their own thing to the point muthafuckas don't even know what they look like under all that shit and the bright eyes, and niggers in space never created a 'nigger republic'? There is no niggerdom in space, but the whole premise of the Star Wars universe(s) is that much of the story lines revolve around people being oppressed or not able to freely be themselves because of a dominant group. Then that people liberates themselves with assistance of Jedi Order (i.e. Holy Ghost Prophets/ Warrior Priests). The Jedi order helps them liberate themselves as a matter of penance? But there is no Niggerdom in space 50,000 years from now. 50,000 years from now, little Black girls are going to be content to either watch Princess Leia do her thing or participate in a re-make of movies where princess Leia does her thing but they let a Black girl play the roles during the lifetime of Princess Leia? This many niggas would call progress. Damn we are deluded Negritude.

Apparently, niggers in space 50,000 years from now are beyond niggerdom...or is that just how they 'represent' us in space. Fat Black liberal Lizzo running a dysfunctional planet where they love music, the arts and leisure; the slave class now being robots controlled by one dude. And they want the Mandalorian to do something about it, instead of them taking responsibility for doing something about it and taking on the crime. Oh, what ironies former slave masters spring upon unsuspecting post-modern former slaves. Imagine the surprise...fat Black women in space, literally married to White men. What a stretch. But oh, every time, they 'represent' us and give us a 'seat at the table' that fits their dependence narrative and our self-imposed dependence narrative, we jump at the opportunity and treat it like not only a financial plus, which

I cannot deny, but that it also necessarily means we are being affirmed and appreciated when we are 'represented' and that is not true.

Part III

Oh, what ironies our former slave masters weave, in an effort, to deceive? How indeed could Ice T, the thug, the pimp, the hustler, cop killa, end up a suburban dad with a 'White wife' that has made a career out of playing cops? He loved the music, loved hip hop, gang culture, pimping, selling dope, and I'm sure he loved his cop killa beliefs and the motives with which he undertook such things, but guess what. Or rather you don't have to guess. The White man pays more, and the average nigga will say anything and do anything somebody will pay him to do completely irrelevant of culture, music, pimping, colors, the hood you reppin and sets... He went from one form of pimping niggers to another, only the people paying him changed to the corporate entertainment industry. LL cool j now has a real job and for all intents and purposes has stopped rappin and is now more or less not only an actor but actor who has made of career of playing cops. Nigger they own us. And our former slave masters are content and exponentially well paid off these niggers. They have gone from owning us outright to owning our 'representations'. How much difference is there really between 1850 southern census showing unnamed slaves listed by age, skillset, sex and monetary value, and the NBA, NFL, draft? Slaves were expensive; walking, talking, human capital. Their skillsets and bodily characteristics make them even more valuable today, running and shooting that ball, blocking, and tackling, trying to get paid by 'representing' some NFL, NBA or MLS team as one of their second tier of mascots, one of their human mascots; one of their contracted and contractual 'representations'.

Marx asked who 'owns the means of production', I ask who owns the 'means of representation'? And the only Black people in America, who own the 'means of 'representation' in America are Oprah Winfrey, Post-Modern Mammy, and an effeminate Black man, pretending like he's not for the purpose of 'representation' (Tyler Perry). There is a thick line between the so illuminati and conspiracy theories, and a magic coincidence those Black people 'own the means of 'production'/'representation' in Black America. Those are the only people allowed to 'own the means of 'representation' in Black America and White people's intentions and interests notwithstanding, no one is going to 'give' us the 'means of our own representation'. Until we make movies for domestic and international consumption, we will look like however 'others' choose to 'portray' (that is to say 'represent') us.

Furthermore, I'm barely able to watch the NBA anymore it is so filled with nigga shit 'representation' and other convenient ironies of our former slave masters as well. Who told White people all Black people love hip hop and would prefer to hear it in all times and places above other forms? What have we to hope for as Black people in terms of dignity when some of the 'richest' Black people we produce, make Subway commercials (like Jarrett) and Doritos commercials acting like subs and chip, McDonalds and Burger Kings are the best thing to happen to the Black culinary experience since the acquisition of grits from Native Americans. Really, niggas selling Doritos and Steph Curry selling the car company like it's the greatest thing since grits and niggas is killin' each other every day. But there you are on your commercials, shooting threes and free-throws listening to hip-hop, but happily ensconced away from the violent dysfunction of poor and working-class urban Negro communities because you live a White gated community.

Rich niggas will be on commercials doing dumb shit in the name of 'representing' the products of White mainstream corporations; corporations whose executives would shoot themselves in the foot before they live around you or sent their children to school with yours (as in Black people generally), but they have made Steph Curry, Michael Jordan, Charles Barkley, Jalen Rose, Shannon Sharp, their spokespeople? Are we 'representing' ourselves? Is Stephen A. Smith 'de rigour' in Black men's aesthetics and tactics in debate and argument? Why has ESPN paid him so much? At what magnitude does Disney think Stephen A's style resonates in Black America, or that we want Stephen's attitude 'representing' Black people's level of engagement and debate about sports, politics, or anything else? Are we 'representing' ourselves, our corporate, entrepreneurial, and individual initiative, or are we allowing 'ourselves' to be 'represented' on behalf of the highest White mainstream bidder whether it is Disney, the Turner Network, Subway, Fox Sports etc?

Let us play one last representation game, alluded to briefly earlier. It is quite common that organized entities have mascots. Nearly all schools, colleges, and universities have mascots. We know UGA is 'represented' by the Bull Dog animal. 'Ugga15' is a bulldog. He doesn't know how his image is being used to 'represent' UGA, certainly no more decisively than any other college symbolism like UGA's colors Black and Red. No idea. Ugga15 has a great life, excellent health care, the best food, eventually someone will direct him to opportunities to mate because Ugga15 will need to exist in promiscuity in perpetuity provided the University of Georgia mascot family line is to survive another 150 or so years. The line of Uggas must continue. That is taking into account and making concessions for 'dog year' lifespans. Uggas owners make millions off merchandising and licensing, and a 'peculiar' relationship with the University. Ugga15, one dog amongst 30 or 40,000 screaming human fans happy to see him trotted out and running up and down the sideline, even though he doesn't have a fucking clue what he is running up and down the sideline about, and why all these humans seem to care so much. And Ugga15 runs and prances on the field at the appropriate times.

Is Ugga15 'representing' dogs? How many dogs live like he does? Well of course, inasmuch as he is a dog, he represents dogs. But he's a dog being used and manipulated, to completely human purposes and ends, and for human understandings of 'representation' and financial compensation. He's not himself, he's the self the University of Georgia, the fans in the stands, the alumni, the media, the current students, and opposing teams and their mascots need him to be....a 'representation' of what human (all too human) needs want him to be and symbolize.

He does not belong to 'himself' inasmuch as his 'representation' does not 'belong' to him. It (his 'representation') is largely a caricature of what his/her former and current slave masters think of him to justify their and their ancestors accidental slips on the wrong side of moral and theological history.

...look at the Black athlete, a mascot, a 'representation'. He runs and prances up and down the court, the field, throwing and shooting the balls, blocking, and tackling, doing tricks like back flips when they score touchdowns, all to the amusement of the fans in the coliseum. It's even more powerful because the spectacle and the pageantry is being broadcast by traditional media and social media components. 5 Ugga15's on the Basketball court, 12 Ugga15's on the football fields, beasts surrounded by the howling roaring fans and the din of noise of screams and shouts, the Black athlete the same. But in the case of the Black boys and men that play high level collegiate and pro-ball, the fans are nearly always White; a sea of White faces, cheering on their mascot. Yes, how the horses run! Churchill Downs, the Preakness, Saratoga, fine breeds, breeding, and bloodlines; thoroughbreds and pedigrees. Best scientific diets and exercise, built and bred for speed...and yet recent deaths at major horse racing events have cast questions on the whole enterprise. Does this not sound familiar?

Black man, Black woman, we must define ourselves in larger terms than simply what we observe White people doing, and what they 'represent' us as doing, and being about it simply because they are willing to pay. We will always be enslaved, always be 2nd class citizens, always need to be affirmed into action, always need set asides, always need remedial programs, always need philanthropy, always need handouts, always need alms and donations, always need reparations and always have to entertain our former slave masters and others by simply doing what they expect and 'represent' us as anyway, rather than doing our art and our own thing. It is about anger and resentment or hostility to anyone, but the kind of freedom that precisely comes from peace and forgiveness towards those who formerly oppressed and repressed you. Then you will be 'what you 'represent' you as. You will truly be free because your picture of yourself will not be dependent upon what your former slave masters thought about you, and whether he gives you affirmation and reparation. You will be equally free in that because you are not operating out of anger and resentment, you are truly free to express yourself independent of prior traumas and experiences, powerful though they might have been. Our freedom is quite precisely in not, yes not, being angry and resentful against White folks. If you are angry and resentful 'they' still control you. I may seem in my writings to be angry and resentful, but it is simply to illuminate truths, it is not because I'm using 'history' or 'weaponized history' as a means of extracting guilt-based reparations and behaviors on White people, White corporations, White institutions, or the government? Do your art and 'represent' yourself independent of what sells, or what 'they represent you as' or are willing to pay you to 'represent yourself as'.

We must not be content to simply be 'represented'. We must produce our own authentic product, a religious, cultural, economic, and political human art on a galactic scale, let alone global, continental, national, etc. Let us conclude these matters with the following reflections. We were told what a great thing Barack Obama was for 'representation'. Little Black boys and little Black girls were to have an example that they can grow up to be president of the United States. And yet, post-Obama Black on Black crime is worse, urban academic performance is worse (pre or post COVID19) and everything the Obamas were supposed to 'represent' for Black families, the Black marriage rate is still ridiculously low and showing no impact or post-Obamas bump. Wedlock births show no signs of improvement! There are probably less employed marriageable Black men today than it was before Obama. Would God, that like Sasha and Malia, all little Black girls could go to private schools, sleepovers with their rich White, Asian, Jewish, and Arab friends and date rich White Ivy League educated frat boys. That's my muthafuckin take on whether or not Black people should be enthused simply by being 'represented' and 'having a seat' at the muthacfuckin table. When

Tiger Woods was at his height the commercial had little Black girls and Black boys, chanting for the Nike apparel company, 'I'm Tiger Woods'. For all the 'representation' that Tiger was supposed to be doing, I'll bet less Black kids play golf today than played before Tiger Woods from impoverished or underserved communities and backgrounds.

Like my request to the Hemmings family, to honor their Jeffersonian ancestor by doing for Black people what Jefferson did for White people in America. Obama being the first African American president is not impressive. Being the first President of the United States of Africa...that would be impressive, maybe even eternal in terms of World History and not just American or Black History; and that you can never get by letting other folks, your former slave masters or not, be responsible for 'affirming' and 'representing' you.

17 Idiocy Made Flesh: Notes on the 2023 Rick Ross Car Show

Do not send me items about how Rick Ross owns numbers of 'Wing Stop' Restaurants, or how many Checkers and Rallys he owns scattered throughout the Negro urban landscape. Do not speak to me of 'Maybach Music' which, despite its name, can hardly be said to be producing high quality elitist Hip-Hop. Do not tell me he has his own Tequila Brand (unless you send my agent some). I am damn sure not going to take anything away from an enterprising young Black man, and I'm happy for him to be (as it were) 'handling his business'. For that reason, I'm not going to even speculate where he is on the GOAT rapper's list. Suffice it to say that any ranking outside the top 15-20 would be charitable, and the whole question becomes oxymoronic and a contradiction in terms. I'm not going to criticize him for promoting and addicting generations of urban Black children to fast food. I'm not going to criticize his 'Maybach Music' for not putting out a relevant artist, let alone groundbreaking artist...ever (including himself). Nor will I criticize his Tequila brand and wink and nod at whether or not he is a creative entrepreneur, or is merely copying off Puffy (Cîroc), Kendall Jenner (818), George Clooney (Casamiagos), Ryan Reynolds (Aviation Gin), Matthew McConaughy (Wild Turkey Bourbon), Drake (Virginia Black American Whiskey), Justin Timberlake (Sauza 901 Tequilla), Jay Z (D'usse Cognac), Ludacris (Conjure Cognac), Channing Tatum (Born and Bred American Vodka), Robert Dinero, Pitbull, Cameron Diaz and Katherine Power, and even Angelina Jolie and Brad Pitt. Can you call Rick Ross a pioneering entrepreneur, or might he best be referred to as pioneering in bandwagon hip-hop mediocrity in business and in music. But I shall not digress any further from my original topic.

There is a saying that you can't 'separate a fool and his foolishness'. This is a translation of Proverbs 27:22. Thus, while Black teen violence and death is spiraling, Black K-12 education is worse than it was during Jim Crow, out of wedlock births have consistently been around 70% and even higher in some communities; as urban communities suffer economic underdevelopment and foreigners own most of the functional businesses, and race relations and polarization (at least politically and culturally) are worse now than it ever been; which is saying a lot considering America's history of race relations...as in how could it be worse than Jim Crow and Slavery? When you are killing and oppressing yourself through ignorance, violence, dysfunction, and family chaos, that is worse than being oppressed by a foreign master. And a foreign master that purposely keeps you ignorant and backwards and loves plastering you all over television and the media in your dysfunction, is hardly your friend or the one you need to be looking to for affirmation like a mentor or something. We should be much more selective about our mentors in Niggerdom. That is why our communities are filled with violence, dysfunction, and family chaos amongst us. In the midst of all of the above, Rick Ross is worried about a damn car show...to the point that he is willing to defy South Fulton County and Fayette County political and law enforcement authorities, who were correctly concerned about traffic and the possibility of violence for the most part. Because of threats of being called racist and classist, even Black South Fulton and Fayette County authorities were loathe to admit their fear of the rowdy alcohol and drug infused and induced participants, animated by the pretty cars and pretty women, and 'competition' over cars and women. Combine that with rowdy raucous hip-hop music that more often than not, glorifies crass sexual behavior, illegal behavior and violent attitudes and activities, and any sane county or city government would have many concerns about such an event and voice them. But our liberal Black political elites won't call a spade a spade because they are accused of being racists and hating on Blacks from the lower socio-economic sectors. They won't call a spade a spade as well, because many of our Black liberal political elite, such as Dickens, were educated in White mainstream academic institutions, worked in White mainstream America, and even live in White mainstream America and send their kids to White mainstream private or public schools. Knowing that about themselves, but still wanting to claim how hip, how street and how Black they are, they refuse to criticize nigga shit because they want the lower classes to think they are hip, instead of leading the lower classes to improve their quality of life. It is the same phenomena the Black community is experiencing writ large, in generations of parents that want to be their children's friends and associates, instead of being their parents and leaders the first 18 years of their lives.

Very similar to their male Latino counterparts, who transmitted the Lowrider culture to Texan and Western poor migrants, Negro male communities springing up in the post-World War II period self-identified with cars and they have taken on a cultural and artistic significance that the folks at Ford, Cadillac, and Chevy never imagined. 'Cruisin down the street in my 6'4'. Lil Boozie and his 'Tight whips', Public Enemy's 98' Oldsmobile, Cypress Hills Lowrider, Sir Mix a lot's Hooptie, Throw some d's (Daytons rims and tires on it), Sittin on Crome, Ridin Spinners, Just two dope boys in a Cadillac, 'lex, beemers and the benz'. It was not just Blacks and Mexicans falling for car culture. Southern White and Midwestern Whites, usually rural, poor White men, have romanticized Chevy, Ford, and GMC truck culture, ATVs, and Motorcycles. Throughout the history of country music there has been odes to the truck because it was the 'vehicle' that rural poor White men choose to represent themselves and symbolize their sense of beauty and power. Poor urban Black men have their own peculiar 'Freedom' symbolizing relationship with cars in hip-hop as do rural White men with trucks and country music. Parenthetically speaking, it is this aspect of it, that poor White men, who don't have a lot to be proud of, chose in the past to represent themselves with Budweiser products and symbolism. That is why when Bud Light decided to go 'Woke', based on the lives and predilections of InBev executives that never have been broke, poor, or needed consumer items to feel good about themselves, they missed the 'blowback' from the Dylan Mulvaney endorsement fiasco. Sure 'brands' belong to the corporations that own them, but corporations do not 'own' what their 'brand' represents in the culture.

So, when a company wants to 'rebrand' in the name of 'wokeness' or anything else, the blowback can be a mutha! But I digress.

Urban poor Black men like Rick Ross have their own romantic relationship with cars. It is a very ancient psychological phenomena, we males do. Many cultures had a romanticized (of course not in a sexual way), relationship and special bond between a boy/man and his dog or horse. Post-modernity has simply transmuted and transvaluated this into cars and motorcycles. And of course, it is transmuted and transvalued notwithstanding eras or time periods. While countries with horses romanticized horses, countries or cultures with camels, romanticized camels. Just today I read of a quote by the prophet of Islam, comparing something of very high value to a 'Red Camel'.

However, my critique of 'niggerdom's' appreciation of cars, trucks and motorcycles is because in the old days, if a man really liked horses, and developed an expertise at such considerations as made a horse great, he would nearly immediately endeavor to mate and breed horses. Similarly, a man into camels of a certain wealth, status and knowledge of such matters as made a camel 'great', would nearly immediately endeavor to mate and breed camels. Japanese, German, Italian automakers compete and build cars and engines to be tested in Formula I Am racing, Indy 500 racing, Baja Races and other endurance and extreme racing environments. Presumably, the Blacks love cars, at least Rick Ross's behavior would suggest niggers love cars. But apparently not enough to breed them or nay, even desire to develop the industrial prowess and expertise oneself to consistently repair, build and even modify them. Or how about just opening some dealerships and employing all these niggas who you claim love cars so much that 15,000 of them are descending on South Fulton, Fayette, and Clayton Counties to celebrate cars. Even better for the Black community would be if our celebrity hip-hop lovers of automobiles opened highly professional repair shops and paid to educate younger Black men with the knack and a love of cars to go to trade schools or car brand-based certification schools to provide good quality car repair services in underserved Black communities, as there are hardly any dealerships in Black communities. There are a plethora of 'buy here, pay here' used car lots in the Black community, selling more lemons than Florida but Rick Ross isn't interested in any of that, just shiny cars, that bounce up and down like lowriders and that have TVs in them.

One unfortunately unique feature of African American life is that we are one of the few peoples whose loves, make everybody else rich. A Jew must eat Kosher, a Muslim Halal and of course Chinese Restaurants, Thai restaurants, Brazilian Steakhouses, etc., most peoples besides African Americans use their individualism and unique 'loves', to make them rich as they must develop business, industries, and corporate bodies for governance to produce the 'beloved' items. Black people do no such thing and are quite content for our 'loves' to make everybody else rich. Maybach appropriation music for our music to be controlled by White record labels. There is no such thing as a Black owned nationwide restaurant even though we are told every day that 'soul food' is a 'real' thing. We buy gas every day for the cars we love from Asian immigrants who seem magically to own all of the gas stations and convenience stores in our communities. The lesson here is, my beloved brothers and sisters, God has dispensed opportunities, even equal opportunities to every people; what he has not dispensed so equally across humanity is priorities, and the consciousness of 'priorities'. The opportunities are the same, even considering 'history', but the 'priorities' are different, and that shapes outcomes. It is thus possible for a person or people to be deficient in their number, quality and intensity of priorities, and it negatively shapes what they will be in the future the same way an individual's priorities in his or her youth, shape his or her later competencies and opportunities as an adult. What Lebron James was doing between the ages of 6 to 8 (presumably) to 15, the competency he developed focusing on those athletic priorities enabled and ennobled his 'game' and his near immediate ascension to and dominance in, the NBA.

Saints of God and Niggerdom, am I wrong to argue Rick Ross (and by extension all of us) sense of priorities leave much be desired as Black people? Am I wrong to argue that 15,000 of us, with money to spend, might spend our time and money better than making the liquor stores and gas stations (mostly Asian owned) along Old National Highway rich, and the fast-food joints rich, in the name of our appreciation for cars? Beloved, what would it look like if we appreciated each other as much as we appreciated the cars, that we spend thousands on accessorizing, and that some desperate ignorant ass niggas are willing to jack you for at the gas station or a streetlight? I know people personally that baby and infantilize their cars, more than they do their children. How many of us ever called our car 'baby', most especially when it is breaking down or about to break down, as in 'come on baby'! Back in South Carolina, I knew a dude that washed his car more than he washed himself because the car was so symbolic of his self-esteem and desire for the esteem of others who admire his shiny car with the chrome rims. How many of us have named our cars? Ladies and gentlemen of Negritude, there is nothing wrong with any of that. What is wrong is not having a mature, responsible attitude towards your cars, such that at every level of ownership, repair and accessorizing, we make other people rich!

18 Idiocy Made Flesh pt. II: The Migos trip to the White House

I've never listened to the Migos. That's how far removed I am from contemporary Black popular music and culture. Other than the 'bad and bougie' reference and song, I would not know a song was by them. That is, unless in the song they repeat their names and the name of the band frequently. So clearly the critique I'm about to make is not based on anything personal. I haven't been on the forefront of hip-hop listening, (or thought I was or attempted to be) since the 90's. So clearly the critique I'm about to make is not a musical assessment or an assessment of their music's value or perceived value.

The critique I'm about to make is based solely on their visit to the White House to hang out with 'Killa Kam' Harris and put their names on some anti-Negro violence legislation in the works, sponsored by the Biden Administration. As the old phrase goes, 'niggas clean up good, don't they'. Dressed to the nines, dreads oiled, moisturized, and styled, they got a chance to go to the 'big house'. I saw some of the pictures of the event on television. All my readers know my angle in advance. This is a sign and symbol of **everything**, and I mean **everything** wrong with how we of Niggerdom look at ourselves at an existential level, and perhaps more relevant, how we look at our problems and their solutions.

We have no other option than to know that the remaining Migos must be sincere in their anti-violence campaign. Their visit to the White House was prompted and precipitated by their sense of loss when their brother was murdered in Texas. Thus, we cannot question their sincerity or the deep heartfelt emotions which are motivating their desire to stop violence in the Black community. Motivated by such strong personal sentiments, instead of talking to and addressing their remarks and feelings to the proponents of Drill Music, gangster rap, gun rap for the niggas who them 'match sticks'. Instead of addressing their concerns with their fellow rappers who rap for the traps where drugs and prostitutes are sold, rap for the playas, the pimps, the hoes, the hustlers, the dope boy fresh niggas, true-e-fied niggas, pill poppers, dope smokers, lean drinkers, ballers, street shot callers, bottle poppers, lean drinkers, the Migo's went to the White House to talk to 'Killa Kam' Harris and 'Sleepy/sloppy Joe Biden'.

The Migos did not tell the streets about the mechanisms, reasons, and ways to be about other subjects than hip-hop's current violent, sexual, and drug endorsing content, and not encourage violence. The Migos went to the White House, presumably to get 'Killa Kam' Harris and 'Sleepy/sloppy Joe Biden' to direct government money and resources to the problem of Black youth violence and violence in the Black community in general. Presumably, instead of talking to and holding their friends accountable, the Migos went to the White House and tried to make the White mainstream and the White mainstream government accountable for decreasing crime and violence in the Black community. The Migos went to master and his favorite nigga wench to get master to help us get enough self-esteem not to slaughter each other in the streets of major urban centers all across America every day. I presume the Migos did it because if 'massa' doesn't help with our problem(s), our problems will never get fixed. Do our problems necessitate White mainstream or government intervention, or are they not in the main something we can handle ourselves with a little accountability, elbow grease, investment instead of conspicuous consumption, and sincerity. That is a fundamental question, and Black liberals, social elites and social justice lawyers answer it wrong everyday by their actions in trying to hold White people and the government accountable for what we ourselves should be doing. We got the dreads, the talk, and the walk, like we are revolutionary, Afrocentric, and don't give a damn about White mainstream or European culture and approval, and then walk right out and beg White mainstream culture to fix us every day. We don't even bother to ask them to help us fix us, we ask them to fix us. Brothers and sisters that is insane, to ask, nay even demand that your former slave master and oppressor fix you, because you are so criminally unbearable to yourselves in your own communities, with the Black on Black self-inflicted violence and chaos going on. "So weez nigguz is got to go to the 'big house' to see master and his favorite nigga wench and may even master himself, 'Killa Kam' Harris and 'Sleepy/sloppy Joe Biden' to get our problems back in the slave quarters (ghetto) solved. But it is all a photo op for 'Killa Kam' Harris and 'Sleepy/sloppy Joe Biden' and the Black and White socialist-atheist-LGBTQIA Democrat political and cultural elites, to have photographic evidence that they give a shit about problems in the Black community. They don't give a shit but don't say shit about the impacts of broken fatherless homes because that would impact their LGBTQIA agendas. And there the Migos are, sitting with them on the big house lawn listening to hip-hop in proof that the White House is sensitive and inclusive, and concerned about nigga problems back on the plantation ghettos in the slave quarters.

If this is painful to read, it was even more painful to watch as 'Killa Kam' Harris sat with the Migos on one of the White House porches, verandas and lawns bobbing her head to the throbbing hip-hop music in the atmosphere. It was as awkward looking as the entire occasion. Bobbing one's head to music is theoretically a sign of satisfaction, en-joyment, and appreciation. Technically, when one is really grooving to something, one does not even notice one is doing it. It feels natural and rhythmic, and this is why more often than not we find ourselves doing it subconsciously when we like a song or groove. Poor 'Killa Kam' Harris, despite her hip-hop sounding name, the fact that she graduated from Howard, and the fact that she was in the AKA sorority, looked like she was awkwardly calculating every single head nod or bob. I wouldn't be surprised if to her it was like physics trying to figure out not just the pop and snap, the rattle and hum of the beat, but where the groove lay, which is what you are grooving to when you enjoy a song. What's all the more logical and biologically reactionary is that if one is really enjoying a song, one closes one's eyes and really grooves to it with the head nods and bobs. Duke Ellington will show something of the process, if you have not seen video of one of his concerts where he shows White people in Europe, who innocently but habitually clap on the 1 and 3 of the beat or rhythm, to clap on the 2 and 4. It was good 'Killa Kam' Harris mostly stuck to head bobbing and nodding, clapping and the snapping the fingers because when she got up to dance, the spectacle of her dancing liabilities were painfully evident.

This reminds me of an industrial techno concert I went to with my White friends from work a few years back. During the concert, one of them leaned over in my ear (as that's the only way to be heard in such circumstances) and said, 'wow man, you're the first Black person I've ever met that didn't seem to know how to dance'. I was flattered, and did not mention, that while not the best dancer, I know how to dance loosely in the style that most Negroes of my age group tend to dance. Thus the issue was not that I couldn't dance. The issue was that having hung around different types of White people as long as I have, I dance more or less like White people when I am at the performance of White music that I enjoy. From the Grateful Dead/Jam band type shows, to industrial techno and metal, White people dance differently (in a sense). Shit I don't mind doing a polka dance during Oktoberfest. What my White friend was telling me as something that could be perceived as a micro-insult, was that I did not look out of place. What would have looked out of place would be if I was at the Oktoberfest polka concert, the industrial-techno concert, the bluegrass concert, the alt-rock European and British bands concert, or the heavy metal show doing 'the polo', the 'electric slide', 'walkin' it out, the 'stanky leg', the 'nae-nae', the 'tootsie roll', 'da dip', 'the Dougie', 'the humpty dance', the 'crank that', 'the wobble', and 'the cha-cha slide'.

And so let us close on 'Killa Kam Harris'. Every Black person with friends of other races knows that there is no substitute for earnestness, sincerity and putting the time in when it comes to dancing in social settings (which I don't do); all of which 'Killa Kam' lacks instinctively. We can tell when we are being imitated out of love, sincerity, earnestness, and the person having spent quality time experiencing and trying the dance art forms. We can also tell when we are being imitated in a patronizing way, or in a way where White people will allow themselves to be laughed at trying to fit in, but we know they will go back to other

Whites and their communities, and crack jokes with their fellow White folk about the menu and dances at nigger picnics and social gatherings, and how we dance at office parties. Without that earnestness and sincere love, they think of it as one of the prices of going slumming. That is to say not being able to 'dance' according to Black people, and as they do in the slums. Those are the feelings I got watching 'Killa Kam' Harris try to bob her head to the hip-hop and dance in a stereotypical and yet age appropriate and dignified in front of White people way. It was horrifying.

As I close, 'Killa Kam' Harris's dance was worse than the White girl from the Midwest at a Black party dancing awkwardly, hesitantly, spasmodically, like she could get hurt; emotionally, physically, and sexually if she doesn't watch out. That is where that jerky look and sensation in White girl dancing is coming from, like Elaine from Seinfeld. The White sister is scared and distracted by the strobe lights. It is the product of overthinking, like the difference between knowing where you are, and thinking that you know where you are, is better than actually knowing where you are; which is just variations on the theme of being lost. You're never lost at home. If you're at home, dance like it. Keep in mind all this came from a person that can't dance, and if I were pressed, around Black to dance, I'd probably dance worse than Kamala Harris out of nerves and fear.

Four

Kind of Blue

19 They told us Sexual Freedom would make our sex lives and relationships better

Love is not freer now than ever in human history, but it is just as cheap and demeaning as ever in human history on a group/mass scale. Presently, in the American government and nearly all the mainline Christian denominations, you can have 'legal' sex with men, women, in a group or serially. Theoretically this would double the propagation of children and religious children, but in fact, as liberal as it is, with no rules barring entry, organized religion and religious individuals is weaker than it has ever been in America. Monogamy is weaker than it has ever been when once it was assumed to be the rule and the standard, not the exception individuals. Porn is available 24 hours a day on the internet (which at least theoretically should encourage us to be sexier and more sexual). Apps on our phones can identify people of the 'algorithmically chosen' correct sex, height, weight range, hair color etc., who want to fuck and are willing to 'hook up'. All this love and encouragement of love and technological supposed easement of and facilitating and encouraging of physical love, but marriage and birth rates are falling. While the sexual freedom movements are at a fevered pitch and fill the airwaves of regular and social media, the AJC announced in a recent June 2023 paper that the birth rate went down during the pandemic, but has not returned to pre-pandemic levels. Just like companies realized that there was only 'so much' benefit in teleworking and conferencing, at a point it becomes less effective. People got used to it however because there is a level of laziness involved, and marketing will tell you it is not that hard to convince people they could be, and deserve to be doing less and working less hard. I know people with part-time jobs who claim they need a month-long vacation every year and some sort of recreational activity. Half your fucking life is a recreational activity, and you think you need an additional one because 3-day cruises are on 'sail' (bad um dump cymbal crash) for $169.00 plus tax. Part time job or not, just put it on your credit card. You deserve it. Half the Black Americans 'cruising' to Vegas, to Jamaica, The Virgin Islands, etc., on pre-paid packages, have been convinced that they deserve a vacation instead of investing that money in a relevant business model or idea, even if it is basic enough to buy back some of these convenience stores in Black communities that are owned by foreigners that don't reinvest in the Urban communities. But I digress. I suspect that the reason birthrates are down is because during the pandemic, a lot of people got used to self-satisfying themselves using porn as opposed to actively dating, by cruising bars and engaging in proximity and promiscuity based social behavior. In theory this might make people more gung-ho about going back out as the pandemic has lifted but apparently according to the AJC the opposite has happened, and birthrates are lower.

But wait a minute, all this free and cheap sex and its encouragement in America and birthrates are down? Is that not counterintuitive? Ain't we so free and sexy in America, it's on every corner, every hip tv show? If that were not bad enough, today with all this free and cheap sex, more people self-report being lonely and relatively unfulfilled in their 'personal' relationships and friendships and their sense of security, stability, unconditional love, permanence, and trust have fallen by the wayside. All this freedom has engendered a world where friendships, families, spouses and even children are disposable if they are not a part of our 'truth' and the 'truth' we want to lead at that time. Bruce Jenner relinquished his entire 'career' as an athlete, entertainer and father, his very identity to his children for all their lives, because he woke up one morning and decided living as a man wasn't 'his truth', and he needed to live his truth at absolutely any expense. The implications of this disposable sexual culture are startling in their variety and power. Aborting children at will, based solely on the 'truth' of the mother, when at least for voluntary sex, it is very hard to find women in America who do not know how babies are made, and are confused as to the consequences of ovulation, penetration, copulation, and ejaculation. But her 'truth' triumphs over all. I support legal abortion because I do not want to send women back to root doctors and back-alley clinicians and surgeons, and YouTube videos that show how to give yourself an abortion with a water hose, handheld vacuum cleaner, duct tape and a strong stomach. At the least however, a culture that respected life should find abortion discouraging. Honestly, if the abortion rate were lower it might be probably that our birth rates balances out by statistical error, but inasmuch as we in America are so wed to the concept and practice of abortion, making it easier and easier pharmaceutically, there will always be women in America choosing abortion like it is a flavor or recipe to be done, simply because you have the right to, just another option in life like Publix sells Tabbouleh at the Deli next to the pharmacy. Not coincidentally in the arsenal of women's public health they sell Fried Chicken, hot wings & flats style chicken and Rotisserie Chicken and wait for it...wait for it...subs! And guess what, in addition to all of that, Publix pharmacy sells abortion pills, day after, week after, month after, abortion pills, plan B,C, E, F, G and H. A regular ole health care and chicken one stop shop, which one will I get today...oh, yes, I'll suck the life out of my uterus because I went beyond the time to buy the plan B-H pill, the appetizer. We might even argue that in urban areas, the chicken is a very popular and thriving menu item. Lawd, we are throwing away babies, we just don't do it like the Romans, and toss them into the local ravine/trash heap. Yep, we're much more humane. We go in utero and insert the equivalent of a vacuum cleaner. This we are told is more humane to a woman than the idea of society having 'forced her' to have a baby and she and the father have to take the time to sell it or throw it off a cliff into the ravine. The tradeoff for women, is letting men and doctors in general 'play around' in your vagina and uterus with surgical equipment and devices and sucking out the living example of your DNA and creative capacity because you want to go to college, or keep your job or not ruin your boyfriend by saddling him with a baby or any other idiotic idea, and you have a right to do so, and ladies you do. But how long will we force the miraculous (the creation of a life) to submit to the mundane, (a desire to go to school, establish a career) and the very idea that these things would be that important to a woman, because they are important to men is ridiculous. I am not sure women have figured out that Women's Lib, is not and cannot be found in imitating men; men's pursuits, habits, apparent likes, and dislikes etc.,. There is no freedom in imitation and there never will be. It is merely an illusion and shadow like when you stand at the shoreline, wade into the beach and tell yourself you are in the ocean. In a sense you are indeed, up to your knees and thighs in the Atlantic, the Gulf or the Indian, but the part you see and stand in is only a tiny, tiny, fraction the entirety of the thing.

Ladies and gentlemen, all of this freedom is not making us happy. To piggyback off the previous statement, a young woman gets an abortion at 24 in graduate school, gets her MBA and rises to be VP of Operations, did that automatically make her happier than if she would have had a baby at 24? Granted, it may have, but the question still needs be asked. But guess what, we have proof that in many cases all of that academic and professional successes did not make her happy because when her biological clock starts ticking at 40 and she looks around in disappointment seeing women she went to school with that had kids and took regular or local jobs for the benefit of their families, and they at least on the surface seem happy. They have a man, they have kids who love them...and she has a career and MBA and PHD in Management Philosophy. She oftentimes can carry this in her heart, and no one would ever know it. Yet we see oftentimes older women in this position go to extraordinary lengths to procure babies. They try in vitro, out vitro, Italian dudes named Vito, they try this, they try that, they investigate surrogacy, they investigate adoption, they resort to 'Brat and Judy' techniques. In essence that is proof of how unhappy they are, and how unhappy their lifestyle choices have made them. The Brat and Judy have gone to extraordinary lengths to procure a child...and yet they learned probably no later than the age of 14 how babies were made....and they ignored it acting like they can reinvent nature and biological clocks just because they want to. Perhaps they have had some bad experiences with men early on, that negatively shaped their desires, or they wanted to go to school or experience corporate success, so they delayed pregnancy. And now that they are old and have ignored human and mammal nature for a significant part of their lives, they make all kinds of ridiculous attempts to overcompensate and have a baby. Having a baby is the womanliest thing a girl or woman can do physically, besides have sex with a man. What da Brat and Judy could have both easily done at 24 with a man, they now attempt to do at 48 requiring being pumped full of hormones and other therapies to increase fertility and fertilized with invitro fertilization. To add a kind of insult to injury to 'womanliest' women, Da Brat and Judy then go on a national media celebration tour, and ask to be celebrated and feted for being a 'couple' in their position, and sacrificing all sorts of money, time, research; working so hard to have a baby as a gay couple at 48, when if they really loved children that much, they would have not only done it sooner, but done it the old fashioned way with a man, which of course by default is much more reliable even if it does come with certain liabilities. Consciously or not, we are sending the socialist atheist, LGBTQIA message to our girls that when you live your life as such, you are a liberated woman, and this is what liberated women do...that is to say have babies when and where they want too, for the reasons they want to, that for freedom from patriarchy's sake don't have anything to do with the opinion of a man or his male God. The problem is that same attitude causes them to delay pregnancy until by lifestyle sexual choice, and the vagaries of the post-30's race towards decreasing fertility and menopause, or some notion of professional or academic success, they end up delaying a 'normal' sexual relationship with a man, and waiting until they are physically the least naturally capable of being fertile and having a child without medical, surgical, and technological intervention. This is what materialist socialist LGBTQIA atheism does to birth rates ladies and gentlemen, it attacks the traditional family in all kinds of insidious ways. Lifestyles and freedom, defined as sexual, economic, and otherwise nearly always come at the expense of, and compromise family and children. That is to say freedom, always requires a great sacrifice, even for the socialist atheist materialist LGBTQIA, and what they sacrifice on the altar in the unholy alliance to get their freedom and their truth, is children and families, the traditional bedrock of civilization.

All this sexual freedom is not having the effect of making us any, any happier! They told us it would. Do Da Brat and Judy really look happy. Does Dylan Mulvaney really look happy, Bruce Jenner. Maybe they are quite happy. Maybe you can be as happy as they are on the commercial because they are taking drugs that makes their HIV undetectable. Maybe Jada Pinkett, Will Smith, Jaden and Willow are all extremely happy people. Will Smith did not look like a happy man, on what should have been the happiest of his nights when he stomped on stage and slapped Chris Rock. They promised us all this freedom to live our truths would make us happy. They told us biblical values regarding sex were prudish, old fashioned and holding us back (that is to say repressing us), and that after allowing socialists, social theorists and Marxist atheists to tear the old-fashioned values down it would usher in a new age of freedom, fun, frivolity, and more fulfilling sexual relationships. It has not and as a matter of fact it has done just the opposite. We should not wonder why every damn body, and every time we turn around, everyone has some mental issue. We have mental health issues because the traditional ways we (humanity) ground ourselves (that is to say made ourselves sane and responsible), mating and family, are ignored in favor of absolute freedom. It is one thing for 'Paternity Court' and DNA to be a tool, but it is quite another matter for post-modernity to literally be dependent on court mandated DNA tests, because so many people are having such wild and wooly sex. And what is altogether worse, the sex is so devoid of value and feeling, mutual respect and attraction, that when told they are the father, the father's don't want it to be true and when the mother is told by DNA which of her 'suitors' was the father, not only is she disappointed, but she has spent the past hour and half at court telling her baby's father secrets and how he and his family that he ain't shit. To her they ain't shit or else they would have been more supportive...and then wanting them to be more supportive in the future just because of a muthafuckin DNA test. Everybody knows full well all they'll get is the bare minimum unless the kid is like Jephthah, Michael Jackson, or Lebron James. Then every potential daddy will want a DNA test so they can get some that money for nothing like reparations for what you did in a completely different life with completely different intentions.

II

Have we not created a nation of sugar daddies and whores? Ladies and gentlemen, 'Quid pro quo' and 'log rolling', politically is just as much a symbol of a dysfunctional in a polity as 'quid pro quo' and log-rolling are a symbol of dysfunction in a marriage or family, if quid pro quo and log rolling are the ONLY ways they can get anything done collectively. They are not signs of political health or sexual/marital health. The marital and family phenomena of log rolling, and quid pro quo seem to me to be what the Black family, such that it exists has degenerated into. Certainly, if we take post-modern hip-hop and R&B as an example this is the case. Even anecdotal evidence seems to amplify these trends. Long before Erykah Badu told her man he better call Tyrone, the quid pro quo was real. Most of my single male friends, unmarried over 40, father or not, engage women with quid pro quo assumptions, though it would be wrong to call these women prostitutes. A few of them find it easier to simply hire prostitutes. It is cheaper than trying to woo a woman with limited resources (no matter how much you loved the woman).

Perhaps the first level of it, is that while the women aren't selling anything or advertising anything, if an interested buyer comes along, there is nothing wrong with him making an offer, preferably a tacit one, full of assumptions and implications. For it is tacit assumptions that are the easiest to deny in a court of law or anywhere else. I need help with my rent, car note, phone bill, childcare, etc., in exchange, the nigger might get something that resembles sex on demand and sex as demanded, which I must implore you all, is completely different from sex as an expression of love and the mutuality of the experience. But of course, absent authentic relationships many men and women are forced into these kinds of temporary tacit, sexual log rolling arrangements, which to our souls are as unfulfilling as giving a man dying of thirst 3 swallows of water. Survival vs. starvation.

In other ways these temporary quid pro quo arrangements are not only unfulfilling, but they are dangerous. Half the domestic violence that happens today, one side fell in love and had assumptions (often tacit and implicit at first) about the relationship the other didn't have. Feelings of public embarrassment and humiliation grow stronger as the breakup first looms and then ensues. Arguments and harassing phone calls are followed by stalking. There is a sense of humiliation when one side put more into a 'Quid Pro Quo' than the other, and then an even higher bidder comes along to our beloved, or the idea of 'freedom' gets presented to our beloved as a 'value in itself', and the spurned lover reacts emotionally, viscerally, with volatility, and yes more and more often violently. That is why domestic calls are the most dangerous for a cop, the EMTs and the Fire Department. Two calls come in at the same time, one is an armed bank robbery in progress carried out by a notorious gang, the other is somebody baby daddy nutting up because his bitch got some other nigger living with her, giving his baby mama and his two-year-old daughter baths, and putting them both to bed. That will drive a sane nigga crazy and a crazy nigga very sane! Every woman that read the previous line is thinking to herself, 'he just better deal with her new boyfriend, for that's her new truth'. Nearly every man is thinking to himself, so deeply he gets religious like his grandma, that 'the devil is a lie, ain't no way in hell I'm letting some nigga she just met, two months ago, give my female little daughter a bath'! But of course there is nothing he can do about it because your baby mama will call the police on you, not her new boyfriend when you show up unannounced. What type of not doing one's due diligence led to this volatile misrepresentation of what the baby daddy and the woman thought they were getting in the relationship for? Perhaps then, the 'devil is a lie' and not coincidentally, so is this post-modern rationalistic liberal legal fantasy we live in that people going in different directions can 'co-parent', and 'share custody'. How can this be when the father's new wife is dressing her step-son up like a girl D-Wade? I can't tell you much about the psychology of it, even though I try from a religious perspective, but one reason low-income families can't participate in transgenderism is because they can't afford it. What Black mother in the projects can afford to get her son $550 worth of hormone therapy a month and dress him up like Zaza Wayde. Add to that taking him to the celebrity spas Gabrielle goes to and afford to even let him pretend like he is a 'real life' fashion model for a day? Can it really be a spiritual or emotional experience, when over half of it is conditioned by whether you can afford it? If you can't afford it, it's just easier to stay your original sex? Can it be a compulsion or 'how God made you', if whether or not it manifests itself is highly dependent on whether or not you or your parents can afford it? Hmmn.

But back to crazy stalking 'buck wild angry baby daddy's' and stalking crazy angry bitch baby mamas. After being introduced to wild female Orca pods gone wild destroying yachts, other than a mother bear or lioness defending their cubs, White Gladis, Big Mama, and Glorilla Orca can only be compared to a crazy ass baby mama, stalking her once beloved, now victim, and upon finding him, selectively undermining him. Oh yes, she knows how important your job is to you 'emotionally' and your professional aspirations. Yep. So, she called up HR and your boss repeatedly seeing if you were at work crying telling the same peers you ask to respect your professionalism, that she was calling behind you like this because you haven't been home in 2 weeks and you won't talk to her. Your boss's response to that may be concerned and caring, but he may have doubts whether you are the man to put at the head of the new division and give a 12-million-dollar budget. Your boss might be inclined to think you have too many distractions at home to get a promotion of that magnitude. Yep, White Gladis and the other Orca selectively disabled the hull and/or the rudder. Apparently they knew exactly where to hit and what buttons to push just like your baby mama.

Therein lies the unique effectiveness of a 'crazy baby mama' or daddy. Even policemen would rather take on an armed bank robbery in progress than go on a baby mama/baby daddy drama situation where one of the participants is armed. And let's be quite frank, unfortunately that baby mama, baby daddy shit can end kinda well and everybody just goes home or separates. But then 2 hours later it pops back off. I did that, you know. I got drunk and went to my baby mama house raising hell (without weapons of course and her and her new man refused to open the door). The police came and told me to go. For two hours straight, in a foggy haze of anger and resentment, I think I went to every liquor store on Bankhead highway buying 50 cent shots of vodka 4 at a time and smoking blunts like I was Bob Marley's nephew. 4 hours later I had the bright idea to go back and raise some more hell at my baby mama house, here again unarmed, but now rip roaring drunk barely able to stand but quite able to yell public obscenities and threats. The same sheriff that warned me the first time, came out this time as well, but this time I immediately got locked up by Douglas County Sheriff's department. It took religion and another relationship for me to 'after-process' the level of humiliation, anger, and resentment I felt, to the point that I engaged in expensive and self-destructive habits because of my feelings of humiliation and anger. In different circumstances, and absent my religious impulses, my situation might have been as explosive as some the things we see on the 6 o'clock news regarding incidences of domestic violence and subsequent death. It is not infrequent that we hear of domestic situations degenerating into muthafuckas killing their own kids, they baby mama, and her relatives simply to inflict as much pain as possible; set off emotionally and mentally on some straight bullshit.

The bitch/nigga moved on, why the fuck is that so hard to take? Even though we individuals know by default how possible, nay how realistic is the fact we might eventually move on too, when it happens to us, in the immediate aftermath when the pain, anger and resentment is most intense, we inevitably strike a pose like Ru Paul or Madonna voguing, like oh no, I'm a saint, I give and gave my all, my everything, my loyalty, my back, my money, my mind and look what 'so and so' did to me! They sound worse than niggers in 2023 bitching and moaning about what White folk did to us during Jim crow and slavery. Facts are facts, but bitching and moaning about them is a choice, and oftentimes a self-destructive one that leads to a kind of downward spiral of self-pity which is the twin, just prettier and handsomer of low self-esteem.

Is it any wonder then, our quid pro quo/logrolling sexual culture where anything is justified if the participants are willing, and the terms have been agreed to in advance is corresponding with a hyper violent age, much of it domestic. It's funny (well not really), but at this point I would urge any young White woman whose boyfriend says to her, "let's take a trip across the country" (Gabby Petito), to join a convent before she does some shit like that. These chicks are coming up missing every other damn week! And they can't blame it on niggers because they be places like mountains, valleys, gorges, and deserts, places the average nigga don't ne'er go. A nigga is going to kidnap you and take you to the ATM, he ain't going to kidnap you and take you to the Grand Teton National Park to go sight seeing.

The post-modern, sexually free, quid pro quo, AI generated algorithmically exposed relationships are as unfulfilling as the old relationships and way more dangerous to boot. Ask the police. Baby mama, baby daddy drama, or divorced, and the sheriff by judge's order must accompany one or the other party to get their belongings, the very necessities of life, lest all kinds of villainy, treachery and violence potentially ensue. Yeah, post-modernity, that is a wonderful omen and harbinger of the future success of co-parenting, which is like co-driving, an oxymoronic exercise in futility and frustration.

20 African Retentions in Human Sexuality

In my last book, I discuss the Afro-Caribbean take on the sexuality debate and their inherent conservatism as an African retention. But we will take it one step deeper today in exposing the blatant hypocrisy, racism, and trans-mansplaining of Europeans and American White culture. Of course, it is an African retention, and here I dare argue it might be one of the oldest African retentions, nay even so old, it is pre-human, ape, pre-ape and evident in the earliest mammal life on land and sea. That is how old male/female sexual differentiation is, no matter what anybody tells you about sex as simply a cultural choice. Though the fact I must argue this at all is disheartening, we have no other real scientific option but to argue that sex differentiation is a mammal retention, and humanoid African retention. If we make any kinds of arguments at all as to the survival of humanity, we must assume and presume that there are yes, uniquely African humanoid, ape and mammalian retentions upon which the whole exercise (humanity) is predicated. As an example, let us take the instances of rhythm and drumming in every human culture from the most advanced to the most 'primitive' and in nearly every epoch and form of human history and civilization for varying forms of ceremonial purposes as a 'retention'. Every race, every branch of the human racial and geographic families has used drums and drumming in its cultural heritage and legacy.

Other African retentions can be placed squarely in the realm of living DNA and the common characteristics we share as humans. Certainly it is these retentions that unify us, though the texture of human hair, the color of human skin may change, all of these and whatever other racial changes human evolution may have required may change, but ALL of the changes are based upon the old retentions (mammalian, African, emotional, spiritual, rhythmic,), not new outer space or alien DNA as supernatural alien interventionist theorists argue is decisive in human evolution. They are looking in the sky for answers when the answers are in our very evolutionary history; even when it comes to wrestling with theological and philosophical issues.

Let me give an example that shows a modern fallacy. I mentioned earlier that an African retention in all human civilizations is rhythm and drumming for entertainment or ceremonial purposes. Now, if rhythm, that is to say, the speed of rhythm, were merely a social construct, a mental abstraction, we might find the distribution of the speeds of average human rhythms would be all over the place. But that is not what we find. Most rhythms, and certainly the ones that are presented as wanting to be understood are at a walking pace. This same 'walking pace', differs only in marginal ways from the pace of our hearts. Faster than a walking pace is a fast++ rhythm, slower than a walking pace is - -slower than a walking pace rhythm. From Native Americans in the Mohave to Carnatic music and rhythms in India. We can speed it up or slow it down but the basis of it all is the walking rhythm. In the African American tradition, Wynton Marsalis describes it as the 'shuffle rhythmic pattern' or the 'shuffle groove'. These rhythmic patterns are not mere coincidences or accidents of patriarchy or social engineering. They are rooted in the biological fact of mammalian and ape evolution, our gait and it's physical properties, and how that determined what humanity thought was the 'normal' speed of a beat. The normal speed of the beat is not a random construct, it is rooted in the physicality of walking and mobility. That one physical fact became the standard of speed, not just for locomotion, but for doing the locomotion too (the dance).

Which brings us into the irony and hypocrisy part. No, it is too hard for present Arab speaking Egyptians to think niggers were responsible for the buildings and pyramids they covet and control in the ancient Egyptian repertoire, so they must 'Arabwash' the whole of Egyptian pre-Arab invasion, Greek, Hyksos, Nubian, etc., history and at best leave the argument that the niggers were there only providing the labor and land and the real civilizational work was done by White or light Semitic type foreigners. Of all the things I've seen Arab people get mad at, including music, I thought the Arab historians and politicians were going apoplectic with anger when our own most famous 'nigger narcissist wench' (not my words) dared make a movie presuming Cleopatra may have been or was 'brown' or perhaps 'blackish'. The Arabs and Egyptians hadn't been that mad (or embarrassed) since the 6 Day War (no disrespect intended as no Black man can joan any other people Black or brown for having had a catastrophically culturally destructive war against White people).

But anyway, recently in the news Kamala, (our other most famous nigga mulatto wench) just got finished lecturing the Japanese on how they need to speed up the process regarding LGBTQIA rights. Fuck the fact the Japanese sell more adult diapers than baby diapers, White folks and their Black liberal representatives are going over there trying to plunge Japanese birthrates even further into a downward death spiral like some kind of kamikaze death wish with their White European and American sexual rhetoric...with friends like that the Japanese don't need enemies. Maybe the North Koreans were wrong all along. They don't need weapons to secure their security and promulgate the North Korean government, they just need to wait until the Japanese birth rate collapses, and they must import poor North Koreans to take care of the aging population. Who knew what 'nuclear power' was, is men and women having babies in 'nuclear families? Then Kamala went to Africa to lecture the Africans on how they need to move forward on LGBTQIA rights. The perhaps unfortunate response of the Africans to Kamala's pestering hypocrisy and harassment I am sure was the exact opposite of White liberals' intent. Some of the African nations responded by making the 'crime' of 'homosexuality' punishable by death. I won't get into whether or not that is or was 'overkill' (for lack of a better phrase) but I see no blame but on Kamala and her tone deaf pronouncements. The decision of the African nations in question was clearly 'in response' to European and American self-righteous lecturing and pestering. We know this because the African countries had never had a reason before in pre-colonial and post-colonial Africa to get on public TV and the media outlawing homosexuality, to the point of death, in order to make a point to the world about their cultural in-dependence, even if their economic and political independence in the international geo-political world is problematic! I am quite sure nearly every African would have wished that in the 15th century when Euro-peans were debating whether or not Africans were human beings, and thus perhaps not deserving of enslavement, White folks were debating what a man and a woman were. It is written Wikipedia style that:

When the 'Age of Discovery' greatly increased the number of slaves owned by Christians, the response of the clergy, under strong political pressures, was ineffective in preventing the establishment of slave-owning societies in the colonies of Catholic countries. Earlier Papal bulls, such as Pope Nicholas V, Dum diversas (1452) and Romanus Pontifex (1454) were used to justify the enslavement of natives and the appropriation of their lands during this era.

The depopulation of the Americas, and consequently the shortage of slaves, brought about by diseases brought over by the Europeans, as well as slaughter of the native populations, inspired increasing debate during the 16th Century over the morality of slavery. One of the early shipments of Black Africans during the transatlantic slave trade was initiated at the request of Bishop La Casas and authorized by Charles V, Holy Roman Empire in 1517. However, Las Casas later rejected all forms of unjust slavery and became famous as the great protector of Indian rights.

Who knew! It turns out White folk should have been debating during that important historical era and time in the world, and indeed it would have made the world safer. The world would be much safer today if Europeans during that part of their pre-Colonial history, spent all that time and energy debating what a man and woman were/are instead of whether or not Africans and Indians were human beings. White people would have thus been completely unbothered by Natives, their lands or their religions and would have spent their time turning Europe into the gay socialist atheist transgender paradise it is today. No pun intended. Too little too late Kamala. You and your White masters in Europe and America are 600 years too late Kamala. That is too late for niggas to be impressed by a mulatto 'nigga princesses' telling them things about White modernity, and how to live 'up to' White modernity, and White modern sexual ideas, when what Africans at home and the Diaspora need is a 'princess of the niggas' inspiring them with hope about what post-modern nigga modernity and Niggerdom can look like. And retaining as many African retentions as possible, that have to do with the dawn of humanoid men, women and children from the wombs of apes and mammals, and the dawn of African Civilizations, which are the original Civilizations. We descendants of Africa should thus be expected to retain Civilizational retentions, the earliest retentions, the most consistent retentions, the most ancient retentions, the most enduring retentions…about precisely what it means to be human. Sometimes I wonder if our disunity as Africans and Africans in the diaspora is an African, humanoid and mammalian retention as there is a push for diversity, disagreement, roaming, expansion, and self-will that acts as hinge on any 'Tower of Babel' type scenario.

I wonder how humiliating it must have been for African leaders to sit through an incoherent Kamala tongue lashing. She needed the damn tongue lashing. Let us state the facts clearly. When Whites first encountered Blacks for the purposes of colonization and slavery, not only were Whites in unity about the difference between men and women, but it was ingrained in their church Judeo-Christian philosophy, the same philosophy they ultimately used to enslave millions of heathen and colonize their lands. Back then White people knew damn well what a man and a woman were, but now they don't? For damn 1000 years the European world has called Africa backwards, heathens, etc., and used such notions to justify African enslavement and underdevelopment. They told us we were backwards, had no culture, no religion worth valuing compared to Whites and other races. And now, because White people have magically come to the conclusion in 2023, that one of the facts, yes facts, upon which human, ape and mammal history and evolution is based, maleness and femaleness, as God's bio-engineering, is no longer of use to White folks and damn if they aren't going to proselytize the whole world telling everybody what the fuck they should believe even though White people didn't believe the same shit they preaching 45-65 years ago? Who made White folks the arbiters and interpreters of 'facts'? Is that why all of a sudden Ancient Aliens' type shows and pseudo-intellectuals are en vogue when White people just 45 years ago would have been horrified and ashamed if anyone thought they not only believed in aliens, but believed that Aliens are the real creative force behind human beings, culture and civilization. Just because you can build nuclear bombs and AI, and fly to the moon does not mean your problems knowing what a man and woman are, aren't worse than your great scientific knowledge...to the point that one without the other becomes meaningless. That is to say, technology without common sense, ain't helpful. Our kids are 'writing' ChatGPT influenced papers and adults are doing ChatGPT resumes, each and the other thinking their perfidy is not only smart for them to do and timesaving, but actually good for the society if they get a job they don't have enough sense to write a meaningful resume for, to show their desire and fitness for the job? Get the Fuck outa here.

To add insult to injury, they (America) sent some mulatto nigga wench down there to lecture the Africans! And here my message to Kamala is the same as my message to Meghan. It would have been better for you to be 'princess of the niggers' and lecture Africans, than it is for you to be a 'nigger princess' elevated by White mainstream cultural trends and lecture Africans on what your White mainstream handlers have taught you to believe and say. Kamala and this current generation of Black elected officials know damn well that if they had the same political positions on LGBTQIA Socialist atheist issues that they do today in the past when they began their career, they would have never gotten elected or gotten Black support, but now all of a sudden that agenda is their bread and butter? That is ridiculous, absolutely ridiculous, and I'm humiliated and embarrassed on behalf of all Negritude.

No wonder White folks are now exporting socialist-atheist-LGBTQIA values in the world. Remember when White folks were all gung-ho about spreading democracy in the world. Yep, we were going to export it to Iraq, Syria, Afghanistan, Libya, et al...how has that 'worked out so far'? What is altogether worse is that since American and European attempts to export democracy all over the world, the American experiment in democracy has proven it is no perfect model.

How can present day American Democracy be a perfect model and Jan 6th happened? And do not let the Fox and far right spin machines fool you, an exercise in democracy and an exercise in chaos aren't the same things whether ANTIFA and BLM are doing it, or not. How can it be a perfect model and Washington is so polarized they can't agree on basic things (agree to stay in existence in a budgetary sense). The public should not be surprised. Once you disagree on basic things like what and man and a woman are, I find it hard to believe you can agree on anything else, participatory democracy notwithstanding. Furthermore, niggers still complain about racism like the shit is worse today than it was 50 years ago in terms of our perceptions of police shootings (all to reminiscent for us of lynching). In what was supposed to be the greatest democracy on earth, women get on TV every day and complain how hard it is to be a woman even though comparatively speaking, I can't think of another culture in which women enjoy such rights and opportunities. Why is everybody complaining, and why is everybody in full complaining mode all the time in America, even though we are telling the world this is the democratic haven and where women, gays and minorities are freest...but all the women, gays and minorities are complaining everyday like shit here in America is just the worst fucking thing ever, and they may as well be living in the Sudan. Wrong. You cannot equate the gay experience in America to what it would be like to be out and gay in the Sudan? There is no comparison, and yet the gay person in Sudan isn't complaining (for obvious reasons) and the one in America is?

Anyway, because of all that, democracy is now problematic to export. So America has decided to export the LGBTQIA lifestyle and stick their nigger wenches and warlocks out there to promote it on their behalf with the minorities at home and abroad. This proves in essence that White people didn't need to enslave us to make us do stupid ass unproductive shit, all they had to do was 'pay us' and invent luxury items. The invention of TV, Movies, diverse entertainments, social media and other technological goods and trinkets, and we niggers will do anything, like the Native Americans that sold Manhattan for a couple barrels of whiskey, and 6 guns (because Jah Morant likes the sound and what they look like in your hand). Three of guns sold to the Native Americans in the Manhattan region didn't work and were minus ammunition, and yes, you guessed it, the Europeans had some beautiful handmade blankets. The Native Americans in North and South America had a hard time adjusting to the White man's diseases. The descendent of Africa apparently proved somewhat hardier, even though of course Europeans post-bubonic plague et. al, brought some 'hellafied' diseases across the world with them to rural places in Africa, Asia, and the Americas with a bacteriological, ecological, and biological imprint tens, of hundreds and even hundreds of thousands of years old. But we niggers are happy to run that football, shoot that basketball every night on TV as the rich White men in the audience howl and roar with the same delights as if they were at the Kentucky Derby or the Preakness, cheering on their favorite horse or the horse they bet on. They bet more on the horses and nigger athletes than the yearly incomes of the families of the nigger boys on the basketball courts. And then even the highly paid athletes in America complain that they aren't getting enough. Shutting up and playing is too much to ask, they want to be respected like politicians, public intellectuals, and historians (Kyrie). You get more than any other nigger in the world, for far less (let us be frank if we consider the woman in sub-Saharan Africa walking a half mile to the well every day, cooking, doing subsistence agriculture, and watching children). Or compared to the person that makes subsistence wages, but Kyrie tells us he is suffering under the White capitalist system? Huh? There are boys in Africa, the Caribbean and central and southern America that can't afford school or three meals a day, and Kanye and Kyrie are complaining about White people and Jews (to whom it would not be an understatement to say they owe their whole careers and lifestyles to).

How can we in America export this new democracy, presently construed post January 6th. White men are complaining and tearing up shit about how unhappy their are. LGBTQIA complaining things haven't gone far enough, feminists complaining things haven't gone far enough, niggers complaining things haven't gone far enough, the labor unions/socialists/atheists/materialists complaining their rights are being trampled by corporations, lobbying and 'right to work'/pro-capitalist public policies, and the only thing they all have in common is that they feel they are suffering under the weight of the American Democratic government in Washington and that something is fundamentally flawed and wrong with it. Thus, the swamp must be drained, the bums must be tossed out, etc., ad infinitum. In such a state of damn near complete political polarization and dysfunction, it is to the point that very few Americans even recognize that this is the greatest nation in the world. Thus, for the U.S. government's current international public policy and political strategy, of course it is easier to promote Democracy and the dominance of western values in the form of the socialist atheist LGBTQIA agenda. It is easier to act confused about what a man and woman are, than it is to justify January 6th, Antifa, BLM, radical LGBTQIA democracy and culture in its present state to the world, which is largely far more traditional in its sexual values and mores. It's too complex to export democracy and reveal our hypocrisy. Democracy, get your version today! Except the American version has an 83-year-old dotard president who can't remember all his grandchildren, or even worse has decided to selectively forget one or two, and the other presidential option in 2024 is Donald 'grab em by the pussy' Trump. Are we telling the world Georges Santos is the rightful product of 247 years of post-1776 Democracy? These are America's choices going into 2024. How can we tell the world with a straight face, democracy as a system, automatically produces the best candidates and the most stable system. The very examples of choices in the next United States election in 2024 prove that democracy in itself, is not a guarantee that the best people for the job are chosen, intellectually, emotionally or temperamentally. Social media and foreign bot manipulation between the election period of 2012-2020, manipulated the Brexit vote, manipulated the debate on Black social media encouraging Black people not to vote for Hillary, and to do a protest vote by not voting at all, and manipulated white alt-right social media encouraging division, fringe candidates, extreme candidates and bizarre Q-anon conspiracy theories, all to the detriment of American democracy. The Q-anon style, alt-right, proud boy, etc., trumps the good old fashioned republican conservatism and conservative values like fiscal conservatism, social conservatism, vigorous intellectual conservatism in the style of Buckley, and traditional Americana. It just can't compete with Trump and Trumpism, bluster and hucksterism. Not coincidentally, this is the same reason Asa Hutchinson's campaign is doomed and will not go anywhere. The girls on The View do not take him seriously enough to really attack him, and neither do the other Republicans; proving that in post-modern American politics, not only do nice guys finish last, they will get ignored, mocked and humiliated by the front runners for being nice guys. That's the kind of America we live in, and that's the kind of reality tv show values that dominate American politics. We are not breeding good people and candidates; we are breeding people who would win a reality show tv show contest a la George Santos. George Santos fabricated damn near his whole life and rode it all the way to political victory, and it's still proving hard to get out. Yes, my friends, Whites ain't going around the world hollering about transformative democracy with all this bullshit going on over here in the home of democracy. The Americans, Trump included of course will tell you Washington is a cesspool, a swamp, that needs to be drained. This is how today's politicians' campaign. Biden will tell us MAGA people are the enemy, the destroyer of the true American values he represents.

According to Biden, it is a fight for the soul of Democracy. Vote for him, because if you don't, the very soul of Democracy will be ripped out by Trump and the MAGA forces of evil. Should such things ever be said in a Democracy?

It is easier to promote nebulous liberal Hollywood values in the world like inclusion and free sexuality than it is to promote real democracy. Real democracy is ugly. America found out how ugly it was the hard way. We introduced Democracy into the Muslim world and they rewarded us by voting extremist Islamist parties into power in places like Egypt, Gaza and the West Bank. There are real politique reasons for picking your nigger wench to send to Japan and Africa to holler and fuss at them about LGBTQIA pride and rights. It is far easier than critiquing your allies and foes about their level of democracy. America can't critique folk about human rights, after playing cutesy and cuddling with MBS, fist bumping him, to the point I wouldn't be surprised if he and Anthony Blinken played footsie under the table like little kids. America looks impotent in the clear face of authoritarianism. America has been cuddling China since the Sino-Soviet rift days and China has repaid American love and affection by confronting American planes and ships in international waters, and floating varying forms of surveillance and spy dirigibles, planes and running satellites over American airspace. Is that what friends since the Deng Xiaoping days do, who we exported technology and jobs to, that White America probably would done better investing in the economic productivity of inner cities and rural areas.

After George W Bush claimed he looked into Putin's eyes and saw his soul, and Trump all but pulled Putin's dick out and sucked it at that infamous press conference where American President Trump said with a straight face that 'the man (Putin) told me he wasn't doing anything nefarious or to undermine the American election and I believe him? Putin is a former professional KGB agent; Trump is a former beauty pageant judge and casino operator. Trump believed it was perfectly rationale to have sex with Stormy Daniels without a condom; proving without a doubt and conclusively that you don't need a gun to play 'Russian Roulette'. Then when the issue came up about how wise it was (or wasn't) to have unprotected sex with a porn star, the president of the United States, here again with a straight face, said that he felt safe because 'in that industry' they have to take tests every month. America, how the fuck can we export this shit to the world, no wonder Kamala and Joe have figured it's just easier to invent shit like the LBGTQIA agenda and promote that, than to promote that the international community needs to imitate American democracy and democratic values as presently construed and exemplified. American democracy is unstable and the only thing holding it together is a kind of centrifugal force based on mass and the manipulation of gravitational fields by altering the course of the roller coaster....but it is a roller coaster ride and it will fail eventually because the skills and engineering it takes to keep it going are being lost in a wake of engineers who not only got ChatGPT to write their resumes, but chat GPT wrote their papers in Engineering school too. Half our politicians are just different versions of George Santos and the other half look like Trump. In a 'democracy' like that how the fuck can any good decisions be made? How can we export our version of democracy. Half the American public either believes Trump can declassify materials with the flick of a synapse in his brain, and the other half believes it doesn't matter if he was wiping his ass with classified documents and using them as toilet paper for his guests in the bathroom at Mar-a-Lago, it wouldn't matter (legally or as sign or symbol of good judgement and probity).

So that is probably why there is this sudden switch in American foreign policy as White mainstream America has done where instead of traipsing the world trumpeting the inherent health and value of Democracy, they have taken to distinguishing themselves from the rest of the world by being so advanced, intellectually, biologically and theologically that we no longer know and can easily describe or discern what a man and woman are independently or in comparison. This is White cultural superiority now, acting like you don't know what the fuck a man and a woman are, even though for millennia, the question has been considered more or less obvious and resolved...but apparently not obvious enough for White groomers. And now they send Kamala to Africa to explain to them how backwards and retarded the Africans are, because they don't take on and uphold the new White European and American LGBTQIA version of what a man and a woman are, in a kind of new intellectual racism worse than colonialism, because it is effected by a mulatto wench as the face of good old fashioned Western cultural imperialism (albeit sexual as opposed to land and resources), the first Black female VP of the united states. Is not the developed world asking, gee how high the price of success with White people is, you have to act like you don't know what a man and a woman are? Maybe that is the definition of acting like a monkey. The point is not that you hoo-hoo and ha-ha like a monkey, the point is that you 'act ignorant' (of what a man and a woman are) and do and 'say' whatever you were trained to do and say, and they reward you by sticking a treat in your mouth. So you get used to doing tricks and performing for 'treats' and jobs in the White man's world with fancy titles and lots of money.

How can we export democracy. Republican donors are sending Clarence Thomas grandchildren to private boarding school and gifting him expense paid vacations. How wonderful and convenient Clarence, to have such friends in lofty places. Lobbyists for big pharma and other big industries donate large sums (to both parties) in an effort to shape, if not determine the outcome of the debate regarding the public policies that affect them and their products. Democracy in these circumstances in post-modern America is too hard, let's just make some shit up about sex that has little or no basis in the history of humans, apes or mammals and try to sell the world that shit, and accept our leadership. Oh yeah, that and the environment. If they follow and they accept our White mainstream cultural leadership, that is all that matters and the quality of the leading or the specific ideas don't even matter anymore. Mere following and engaging that gender pronoun stuff other than what you see, you're accepting the White European socialist-atheist-LGBTQIA agenda.

21 Oh Atlanta So Much to Answer For

It is with great trepidation that I undertake a discussion B E. Mays student Bre'Asia. I was born in the 70's, and if I were to be honest, I couldn't count the times I loitered at an unauthorized gathering at Mays High, Therrell, Ficket, Adams park, John A White, etc. We called ourselves socializing, sometimes drinking a little alcohol and/or smoking a little weed. If I had to put a numeric value to the number of times between the age of 15 to 18 I loitered like that without supervision it would have to be just shy of 50.

As a matter of fact, we teens were always looking for 'cuts', 'fades', dead end streets that offered a little privacy, where presumably we would be away from the prying eyes and ears of adults. When I got a car as a teen, I got my first 'handjob' from a young lady in B E Mays parking lot, parked right by the track about 11 pm, after I had taken her to the movies and the Chinese restaurant but before I had to have her home. I say it was my first handjob, but more specifically, let us say it was the first one I had not given myself. In reflecting, I'm amazed how little fear we had then. We didn't feel vulnerable at all hanging out in school parking lots and unauthorized places late at night, the more remote, the better. In today's times it's like asking to be robbed, raped, killed, mutilated or sex trafficked. But then we had no fear and I never remember being harassed by the public (unless it was concerned homeowners or parents). None of my friends had guns or were interested in them and I made it through Douglas High without ever having heard of one on campus or seen one, though that does not mean it didn't happen. Oh yeah, this dude named Carlos said he had one. And he sold weed. And he was built like a grown man. I do not mean this to suggest he was athletic, muscular, or robust. Carlos had a 'dad' body and mannerisms in the tenth grade. But Carlos is the only person I ever knew in high school that even suggested he had a gun but I certainly didn't see one.

On the night in question, I'm in B E Mays High School Parking lot and for lack of a better phrase, the young lady is started to 'get the hang of it,' after a shaky start. Ladies and gents, time I leaned my head back in a somewhat feigned posture of ecstasy that I had seen on the limitedly available porn tapes from those days that are probably considered R rated today, blue police lights flashed with no sound behind me and in all the mirrors. The officer walked up to the car so quickly, I had no time to put my 'equipment' (here again for lack of a better phrase) in my pants. He walked up and started fussing at us. "We're not doing anything wrong," stumbled idiotically out of my mouth as the officer's flashlight shifted between my face and my poor 'blue balled' manhood. "How can you not be doing anything wrong your pants are open," he said defiantly. I felt worse for my girlfriend because the last thing a respectable girl wants to be seen doing by anyone is something disrespectable. I was embarrassed for her, not myself, and that I had gotten her into this kind of predicament of being seen in public with my 'wood out', like it was really disrespecting her to have her out there in public like that. A little more fussing about being home at appropriate times and he let us go, saying 'get the fuck outta here'. We happily and humbly obliged, however it must be noted, that the wind was completely out of the sails (and my blue balls) of our amorous intentions and romantic encounter.

More memories flood my mind as I wonder how Bre'Asia died at Mays High school, someplace I lived not too far from and that played such a part in my childhood and adolescence. Bre'Asia lived in the Adamsville/Plainville community of Southwest Atlanta. It was one of the first areas developed for post-Civil rights era newly educated and middle-class Blacks that wanted to own their own homes. My father taught for years at Adamsville elementary/middle and L P Miles, Adamsville area community schools. Consequently, I spent a lot of time up there with him from the period of the 70's, early 80's. My ex-mother and father-in-law have a lovely home in Adamsville to this day.

Yesterday, Saturday 6-3-23 I was there in Adamsville, two doors down from Bre'Asia's home and the assembled funeral cortege. The mood was somber and solemn as neighbors gathered quietly on their porches and watched the goings on with dour expressions... it must have been dozens of cars lining the street and in addition to the customary limos for the immediate family there were about 2 or 3 Mercedes vans, some which had TVs in them. I think the vans were for Bre'Asia's friends and other Mays students that wanted to participate in and go to the funeral. When I walked up, my boys were smoking blunts and talking quietly about the situation. As one passed it to me, more surreptitiously than usual, I hesitated out of respect for the assembled cortege but it was so much going on, I'm not sure anyone would have been able to tell if it was us, or a member of the procession in their car, doing like Sharri Jackson the sprinter and using marijuana to help deal with their grief.

Current Atlanta mayor Dickens is from Adamsville and never hesitates to at least imply that he still lives there, though I find that hard to believe. Deacon Dickens, in addition to mayor Dickens. If he went to Adamsville elementary or middle school back in the early to mid-80's, and was 'bad', my dad probably taught him. Even as a child I noticed something about my dad's career. I thought my dad was a genius, certainly everyone treated him with the utmost respect and that thus, he only taught the brightest kids. But as so often happens, women and homosexuals teach the 'brightest' (read smartest and safest from good homes kids) that cause fewer discipline problems. They make male teachers like my father, and with all due respect, they also make female teachers that have a reputation for being disciplinarians and have a more imposing physically presence get the bad students and students with discipline problems. I only rarely remember my dad complaining about that situation and he seemed to accept it as natural.

In any case it was good for me because the students I was exposed to hanging out in my father's classroom and on field trips had lots of 'personality'. As a matter of fact, after the Norman boys, the next dude that really impacted my sense of adolescent maleness and manhood was a dude in my father's class named 'Swisson'. That's who I got the name from. I could be wrong, and his name was totally different, but that is what I seem to remember everyone calling him, including my dad. He was athletic, apparently attractive because the girls loved him and dudes wanted to hang out with him. Oddly enough, it didn't seem to go to his head. He could have very easily been a bully, but he was actually kind of nice. His innate kindness was even extended to me, his hated teachers' child. I would have been happy and quite content to let him bully me, seriously, he was 'that' nigger (in a good way). But more often than not he'd talk to me, slightly amused by my obvious admiration, and I think he took some kind of pride in the fact that the teacher that's the hardest on him and others of his ilk, and that he 'hates' as young people do adults that make demands on them, son thinks he's the greatest thing since the invention of grits.

I was so convinced Swisson was the greatest invention since grits that I mustered up the courage to ask my father what he thought of Swisson. Surely as intelligent and as bright as my father obviously was, I thought he would recognize Swisson's obvious gifts. I think in my heart that is the conversation I wanted to have with my dad, though I knew I could never have a conversation with my dad like that, but I could imply dad should give Swisson great grades. That was what I really wanted to say, but in my 12-year-old passive aggressive mind, I didn't think starting a conversation off with my dad with...'that Swisson is a great dude isn't he'; was a good idea? My dad's one line remark shocked me so bad I had no follow up. My dad said, "Swisson is a fool". I remember being startlingly surprised. So surprised I had no follow up. In the name of Swisson I almost wanted to cry. Indeed, I honestly hadn't given much thought to whether Swisson was smart or not, just that he was cool, all the girls loved him and the dudes wanted to be him, and on his team in any pick up sports games, even the card game UNO.

When I was in high school, believe it or not we had a violence problem too, even though compared to today our problem was miniscule. Many of the South Atlanta and South Fulton high schools were embroiled in rivalries and fights, and would fight each other after football and basketball games or large parties at varying homes in feeder neighborhoods. Teens from different high schools would be drawn to stadiums like

Lakewood, Cheney and Grady (now renamed out of fear that if a Black child goes to a school with the name of a former Confederate or racist that automatically means the poor little nigga child cannot learn). That is even though thousands of MLK Jr, elementary and middle schools are cranking out kids reading 2 or 3 years behind grade level every year all over the country, and the liberals aren't complaining.

Anyway, when I was in high school some doo-gooder-goober liberal with a nonprofit collecting money to stop teen violence, seized upon the trend and created an organization called 'Black Teen Advancement' (BTA), presumably to stop the violence amongst Black youth. However, it did not stop teen violence (clearly). We grew out of it (violence). BTA hosted plenty of pep rallies at different schools where we teens chanted 'stop the violence' slogans and gave out T-shirts with 'stop the violence' rhetoric written on them. Douglass and Mays High schools used to fight regularly; Therrell, Washington, Tri-Cities, South Fulton, every school had brawlers. My favorite 'battelrama' spots were Krystals on Campbellton Rd and Burger King by Greenbriar after parties or sports events. But of course, brawls are different from gunfire and to be frank, with the physical energy it takes to brawl effectively, one can just as easily run, which at least temporarily offers reprieve. When guns are involved, they make running and running from fights efficacy quite problematic. Only superman and 'the flash' can outrun a bullet and with repeating fire and high-volume cartridges your aim need not be that good. Perhaps that is the salient here. You cannot run anymore. Weapons technology is at a point where merely running from confrontations won't do. To use a biblical phrase, 'fleeing before the face of' somebody enraged is not an option. But enough about me, I'm 100% non-violent, no weapons, but there is nowhere to run or hide in America. I am told lil baby, who is different from da baby has beef with gunna.

22 Atlanta: Please Don't let Bottoms, Dickens, Abrams, and Warnock Fool You!

It is with utter disgust that I watched our Negro former and current mayor(s) pat themselves on the back for their 'tireless' work to document, reinvestigate and memorialize the Atlanta 30 to 35 Atlanta Missing and Murdered Children situation from 1979-1981. And yet at the very same time in 2023 there are many Black male and female teens that are murdered, but they aren't missing and the perpetrators are quite known, that is to say, there is no need for conspiracy theories about the KKK, FBI, CIA, and the same people that introduced 'crack' to the Black cities in the 80's during the same time, because it is the Black children's own Black and brown peers that are killing them! And yet, even though we have way more facts about the disturbing current trend of nihilistic Black boys than we do the 'Missing and Murdered Black children 1979-1981', Dickens and Bottoms treat the current problem like it is Churchill's famous description of Russian policy and politics as a 'riddle, inside a mystery, wrapped in an enigma'. They have nothing to say except 'we've got to do better' (Bottoms) and 'this has got to stop' (Dickens). But ask them to speak on LGBTQIA rights and they show up to every parade and every elementary school drag reading hour their handlers can schedule them for. 'Slickens' and 'Bottoms' make quite definitive statements about the value of LGBTQIA persons and rights, but they can't make one or two definitive statements about the value of our youth and why we shouldn't treat it like a simple fact of life when they kill each other. And yet they can waste time and money investigating whether the 'Missing and Murdered Black children 1979-1981' was caused by the CIA, FBI, mob/mafia, KKK, some rogue White sexual predator(s), some rogue Black sexual predator(s), 'the illuminati' and/or 'the elders of the protocols of zion'. As long as they can wax philosophic how justice must be served and use platitudes like saving and loving the children, combined with memorializing the children that died during the 'Missing and Murdered Black children 1979-1981', it will work fine for Dickens and Bottoms. However, do not expect them to have anything sane, credible, intelligent, practical, or effective regarding the problem with Black teen violence or adult violence and economic dysfunction today. No disrespect intended, those problems are way greater than the dynamic incurred in the Black community when some random entities killed 30 to 35 children and young adults during the height of the 'Missing and Murdered Black Children 1979-1981' incident. How the fuck can it be easier to solve crimes and problems where the children were 'missing', than it is when the bodies of our children today are quite 'found', and we know the perpetrators because they are our children's peers? And yet 'Bottoms and Dickens' (no pun intended) have nothing to say but 'this has got to stop' and 'we're better than this'. What the fuck are the citizens of Atlanta paying them for and why is the White mainstream socialist atheist LGBTQIA Democrat party plying them with positions and gifts?

And the real crime lies in the fact that after all the re-investigation and memorialization of the 'Missing and Murdered Black Children 1979-1981', no one still really knows or agrees on some or all of the facts of the 'actual' crimes and the responsibility for them, and this is why 'Bottoms' and 'Slickens' can delude themselves (and the Black community in Atlanta), and pat themselves on the back for wasting more money between 2019-2023 than was wasted in the entirety of the effort to blame everything on Wayne Williams and close the case and that chapter in Atlanta's 'City to Busy to Hate' life. If you remember, the whole case hinged on the famous 'carpet fibers'. If it weren't so sad, it would be laughable. Where is Columbo, where is Monk, where is Will Trent, where are the other investigative neurotics and retarded geniuses like 'the good doctor'? Where is Mrs. Maple, where is Agatha Christie, where is Poirot, where is Nancy Drew and the Scooby gang (somewhere having existential breakdowns and sexually experimenting) when we niggers need them to solve the Atlanta 'Missing and Murdered Black Children 1979-1981' and if they have any spare time in such an endeavor, can they please tell us what we can do about our wild ass children in 2023 besides police and legalism enforced curfews; which have the intended or unintended effect of further criminalizing our children.

But let us continue my bizarre metaphor. Where is the character Samuel Jackson played in Pulp Fiction, how the fuck could he see some kids do some crazy shit and not speak the fuck up? Where are Kerri Washington super smart investigative public relations genius negress and Shonda Rhymes? Sure they can solve the 'Missing and Murdered Black Children 1979-1981', and solve our current 2019-2023 'not at all missing but quite murdered', teen mystery of why our children are behaving as such? But oh yes, the only way Kerri Washington's character in 'Scandal' would have solved either crime would be in the context of there being some rich and powerful White man that had to be fucked in order to solve the crime. Then she would have been 'point on', however those circumstances notwithstanding, this is what we get from Black leadership and the arts community. Where is Tyler Perry and Alex Cross? Where is Madea in our present crisis? To let Tyler Perry tell us, which is the same story he has been telling us for 40 years, all Madea needs to do to solve the problem with 'these bad ass kids' is smoke some weed and talk trash to our children and threaten to and actually beat them every other sentence out of your mouth....Clearly, that is not working, as I think that style of child rearing is already more popular in Black communities than it is in the communities of others, unless they are just as poor, just as ignorant and/or just as Black and brown as us.

There are other tragedies of this Andre Dickens, Keisha Lance Bottoms public relations and public common-sense fiasco. At the same time we are bitching and moaning about the conspiracy theories surrounding, and the memorializing of the 'Missing and Murdered Black Children 1979-1981', every day in Atlanta and urban centers all across America we are still producing murdered children, and it ain't no damn White conspiracy theory how are children are dying, for they are dying at the hands of their gun toting Black and brown peers! We know the accused and the culprits and unlike their more favored White and

Cream-colored criminals, don't know how to hide their crimes as good and make their crimes even more obvious. It seems in such regards they tend to trust numbers more than skill and dexterity when it comes to smash and grab, car burglaries and break ins, and other random acts of chaos and violence etc. And in such a context all Keisha and Andre have to say is stupid ass shit like 'we're better than this' (when clearly, we are not). 'This has got to stop' (when clearly it doesn't and that is why it is not stopping, and senseless youth and young adult violence is getting worse.

Worse still, all they must do is claim they are doing something (anything it doesn't matter if it works or not) about the Black youth nihilism, crime and violence problem. Talks about programs, then curfews, community-based cops; holding parents accountable, further criminalizing children you know damn well don't need further criminalization. But these part time Negro intellectuals, are full time players and parlayers, flipping Black people's problems into fancy positions in the Democrat and Republican parties. So with absolutely no creativity, no reliance on the Atlanta University Center, Georgia State, the Black Church and the Black bourgeoisie, you do the same thing White folks do to get tough on crime, and crackdown on your children in a way if White folks were doing it, you'd call it racist. But 'Dickens' and 'Bottoms' (here again, no pun intended), can do the same idiotic old legalistic and law enforcement personnel-based crack down on crime that White policy does out of ignorance, insensitivity, and a lack of creative ideas as to how to really solve the problem. And what complicates this is that if God, traditional values and families, fathers in the home, strong nuclear and extended families are the solutions, but our Black Democrat politicians are wedded to socialist, atheist, LGBTQIA policies that is why they must support and try everything under the sun (even slogans that make them look idiotic like 'this has got to stop' and 'we're better than this'), but strengthening traditional families. That is why they will preach that socialist-atheist LGBTQIA stuff in great detail, but all they have to contribute to the discussion on 'the enemy within' is 'this has got to stop' and 'we're better than this'. The truth of what needs to be done to help urban Black communities is strengthen Black families, but out of 'Dickens' and 'Bottoms' loyalty to their real constituents, the White mainstream Democrat socialist atheist LGBTQIA agenda driven party, the urban poor and largely working class Black city 'Dickens' and 'Bottoms' claim to represent is suffering, so they can rise and get big time fancy jobs and titles in Biden/Harris administration and the Democrat party higher offices(while they are in power).

As this ridiculous level of violence is going on daily in urban American and largely African American communities, we hear silence, crickets and frogs from Stacy Abrams and Raphael Warnock, who told us as niggers, they needed our support because they could solve niggas and White people's problems (running for statewide office). But ironically (counterintuitively speaking), they can't solve Black people's problems, even to the magnitude of our babies and children killing our babies and children (the supreme absurdity in a civilized people's life). I have a hard time believing Stacy Abrams and Raphael Warnock can fix White people's and America in general's problems too, even though I guarantee you the both are positioning and parlaying themselves in the Democrat party to run for even higher (hire) offices than they presently hold. And as much as I hate to say it, Trump was right about Elijah Cummings and John Lewis. During their late careers they were busy as shit attacking Trump and everything Trump was about and did. Meanwhile their 'shit hole' districts (and the only thing that would preclude them from having wholly shit hole districts is the fact there are Whites, others, and middle-class Blacks in some of it), were and are more violent, poorer, more dependent on government, than when they inherited their districts and when they died. That's a hell of a legacy isn't it; along with the legacy of MLK Jr that you can go in any urban area in America on MLK and the likelihood is that it is a shit hole, and 5 steps away from Haiti. As is the likelihood that any school in a Black community called MLK Jr., is a shit hole of poor performance too.

Black liberals and the White LGBTQIA feminist socialist atheists that support them, that honor and memorialize our great Civil Rights era figures like Elijah Cummings and John Lewis and are only too happy to build them statues and monuments, but they wouldn't dare live in John Lewis or Elijah Cummings District's or send their children to public schools in Elijah Cummings and John Lewis Districts. That is, notwithstanding my earlier comment (and the only thing that would preclude them from having a wholly shit hole districts is the fact there are Whites, others, and middle-class Blacks in some of it). Other than that, they wouldn't dare. The White mainstream socialist atheist Democrat LGBTQIA party is all too happy to tell minority women that abortion helps them financially and in terms of freedom, but the kids they have they wouldn't let play with yours, like Beyonce and Jay Z avoiding 'playdates' with Kanye and Kim even though the latter greatly desired such a thing. Jay Z and Queen Bey would love for Blue Ivy et al to have been friends (age notwithstanding) with Malia and Sasha Obama, but we all have standards don't we, and your White liberal friends would be happy to have a transgender woman read story time to your children, but that same White transgender woman, an adoptive parent, wouldn't let their children play with yours regularly. I'm just telling these Black liberals who have risen high in the Democratic party that those you think are your friends aren't as wedded to you as you think, politically or ideologically; and I hope it doesn't hurt your feelings too bad when they shit on you and let you go.

Part II

Ladies and gentlemen, what we witness in 'Slickens and Bottoms' parlaying the Atlanta 'Missing and Murdered Black Children 1979-1981' issue into fooling urban Black and White mainstream Atlanta that they are really concerned about 'Black youth' and desirous of righting wrongs and injustices. Only because the injustice is speculative and probably being caused by the KKK, rogue racist White police or the illuminati or the same CIA/FBI group that introduced crack to the cities, it is safe to score some perceived 'cool points' addressing the

'Missing and Murdered Black Children 1979-1981' issue. But dealing with the reason exponentially more Black children are dying at the hands of Black children today, and their homes and families are un-stable, currently is not safe to address because in that issue, there are some fundamental assumptions and critiques you have to make of Black people themselves and their habits and predilections and people find themselves getting offended. And many of these people who get offended are dumb enough, crazy enough and violent enough to cause real harm. These are not speculations and hypothetical critiques of fantasy land illuminati White people, the mob, the FBI/CIA, rogue White or Black pedophiles and a diatribe on the effects of what White folks have done to us in the Western Hemisphere for 500 years. No, my friends these are not random assorted, all and sundry diatribes against White mainstream global capitalism and the new world order or post-modernism itself. This is not simple talk about what the White man owes us. No, talk that shit around Black people and they will applaud you and pat you on the back. Start telling Black folk they need God in their lives, and to honor their trusts and kith and kin, be academically studious and encourage studiousness, encourage commerce, industry and finance, and go on to suggest that it is damn sure not White folk's or the government's responsibility to provide you with those values or model them for you (first) or opportunities for you to practice them. It is our responsibility. No one else. No one owes us anything, if for no other reason than I don't want anybody telling me they are responsible for me or my success. These are Black people critiquing themselves and saying are our values in the right places. Do we value God, family, education, commerce, and industry or.... other things like Rick Ross Car shows, Real Housewives of Atlanta and some kind of Tyler Perry nightmare where nearly everything on every Negro channel in America is somehow either one of his shows or the model of it is influenced by his shows.

I'm arguing here that even though 'Slickens and Bottoms' bodies are in Atlanta presumably concerned about urban nigga problems, their minds and spirits are parlaying for their next gig and if they kiss Joe and Kamala's ass enough, they might get a real 'gig' in the Democratic party machinery where they can stop even pretending like they are representing niggers, and simply live their lives of independent wealth and means. Dickens, Bottoms, Abrams, and Warnock are completely irrelevant in this issue of Black youth violence, as important as it is. And we know that if they could prove Whites were killing Black children and somehow responsible, they'd be right down here leading us in protest, but they know damn well it's niggers doing the killing and thus there is no 'blame Whitey angle'. They do not know what to do politically with that hot potato, so they avoid it completely. Completely! They are out of touch with the urban middle class, working class, and the urban poor (proletariat lol). This current crop of Negro elected officials are Democrat Negro talking animals, that they (the White mainstream Democrat socialist atheist LGBTQIA political elite) stick up in front of us and say, 'behold your new fearless Negro leader'. The drawback for urban America is that they are 'feckless' and not 'fearless' and have no more intention of 'solving' the problems of urban America or the urban Negro that then man on the moon. No, that's not the hustle. You didn't know most bourgeois elites are hustlers did you, just like their counterparts from the lowers socio-economic strata of Black America? But the hustle doesn't revolve around selling dope, prostitution, robbing, thugging and steady mobbing. Naw, it's a different hustle. The first hustle is graduating from a White institution (economic, professional or academic) and talking at least halfway standard English good. And with a little luck you can parlay that into convincing people (Black and White), usually less educated than you and without an understanding that there are other choices, that you are indeed their 'fearless and exalted wise leader'; and that you are genuinely concerned about them and will protest to White people for them to help you, for a small fee.

Then these bourgeois elite hustlers go to their White masters in the democratic and republican party and say, see, I lead the niggers (I'm princess of the niggers and I Meghan will through my podcast liberate generations of young #Blackbrown and #blackgirls, #blackgirlpower, #blackgirlmagic. These are largely mulatto hacks that want to parlay a little education and talent into being a 'real' nigger princess....as opposed to 'princess of the niggers'...which is too hard). Now they want the White mainstream world, Spotify, Netflix, Apple, and any other large White mainstream platform podcast world, to give them a job and platform in the White mainstream world and the democratic and republican parties, so that they can say that they somehow lead and 'represent' the niggers on the strength of some tricked out highly White mainstream influenced conception of nigger identity. And lead them in the argument that the White mainstream world owes them something. Really? What they fuck kind of leadership is that? Leadership that leads you to a new master and says, 'he owes you something, you better protest'. And this is why no Black Democrat or Republican ever said to himself, my goal is to create competitive, strong, thriving urban schools, families, cultures, and economies of scale. No, that is not what they are selling. They are selling, I'm going to get the White mainstream government and polity to help you. Those are two different leadership strategies and frankly, the present chaos we are living in as Blacks in urban America is due in large part to the prevalence of the latter in defining what are the expectations for Black politicians and politics in America.

If you ask Keisha, Andre, Stacy and Raphael, Black people don't need God, fathers in the home, and strong families, that might anger our socialist atheist white mainstream LGBTQIA and feminist allies...we need more government and more lucrative government programs and reparations. We need living wages and unions and government mandates. We don't need strong extended families to support the schools, and strong local community businesses and industries to provided additional funds and booster support to schools, we need more government programs government curricula that undermines family and religion. That is their strategy and they have made a career off telling Black people that the solution to their problems is holding White folks accountable for what they owe you (presumably because of your ancestor's 'service'). If you ask them, they will say the solution is for White public and private schools to import more niggers and have more niggers 'represented' in the student body and staff. Whites are ok with that because with one stroke it allows them to both humiliate and underfund urban education to the benefit of their educational institutions, which continue going from strength to strength. Their schools go from strength to strength in that they cream the smartest, fastest running, and best basketball shooting niggers right off the top of the Black community (alienating them in the name of liberating them) and make them run balls for their schools and improve the overall test scores at their schools, and then they can use Black students statistically to tout success of the program and tout their diversity. Then they turn around philosophically and monetarily support political positions on public schools that justify withdrawing support from the urban public school system because of the dismal test scores and behavioral rates...when White folks have creamed the best of the Black community in these urban schools, that is to say highest test scores, run the fastest, the tallest, the shortest (for gymnastics), and the best of the best right off the top of the Black community.

III

Other genius strategies that are completely self-defeating for Black people are reparations. We are debating and protesting White people, and donating and giving niggas with a little education they got from the White man and that talk good money for a full time salary and staff, for the sole purpose of begging White folks for reparations. That is the definition of a counterintuitive revolutionary strategy. Instead of taking up money to start businesses, support marriages and families, etc., we will pay a nigga the White man trained, to complain to the White man on our behalf that we need reparations and if the White man does not give them to us, we are doomed to both lack of self-esteem and perpetual poverty? We may as well in that case start back talking like slaves, 'massa wees is need reparations and affirmative action or elses, we just won't make it; massa not only do we not know what to do with ourselves relative to the global capitalist economy, we can't figure it out without you massa'! You take up money and pay this White mainstream university trained nigga to argue you need reparations and welfare, when instead, your contributions to his salary, advertising and schmoozing in Washington, New York and Hollywood budget, could have bought 2 or 3 convenience stores and gas stations in an urban area presently owned by immigrants.

Then we could give our children jobs and work experiences in our retail stores, instead of affirming Chinese, Indian and SE Asian business and even LatinX Caribbeans that open businesses in our communities because it is a hell of a lot easier than establishing businesses and a presence with White folks. Our urban economies are foot in the door business opportunities for everybody (races and nations of the world) but us? And I still wonder how we beg for affirmative action when every convenience store and gas station in our communities is owned by immigrants. It is like we practice affirmative action on everybody else, the world and its immigrants and then we got to beg muthafuckas to give us some affirmative action. That's what the fuck Dickens should be talking about when he says his constant refrain every time there is Black teen and youth violence, 'this has got to stop'. Immigrants are living their 'foot in the door' dream with a business in our underserved Black communities that no one else wants to operate in, not even Black people (go figure...is it because we don't know how to act?) and using it to parlay their American dreams! All while we claim we need reparations and affirmative action from the White man to live ours (American Dream)? They (more or less recent immigrants), live their American dream of business and home ownership and sending their children to prestigious White universities. Guess what, to add insult to injury, the White people at these prestigious White universities don't assume they got there because of affirmative action, but they think yours (our Black children) did, or that they are primarily there to play ball, and treat them accordingly. Only thing is, immigrant children did get there because of affirmative action. Black people in urban poor communities practiced affirmative action on them and sent their kids to school, helped their parents live their American dreams and helped bring their family members from overseas, improving their lives; the very same things we should be doing for ourselves and our family members...go figure. All the while, we niggas and the elite White mainstream university educated nigga graduates they select for us as so-called leaders, beg, bitch, cajole, harass, protest, steal and moan for White mainstream and government help we poor niggers. Meanwhile our children are in chaos.

Part IV Conclusion

Between 1979-81, approximately 30-40 young Black people died under mysterious circumstances, the phrase to describe this phenomenon came to be known as 'The Missing and Murdered Children of Atlanta 79-82'. It got national attention and no less than famed Black author James Baldwin wrote an entire book on the subject of 'The Missing and Murdered Children of Atlanta 79-82'. Just this past weekend in Baltimore, 2 dead, 28 people injured many, under the age of 14. In my beloved Atlanta, the Black Mecca, since January of 2023, 65 people under 21 have died due to youth Black on Black violence, often over ridiculous things, like social media posts and perceived disses, (sacrificing our seed to a technological god Molech in a way). Comparatively speaking, 35 Black youth under 21 died between 1979-82 (a four-year period) in 'The Missing and Murdered Children of Atlanta 79-82' . That deserves 'investigation', sighing, memorializing, and handwringing. But between January of this year and a July, just in Atlanta, 65 youth have died under circumstances no social scientist, nigger, White person, or foreigner in their right mind would say is 'unusual' circumstances. And yet *'Slickens'* and *'Keisha parlay to a position higher in the Democratic Party Bottoms'* are patting themselves on the back and taking celebratory photos and publicity shots about their great work on behalf of nigger children who died damn near 40 years ago. No disrespect to those deaths at all, but why do they stick out so powerfully in the Black psyche, as opposed to holding our politicians accountable for the fact more of our children killed each other this year than in the entirety of the 79-81 Missing and Murdered Children Crime spree? And that lets you in on a dirty little secret of Black politics and Civil Rights lawyering.

Apparently, the only deaths that matter to Ben Crump, Dickens, Sharpton, the NAACP, the Urban League, etc. are the ones that our so-called leadership can directly, indirectly or by conspiracy theory blame on Whites. And that is the great tragedy of Negro life in America. No one will complain or ask existential questions about Black-on-Black violence, which outweighs White on Black violence exponentially. That is, other than lip service and vague inuendo like criticisms like 'this has got to stop' and 'we're better than this' if Blacks kill Blacks. But if Whites or any other non-White agents of 'the system' we call institutionally racist kill us, it is a great national tragedy that deserves protest, anger, throwing rocks and water bottles filled with pee at police. How did all of this work for the 'Occupy Movement'? Remember them, a headless horseman scam, just like BLM. We complain about 'institutional racism', even though Nigerians and Indians are just as Black and brown as us and fill up Med Schools and elite universities far more than 'usses' (African Americans), even though we've been here 400 years. And for that matter Indian people have a higher per capita income in many places than Whites quite because of their academic success, success in Silicon Valley as well as, and yes, in their equally amazing success opening and running varying businesses in urban usually poorer Black communities in the United States and to be frank, poor Black communities in the Afro Caribbean diaspora and the Afro Mexican, black communities. What counterintuitive ironies. The very same Black communities middle class and elite Blacks run from in order to live around and send their children to White mainstream schools, the White parents just think your kids got there by affirmative action, Indians and Asians run to those same Black urban poor communities and put up businesses and send their kids to the same schools where their children are assumed by even White people to be smarter than everybody fuckin else. What ironies?

How do we know middle class and elite Black people run from the very same poor, urban and Black communities Indians and Asians run to, in order establish themselves in America, get a foot in the door, establish credit, and get rich? Even Young Thug's own neighborhoods weren't good enough for him, so he lived in Buckhead. Meanwhile we complain about gentrification and this gnawing often subconscious feeling that White people are stealing from us, but we won't know it until it's too late and we are priced out of our own communities and chocolate city has imported enough affluent Whites, Asians and LGBTQIA et al, to elect a White or even Asian mayor in Atlanta. Not so much a chocolate city anymore, but at best a creamy off-White colored one, which is fine, but I wished we could have fixed 'Chocolate City', the 'Black Mecca' and made it work as an example to other urban areas that are facing many of the same existential, economic, and political problems Atlanta is right now with our youth and otherwise.

Five

Saxophone Colossus

Anecdotes, Aphorisms and Thoughts out of Season

1. One of the cable networks is promoting a new reality show/docu-drama about a Black family with 14 kids, I think. On the promo commercial we hear the father telling one of his children that had the temerity to suggest the family go camping, that 'Black people don't go camping'. This he said with a straight face. This is instructive on many levels. 1) White people realized a long time ago that 'it's not racist if Black people say it'. 2) How easy it is for Black parents to reinforce 400 years of negative stereotypes of being told (by a combination of White racist culture and igno-rant Blacks profiting off 'chaining' Black culture only to what is stereotypically Black) what's appropriate to Black people (culture etc.) and 3) Black people seem to enjoy, revel in and find humor in crippling stereotypes we unconsciously put on our children. As I think slightly deeper on these matters, it (the notion Black people don't camp) must be a lie because clearly 'runaway slaves' have absolutely no problem with camping. Lol White people have been telling us conveniently selective qualities about ourselves for a long time.

2. Do yourself a favor and research the British English phrase 'the nigger in the woodpile'. In short, before the advent of the Civil Rights Movement and the age of political correctness, a British politician, businessman or diplomat could be doing state business and get to a point in the deliberations that a particularly gnarly or thorny problem exists, and the way to the solution to the problem has broken down and is not obvious. And the British leader or one of his subordinates, in wondering what the problem is and the solution, will exclaim in all British earnestness (because being Ernest is important), 'that's the nigger in the woodpile'. The meaning is that something is a thorny problem without obvious solution, a hard to find, hard to track, hard to pin down problem is called 'the nigger in the woodpile'. The answer is there in the 'bottom of the woodpile' White man, you just must dig down deep enough and find it. You may be wondering how indeed the phrase 'the nigger in the woodpile' came about. Apparently, often enough to be of note, African slaves in the Caribbean and America would run away. Obviously, such as great an investment as these niggers, would need to be chased down and returned to something that resembled usable service on the Sugar cane plantations, cotton plantations, indigo, rice, etc., plantations that they ran away from. Obviously, White people in such slave owning circumstances got a lot of experience in chasing down wayward niggers. You might even say they had to develop skills, techniques, methodologies, and skillsets for tracking down wayward nigger slaves that got the bright idea to run away from the plantation. Apparently, this was so much so the case, that it became a truism for White people that when you were chasing down wayward, crazy runaway niggers, that you would often find them at the bottom of, and in woodpiles. This is no doubt the case because finding sanctuary ensconced in a wood pile with dogs chasing you is surely the very last resort of a wayward runaway slave. All other options of concealment, speed, and escape are gone to the slave

and the best he, she or they could do was get under a woodpile. Last resort though it may have been, there is more than enough evidence to suggest that at least some of the time, it worked. It was possible for the slave to conceal himself in a woodpile, in such circumstances that it became nearly impossible for the slave catchers to catch him, or for the dogs to find him. Perhaps this happened often enough to become a trope for White people, that the nigger escaped in the woodpile. However, quite often hiding in the woodpile didn't work, and indeed they found 'the nigga in the woodpile' and returned him to active duty at the plantation. I would be remiss if I didn't add what should have been an obvious question to my more dutiful readers. On occasions when hiding in a woodpile worked, how could simply being in a woodpile make the dogs unable to detect your scent. We could assume the slave(s) ran through some water and slicked themselves down with mud like Arnold Schwarzenegger in the first Predator movie. This was to put the smell of putrid, fetid, swampy mud on them rather than the smell of human traffic. There is another tactic and strategy as well related to the question, nigga how bad do you want to be free? For obvious reasons, I did not hear this from humans or their descendants because the slave's contemporaries and descendants would have thought they were crazy and even if they weren't crazy, they could not in all honesty encourage or tell slaves to reproduce the strategy I will now share with my human friends. I had to hear this from my bear cousins in the woods and their tales of the ancients about this happening during the days of slavery...cue reggae artist Burning Spear...Do you remember the days of slavery nigga? Sometimes, when escaping the White man and his dogs, a slave tried to find him an old bear cave, preferably uninhabited, even more preferably recently inhabited, which meant that the scent of the bear was strong on that cave. Dogs are known for all sorts of bravery and loyalty, but at a certain point rushing into a bear cave, and this the key, when Sounder, Lassie,

Bosco, and Ole Yellar aren't looking for bears, they are looking for niggers, is not a wise move. For the dogs know, no sane nigger (in the woodpile or not) would last long wandering into an extremely recently or currently occupied bear den, perhaps even a mama bear den. Which brings me to the legend of Mama Bear. One winter's day, a wayward (he/she was confused) runaway slave crawled into a hibernating mother bear's den, damn near naked as the Lord birthed him/her. The human was crying, sobbing and even half in hibernation, the mama bear could hear the barking dogs and the shouts of the human men off in the distance. She knew the shouts of human men, especially human White men. An evident fact in mama bear's consciousness was that it was the same exact shouts and sounds the White man uses when he chases and hunts bears too. And yet because Mama bear was in a dream state (Dreamtime), was this reality or a dream? Was the human, the giant naked mole rat in my den huddling against me real, or is this the proverbial aboriginal 'Dreamtime' and the ancestors are trying to show me something? And yet, her cubs, her babies are born more or less naked, writhing and whimpering. Should Mama bear show tenderness to the naked human thingy huddling in fear against her. Was this 'Dreamtime' or reality, Mama bear wondered. The barks of the dogs grew louder as did the yells and chants of the men...tally ho, tally ho, 'the nigger's in the woodpile', (dreamtime 'the bear is in the woodpile'). Mama bear could feel the slave squeezing her tighter, shivering with fear as the barks and chants of the men grew ever louder, ever nearer. Mama bear simply slept. Yawned and slept. Mama bear knew that if those dogs, horses, and men, come up in here, in a mama bear's den, with two cubs in hibernation, all of them are going to get exactly what they are looking for when you rouse a mama bear. But was it 'dreamtime' or was it reality for mama bear. The dogs, if not the men, knew damn well what time it was. Ain't no muthafuckin need for we dogs to run up in a mama bear's den, when we ain't looking for bears, we're looking for niggers. So the dogs moved on, leading the humans with them as they chanted 'tally ho' and "let's look in that woodpile over there"!

3. I should have known that after Cliff Huxtable, the Black doctor on the show ER and the Black people from Grey's Anatomy, White people would feel the need to take the image of the 'doctor' down a few pegs or two the way they had to take the presidency down a few pegs or two by putting in Trump after Obama. You take the presidency down a couple notches by after the smart Black guy gets it, and at least seems to do a decent job, give it to Trump, just to prove that anything the smartest nigger can do, a dumb ass White man can do it just as good. And you take the notion of the Black doctor down by successfully broadcasting the show 'The Good Doctor'. Sure, there are such things as idiot savants and of course, a White one would be better than any nigger admitted to med school on affirmative action and trained without reference to his special needs. Though of course, it is one thing to feel confident enough to let the 'special needs kid' redesign grain feed and slaughtering lots like Temple Gransden or count the cards for you in Vegas like the movie 'Rain Man'. It is quite another matter to let 'the developmentally disabled kid' do open heart surgery...but just to prove anything the smartest nigger can do...a retarded White man can do...ergo the 'Good Doctor'.

4. Beware of diet programs that argue you will meet the love of your life; after successfully completing the diet and looking sexy and fit. If it was the unconditional 'love of your life', you would have met them when you were fat. Typically, when fat people get on a diet and accept such an argument, they know damn well they aren't going to meet the love of their lives, and even if they did, they wouldn't recognize them because 'your' personality is fucked up. Thus, the lens you look at other people through is fucked up, and even if you saw 'the love of your life'/'your soul-mate', you'd see something quite different. It would be like seeing

the most beautiful woman or man in the world, but in a distorted 'fun house mirror', and thus not even realizing it's the most beautiful man or woman in the world. Knowing this fat people accept the argument because they think that when they are 'fit and sexy' they will attract other 'fit and sexy' people, and thus be spared the fatness (symbol of failure and ugliness to them) they once embodied. Thus, they reinforce the very stereotypes they claimed hurt them so bad when they were obese! Liberal Black people and the LGBTQIA communities do the same thing.

5. The Civil Rights Movement was a largely Black Christian political movement, which is to say a religiously themed movement. The BLM and more recent efforts at organizing Black protest dropped the Christianity piece and made everything not about 'rights given to you and secured by God', but 'rights' given to you and secured and guaranteed to you by the secular White mainstream socialist-atheist LGBTQIA state. The default and natural implication of that is the assumption therefrom that for Blacks to improve their quality of life, depends on how adept Blacks are at manipulating White good will, manifested as the state and corporate power of coercion, which if that White good will doesn't seem to be forthcoming naturally, nigger liberals seem all too eager to brow beat and mock White people into believing. Apparently, Black liberals think Whites should be empathetic to us because of our history of oppression, and our opinion that since 1610 we've been suffering, and they owe us. 'Manipulating White good will' I define as caring more about what they say and think about you publicly, than what you think and say about yourself. Does Vogue think Black women are beautiful? Does Disney think little Black girls can be princesses? Do the executives at some big White corporation who when discussing 'Black issues' or issues of cultural import, use the phrase 'Black Jellybeans' as a euphemism for talking about niggers in disparaging ways without actually using the word nigger? We see the effects of

this protesting about what niggers deserve (without any mention of religion or our obligations before God), from the White man, supposedly because of the pain of slavery and its continuing traumas in the lawlessness and crime in Black people these days. We'll rob anybody and be proud of it. Rappers will go on record and on social media videos with lawless beefs about violence, drugs, and sexual license. Gangs of Black youth walk in shopping centers and commit flash mob thefts. That is the result of raising 2 or 3 generations of Black people with no fathers, and who think middle-class Black people, White people and Americans in general owe them something, and is not giving it to them so they must take it. You've heard their attitude before because it is etched on wax, 'It's hard out here for a pimp'. Then they turn around and say they are doing that (lawlessness) to survive because it's so hard for them out there in the real world because they didn't do shit in school; ostensibly because Robert E Lee's statue was out there in front of the school telling little Black boys it's better to be thugs, hustlers and rappers than well educated. The Civil Rights movement was not just about 'rights' and what White mainstream culture and the government owed us, it was also about our sense of the power of Christianity and its ethics and ideals to improve our lives on a macro and micro level. It was equally about holding Black people and our children accountable to what we owe ourselves and our ancestors, provided we have equal academic and economic opportunities, not just sitting around wanting a check for labor our ancestors did during slavery.

6. There is a television commercial popular in Negro markets such as Atlanta, that runs as follows. A young Black woman is standing in a clearly middle or upper middle-class kitchen, presumably preparing a meal. Her little Black child enters the room, with a shirt on (and presumably draws on, but no pants on). As she comes in the kitchen, the little girl says 'rooaar' growling lion like in a 4-year-old girl's voice and raising her hands in praying

mantis style martial arts position. Her mother says to her with a straight face, why don't you have on any pants? And the daughter says in her lion-like roar, and 4-year old's version of a growly voice, "I'm a dinosaur, and dinosaurs don't wear pants". The mother acknowledges the child's logic for what it is, a 4-year old's perception of the power that comes from being (pretending like you are a dinosaur) in the physicality of the child 'appropriating' the 'praying mantis arm position' as an aggressive posture. This manifests in the child's imagination emotionally, and vocally in the child as the child considers and 'appropriates' the 'roaring', 'growling' gravelly voice, the 4-year-old child associates with dangerous animals and monsters. None of us has a problem with that scene in context. It is cute. The commercial ends there but the child will probably eat breakfast that morning 'pretending to be a dinosaur', with no pants on at the breakfast table and then watch cartoons and go back to sleep, all at home where her parents let her pretend, she is a dinosaur. Naturally her mom/parents/extended family would get her books on dinosaurs and tell her about the fields of paleontology, archeology, and things like that. But imagine the tragedy, if that parent sends that child to pre-school, and into the public world in general, with the idea, that the world owes the child to not let her wear pants, and treat her 'like she is a dinosaur, because she roars, growls, and holds her hands in the 'praying mantis position'. Is this level of public acceptance justified on the bare grounds that presumably, the child wants to be a dinosaur, more than a human being... at the age of 4? Would we call those parents 'liberators' of their children that want their children to be treated like dinosaurs at school, by default alienating the other children that happen to not think they are dinosaurs. These 'liberating' parents, who will mutilate their children's sexual organs like a poor Italian family of the early renaissance era, deciding to have their youngest son castrated, so that he can make some money for the family, by singing castrati in the many productions of the Renaissance era Italian church and opera. How far will you liberating parents go to get acceptance for your children? Will you endorse the parents that want their children to be dinosaurs and thus want to eat raw meat at lunchtime? That is what dinosaurs do isn't it? Even the little girl could tell you dinosaurs don't cook. And dinosaurs don't go to the boys or the girl's restroom either, they go out in the woods, or the grounds in general and mark their territory. This should be allowed on the grounds of the child's freedom, and their liberating (liberal) parents who are on a crusade for their children's freedom to be precisely what they want to be, no matter how much, at the very least, lack of natural aptitude the child may present physically or mentally or in terms of humans not having powerful jaws and big teeth like tyrannosaurus rex. That does not matter however because cosmetic dentists can put some fake Wu-Tang Clan style fangs on your child. Thus, the liberating parents would want the school to not only acknowledge that they feed their child 'raw meat', and that it is normal because you are determined to let your child live her life as closely as possible to what a real dinosaur experiences (or what you and your child think of what a 'real' dinosaur experienced or would experience). Ergo, the 'public school system' owes your children a 'raw meat diet option' at lunch time that is presented right alongside the endless chicken nuggets, green beans, and pizza(s). Now because of corporate malevolence, 'Lunchables' are served to children for lunch. Japanese and Chinese societies correctly think this 'lunchable' lunch, must be the lunch Satan serves in 'hell', and view such a lunch as child abuse or neglect to inflict it on children. Yet this is routinely served in many cities in America as valid healthy lunches for growing children. Maybe raw meat is good for growing children. Some Ethiopian ethnic groups eat raw meat and of course the Japanese eat sushi. But would we call the parents who support these 'dinosaur' children eating raw meat at lunchtime in the cafeteria 'liberators' of those children, encouraging them in their youth fantasies and perceptions about being something you don't know a damn thing about? Let them that have ears to hear, hear.

7. I read that Floyd Mayweather spent $7 million dollars at the Gucci store in South Africa. Ladies and gentlemen, boxing is a very dangerous sport...it is quite possible that someone beats you senseless. Let them that have ears, hear.

8. Also in recent entertainment news, I read that investigators in Las Vegas are still spending money on trying to find 2-Pac's killer(s). Honestly, we already know who killed 2-Pac, niggas, and nigga shit killed 2-Pac. Which ever 2-4 specific niggas participated in the cabal that did the crime, there are hundreds of thousands of niggas, if not millions to be frank in America, still caught up in nigga shit, and committed to be thugs, criminals and doing ignorant shit like going to South Africa, the last bastion of White colonialism and oppression and laying $7 million dollars down at the Gucci store, requiring a troop of armed guards to protect you from your own people. While I would never justify violence, would it not be extremely insulting, if a rich Black man from America came to South Africa and spent $7 million dollars at a White/European owned luxury brand store and then hired a whole troop of armed guards and security to protect him...from the masses of poor Black people in South Africa who are still poor some 35 or so years after the promise of Mandela and a new South Africa? And what is altogether worse, Black leadership in South Africa from a Democracy and performance perspective, has in some regards been almost as brutal, corrupt, and oppressive and incompetent at relieving poverty as the former colonial apartheid regime (which of course had a reason to keep Black people poor). But of course, Mayweather doesn't understand all that history, he saw a Gucci store out the window and that's more worthy of $7 Million dollars than anything else or anybody else he saw in

South Africa. To continue belaboring the point, we do not know if Floyd Mayweather has learned to read yet. A few years ago, the rapper '50 cents' (no pun intended), challenged Mayweather to read one page of a children's book. We know 'fiddy' can read because I am told that professional writers wrote all or most of his raps, which of course necessitates him being able to read. Floyd, for reasons only known to him, refused to read publicly. This is why Whites are all too happy to give nigga athletes and entertainers money, for they know damn well they'll get it all right back soon, one way or another, either through the sheer incompetence of nigger financial management skills, or criminal debauchery. Or niggers worried about finding and prosecuting 2-Pac's killer. And buying luxury items, like Gucci, Mercedes, BMW, and high European and American fashion...they'll get it all back one way or the other.

9. Recently I reflected upon the prevalence in medical, psychological, physical care and even hospice situations of 'therapy' dogs. Having had dogs nearly all my life, and missing not having one now, I do not need to be told of the efficaciousness and effectiveness of dogs to provide comfort and care. I am also aware that autistic children and children with Asperger's many times react better to, and are more interactive with animals than they are with humans. I am told that the reason for this is that interacting with humans has way more variables to consider than interacting with animals, who are as it were, trapped in their animal natures and instinct. Humans lie. If they aren't lying, then even a child in kindergarten learns to be suspicious of their motives when a child asks to play with your toy, and then takes off running with it, with the intent to commandeer it for himself. Teachers asking questions and making demands...way too many variables for many autistic children. Clearly dogs are indeed man's best friends. And yet I could not help but wondering, if some of our children, who are clearly having adjustment problems, if they are ending up

academically poor, and in juvenile at dramatically high rates, may need 'therapy fathers'? Yes single mothers, grandmothers, and single women taking care of chillun. If you are having problems with your child, he may need a 'therapy father'. Sisters, you may be wondering if men are qualified for such an important task. If you compare men with dogs, as so often is the case, your fears and worries will be allayed (like you were the night you met your baby daddy). Furthermore, no disrespect intended, your baby daddy was good enough to fuck the first night you met him without a condom, it is a little disingenuous now to argue he's not qualified to be your child's 'therapy daddy'. Furthermore, many a stray dog, met on sight, ends up being the most loving, dutiful, and dedicated dogs, even above full breeds. He doesn't have a college degree. Dogs are uneducated, so what that your baby 'therapy daddy' is uneducated too. Your baby daddy doesn't talk good, and he doesn't sound like Obama when he talks. Dogs don't talk good, they seem to be limited to barking, whining, and howling in pain (wolves howl for real, dogs do it more for play, and to sing bad songs along with their human friends). As a matter of fact, barking, whining, and howling sounds just like human male caregivers and 'therapy fathers' to me. You say your baby daddy been in and out of jail, I know many dogs (some of which were my own), in and out of the pound, and whatever they experienced in the pound, horrific as it must have been, didn't really change their nature towards a good meal, stomach, neck and back rubs, his own doggie bed, some treats, and/or some trim. Ladies, in all earnestness, does your child need a 'therapy father'? For that matter sister, perhaps you could use a 'therapy boyfriend/ husband/' for some of your own neuroses, not just your child's. let them that have ears, hear. As an even more ridiculous aside to this ridiculous subject, I read just yesterday that Kim Kardashian, has hired...you guessed it a 'Manny' (a male nanny). She says she is doing this because of course Kanye is an absentee father (literally and figuratively whether he is in his children's physical presence or not), clearly. When their father Kanye shows up for court mandated visits, I am sure they do not know which 'Kanye' is going to show up either. Will it be the father ranting about Jewish conspiracy theories and the illuminati or will it be the kind hearted sensitive one that so impressed the hip-hop world when he was younger. And now that the children are older, discipline is becoming more problematic. Sisters, does your child need a 'therapy dad' instead of a 'therapy dog' or a 'manny'?

10. How do we know America is fucked up and has ridiculous priorities. The lotto is at a billion dollars but every day we are told how many people need help, food stamps, food banks, diapers, formula, shoes, school supplies, etc. Why the fuck would we Americans contribute anything towards that stuff, or even invest in or start real legal businesses, when we can get something for absolutely nothing, by playing the lotto. Our country will be going to hell in a handbasket, literally, but we won't mind because of the idea that being a billionaire (in hell) is better than working to create a stable society where people have stable expectations about what education, hard work, investment, skill, etc., can bring; this is the new American version of patriotism. Who wants to be a millionaire, billionaire, trillionaire, Idol, bachelor, bachelorette, we all want something for nothing.

11. What the fuck kind of world have we and are we creating for American Black people and our children. Niggas can literally watch Oprah's entire oeuvre 24 hours a day because she has her OWN network. Similarly, we can watch Tyler Perry's entire oeuvre 24 hours a day, in infinite variety. And now, it is very possible to watch Steve Harvey, in infinite variety, 24 hours a day. Damn, we been cranking out college graduates from HBCUs and fancy elite White name brand colleges for over 100 years and the state of nigger entertainment is no better than this? Cue Florida Evans...Damn, damn, damn! As much as I love the sisters, queens,

etc., if I see another television series, docudrama on the intricacies of life for ghetto fabulous women like Real Housewives of ATL, Hip Hop Wives, Hip Hop Children, Gospel Children, etc., I'll...I'll, I'll nothing, apparently this is all we expect from nigger entertainment and if Tyler Perry buys BET I can't envision it getting any worse because he uses every television deal he gets to produce his own shit, just his own shit...over, and over, and over, and over again. One day we will see the Movie 'Madea at the pearly Gates', where 'she' is sassy and brassy fussing at Peter, James and John trying to see Jesus'. The obvious sequel to that movie, because it's such a wonderful idea I'm glad I thought of it (call me Tyler), would be titled 'Madea goes to hell'. The premise is that she gets put out by the devil because of her sassy, brassy, hip swiveling, neck rolling attitude' and finally the devil calls heaven on the phone and says, I repent, get this beg 7 ft nigga-bitch outa here! "I can't take this shit anymore" (up to that point he thought Hitler and Genghis khan were bad). Madea goes to hell and shows the devil and the inhabitants '#Blackgirlpower', and '#Blackgirlmagic'. How the fuck can Negro entertainment be this stereotypical and bad? Look at the list of Black Hollywood actors that went to or graduated from Yale School of Drama; Angela Bassett, Sanaa Lathan, Courtney B. Vance, Winston Duke, Joy Bryant, Yahya Abdul Mateen, Jonathan Majors, David Alan Grier and Ernie Hudson just to name a few. By no means am I arguing the current low state of Negro entertainment is their fault. I'm just making the argument that our shit should be better than it is.

12. Trending on YouTube recently are a series of videos discussing why some rappers are underperforming when it comes to concerts. Apparently, ticket sales are 'slow and low' (Beastie Boys). I have not seen any of these videos but just off the top of my head I'll offer some opinions. Of course, our intrepid band of rappers, proud of the fact the only college they ever went to was 'break-a-bitch' college will not listen. 1) Statistically relevant or

not, the anecdotal truth is that attending a concert by today's rappers is like asking to be killed and assaulted. This will not stop these men and boys from engaging in dangerous behavior or rapping about dangerous behaviors. I know this because statistically speaking, a gay Black man in Atlanta has a 65% chance of getting AIDS and Black liberals still promote the lifestyle as though that statistical fact was some kind of weird coincidence. In the case of hip-hop concerts, you don't need commercials that show the negative side, all you must do is look at the 6 o'clock news every day. Day in and day out fights and shootings happen frequently at hip-hop venues, clubs, and gatherings. Just ask yourself the question, when was the last time somebody got shot at a Bar or Bat Mitzvah? And then ask yourself when was the last time a Black adolescent got shot at a graduation party? Uh, about 3 months ago. If that were not enough, the more successful hip-hop artists seem to relish in beefs, fights, disputes and take a weird pleasure in dissing other rappers on record. Liberal BLM tropes aside, it is no secret that post-modern hip hop in its present form is dangerous. Add to this the celebration of alcohol and drugs. In itself, that isn't necessarily a problem. I've hung out around Grateful Dead fans (Deadheads) off and on since college and gone to cover and jam band concerts, and as intoxicated as I and everyone else was, nary a fight, let alone a shooting or killing broke out. I've been to varying forms of German Octoberfest celebrations here in the states (with the hope to go to Germany one day and participate in the actual event), and Germans and their beer drinking public, sit there talking and laughing, listen to polka music and even classical, everybody having a great time. No fights broke out or shootings. The only drawback is people drink too much and get sick, throwing up in unpredictable places and at unpredictable times. The food is expensive and the lines so long at the 'porta-potties', that when you get out of the line, it's best to get more beer and get right back in the bathroom line.

Similarly, in college and late adulthood, I had many White and Asian friends and associates, and we'd listen to the Grateful Dead, the Doors, Phish, Dave Matthews, and here again, be rip roaring drunk and high off weed, they would be doing pills, but not only did no fights break out, the idea anyone would just casually have guns on their persons was an anathema to that set. It was about love, peace and good weed (whatever else they may have been on I can't tell, but I can say whatever they were on never, ever led to random violence). But somehow when it comes to we niggas, random people feel disrespected by others and fights and shots ring out? Similarly, the next reason not to go to a hip-hop concert, is because, to be frank, it is not an environment that respects women. Every song is filled with bitches and hoes, every video has half naked whores in it, as the rapper throws up a stack of money and makes it rain as she 'shakes it fast, and shows us what she's working with'. No sane Black man, nay, no sane father can take his daughter to that type of shit. R Kelly, Chris Brown and others used to call a woman on stage out of the audience (ostensibly to dance), and gyrate on her, putting his crotch all over her as the crowd goes nuts and low self-esteem nigga women swoon. She'd go backstage and the presumption would be, that she got her 'dream' that night. Every sane Black woman knows that when the hit shake your ass song comes on, every nigga in the concert, like flies drawn to shit will want to dance with you and bump and grind as the sister is expected to 'bow down' like Nebuchadnezzar wanted everyone to do when they heard the music, and start shaking their asses, 'dropping it like it's hot',' 'backing that thang up', 'popin that pussy' and doing the 'butterfly' (y'all don't even remember the 'butterfly' do you sisters). It is not uncommon that women at hip-hop concerts get groped. Not only that, but some concerts you go to, or other events, or in the old days church, and you think to yourself, one reason I might be here is find a wife, husband or spouse. No hip hop promoter, no hip hop artist and no Black woman is dumb enough to enter the arena or concert hall with that possibility in mind. Far more likely, some dumb nigga will think the fact you put your ass on him all night dancing means that y'all are going to hook up and fuck at best. Even though clearly it must be happening, I can't imagine Black women go to hip-hop concerts thinking that they might meet their future baby daddy that night, have unprotected sex and end up in paternity court trying to figure out who the father is, and you can't even present to the court the man you think is your child's father's real name. And what happens to a Black woman at a hip-hop concert, when Nebuchadnezzar's 'bow down' ass and pussy popin song comes and she doesn't dance. She will summarily be accused of being stuck up, and straight out of that 'Dre Day', someone will accuse her of being bougie and needing to be put in her place by dumping a 40 ounce of Old English 800 on her. That's why no sane muthafucka wants to go to a hip-hop concert these days. Kanye says he's more talented than Beethoven, Bach, Miles Davis, Duke Ellington, Coltrane, Bob Marley etc. Shit, Kanye and many other rappers have been living the adage, 'you can fool some of the people, some of the time, but not all of the people all of the time'. Our current batch of rappers is also living out P T Barnum's famous axiom, 'there is a sucker born every minute'. Our current hip-hoppers are determined to prove it, by making self-destructive, family destructive, body destructive killers and fools out of us. Let them that have ears, hear.

13. Recently there were riots involving large numbers of Black teens in Chicago and Philadelphia. I'm afraid we have not witnessed the end of our children running wild in liberal chocolate cities. Our children are bearing the brunt and carrying the foul evil torchlights of the gang and the mob, illuminating our broken families against a night sky of post-modern desperation, despair, poverty, fatherlessness, family dysfunction, crass materialism, and nihilism.

14. I was looking at Bloomberg financial news network recently and Tom Keene (an on air personality/analyst) came on, and said twice repeatedly and with emphasis, 'price down, yield up'. I have no idea what he was referring to except that it was something related to investing and presumably reaping the fruit of the investment in the present or later. Immediately I was reminded (courtesy of Uncle Luke Miami Bass Music) that we of Negritude have a slightly different saying...(Head Down, ass up...that's the way....). Either case requires significant exegesis.

15. Just watched a commercial where a woman says about her (elderly dog), "since I've been giving him this food, he runs and plays like a puppy again." What the fuck is in that dog food, cocaine? And if the dog had a heart attack right after eating, playing, and frolicking around like a puppy is that necessarily the best outcome?

16. Presented with multiple disappointments, I withdrew a little from social and family commitments. In light of this, I was asked why I seemed to be sitting around feeling sorry for myself. I made up some excuse about trying to get things together to get back in action, but I realized the reason I'm sitting around feeling sorry for myself is simply because no one else feels sorry for me.